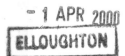

GLOBAL FLYER

GLOBAL FLYER
Around the World in 80 Flying Days

BRIAN MILTON

MAINSTREAM
PUBLISHING

EDINBURGH AND LONDON

First published in Great Britain in 1998 by
MAINSTREAM PUBLISHING COMPANY (EDINBURGH) LTD
7 Albany Street
Edinburgh EH1 3UG

ISBN 1 84018 129 X

A catalogue record for this book is available from the British Library

Typeset in Garamond
Printed and bound in Great Britain by Butler and Tanner Ltd

When the wild ducks migrate in their season, a strange tide rises in the territories over which they sweep. As if magnetised by the great triangular flight, the barnyard fowl leap a foot or two in the air and try to fly. The call of the wild strikes them with the force of a harpoon and a vestige of savagery quickens their blood . . . the call that stirred them must torment all men. Whether we dub it sacrifice or poetry or adventure, it is always the same voice that calls. But domestic security has succeeded in crushing out that part in us that is capable of heeding the call. We scarcely quiver; we beat our wings once or twice and fall back into our barnyard . . .

Antoine de Saint-Exupéry, 'Wind, Sand and Stars'

CONTENTS

PREFACE

Keith Reynolds and I set off to fly a microlight around the world in 80 days. A hundred and twenty days later, I returned to London on my own.

When we set off I had expected that we would have some amazing adventures, but I had not expected them to be quite so bizarre. This book is the story of how it happened.

Every morning I woke up before dawn and wrote or typed between 1,000 and 2,000 words a day. Those journals were the raw material for my story.

I want to thank Keith Reynolds and Peter Kusmich Petrov for flying with me.

I was strongly supported on the flight by Kay Burley of Sky TV, Valerie Thompson, the legendary City trader, and my friend Moira Thomson. I hope you feel, Kay, that your mother's engagement ring has had sufficient adventures for the time being.

I want to thank Judy Leden for the piece of history, a sprig of heather once carried by Amy Johnson, that I carried as my own good luck charm.

I also want to thank Dave Simpson, John Hunt and Graham Slater, all superb pilots who gave advice and help unstintingly. I am also deeply grateful to Dave Simpson for proofreading the manuscript and giving me advice on how to make it more readable.

To those who fought so hard to save the flight in the Saudi Desert: Nigel and Conrad Beale, Mark and Michaela Hurtubise, thanks for the commitment you put in.

There were dozens of people all over the world who helped, and without whom the flight would have been much more difficult. Thanks to you all. These include Mr Al-Nabjan in Qaysumah; Malcolm Hardie in Al Ain; Steve Crossman in Hanoi; Paul Clift in Hong Kong; Onou Senta and Katasuoshi Kawashiro in Japan; Andrew Fox in Vladivostok; Murray D'Ath-Weston, Dennis Wilson, John Stewart, Tanya Berkova, David and Sarah Simerka in Yuzhno-Sakhalinsk; John Russell, Doug Deering, Herb Rossen in

Nome, Alaska; Mike Winecoff in Seattle; Gene and Margie Fincham in Lincoln, California; Robert Palfreeman in Kuujjuaq; and Bert Rose in Iqaluit. As well as a great many others. People like me need people like you.

I want to thank the two young professionals who survived the flight. To Charles Heil, who carried the heavy burden of organising it and who cannot have imagined how difficult it would be, I hope you make it in Hollywood. This has been an appropriate training ground. To Alison Harper, slung in at the deep end, whether brilliantly arranging that first day's departure, or dealing with a media gang-bang on the last day, your future jobs will be wimpy by comparison.

This flight would never have happened had it not been for the introductions within GT Global done by Dallas McGillivray. I am genuinely sorry that we were never able to develop a personal friendship after those early promising days.

To Paul Loach and Prince Philipp of Liechtenstein, though you are no longer involved in GT Global, I am grateful for the stylish way you backed this flight, and I hope you feel that you got value for it. I tried never to let you down, and I do not believe I did so.

I want to dedicate this book to two people.

The first is Fiona Campbell, my wife of 28 years, who looked for and found a new life separate from me. Thank you for those years we did have together. In this book, I have tried to be the writer you thought you were marrying in 1970. I hope our children, James and Jade, see the adventure as an inspiration.

The second is Helen Dudley, arbitrarily elected my muse. Men are odd creatures, that we need one.

Brian Milton
Villefranche du Périgord
2 September 1998

1. ORIGINS OF THE FLIGHT

Deyr fe, deyr froendr
Deyr sjalfr it samr.
Ek veit einn podaldri deyr
Doemr af mannr domi

Cattle die, kinsmen die,
You die yourself in the end.
I know one thing that never dies,
The reputation of a man's deeds

Norse writings from between the fourth
and fourteenth centuries

I had wanted to fly a microlight around the world in 80 days ever since the Australian billionaire Kerry Packer summoned me to the Savoy Hotel in London in 1987 and asked me if it was possible. He wanted me to start and end in Sydney, Australia, to be back in time for Australia's bicentenary on 26 January 1988. At the time I was 44 years old, dressed in a pin-striped suit, and looking forward to a good lunch with a City friend after a morning shift as TV-am's financial correspondent. But as I stared across at Mr Packer, who oozed power and magnetism despite a fearsome exterior, a dream stirred. The dream was not destroyed by the realisation later that week that an 80-day circumnavigation by microlight is not possible except in a northern hemisphere summer.

My then wife, Fiona Campbell, steered me towards suggesting that I could fly a microlight to Australia in 30 days, to emulate the great pioneer Ross Smith who made the first England to Australia flight in 1919. Mr Packer said yes to this proposal, then six weeks later said no: 'too expensive and too dangerous'. The idea was picked up that summer by the food group, Dalgety, and I subsequently flew a microlight from London to Sydney in 59 days – faster than the 96 days Smith had taken to get to Sydney, slower than the 28 days he had taken to Darwin. He had his major problems in Australia; I had mine before I got there. Mine included being wrecked on a Greek island and gluing the aircraft back together again, then falling into the Arabian Gulf on Christmas Day, 1987, 32 miles from Abu Dhabi, in the middle of the Iran–Iraq War. In both cases, the Dalgety Flyer was made airworthy again inside a week – thanks to my mechanic Mike Atkinson, who made the journey on a first-class airline ticket (with many stopovers). It is now in Sydney's Powerhouse Museum, and it is a candidate for its own permanent display stall in the new Bankstown Airport which is being built for Sydney 2000.

For ten years that was the longest, fastest microlight flight in history and was in the *Guinness Book of Records*. But its reception by the British microlight community was appalling. A non-flyer called Norman Burr, editor of the official magazine, *Flightline*, led his letters column with a missive from an instructor called Ted Battersea, which deprecated the flight and asked if others too had cringed at the sound of my name. Burr headlined the letter, 'The World's Longest Ego Trip' – this was his own petty invention, not a phrase from Battersea's letter. Burr followed this up by publishing an article in which David Cook, who had built my aircraft but resented the fact that Dalgety – rather than his own company – got all the publicity, suggested I had made an emergency landing on a golf course in Australia purely for publicity purposes. Cook asked readers to suggest which of my previous problems had occurred for the same reason.

Burr, Cook and 'Cringing Ted' Battersea were not acting in a vacuum. Burr certainly reflected the views of the BMAA's then chief executive, Brian Cosgrove. Sadly, it is a fact that a year after I had completed the flight and nine months after I had returned to England, I had received not one invitation from a British microlight club to talk about it. That was in a year when I was a guest at 617 Dambuster Squadron's annual dinner, invited by Tony Iveson, the man whose bomb is credited by some boffins with sinking the Tirpitz. The contrast between the two sets of values, wartime bomber pilots and the modern microlight community, is a telling illustration of much that is wrong in the world.

If the Norse poet was right and the one thing that never dies is 'the reputation of a man's deeds', then the reputation of my deeds had been traduced beyond any semblance of justice. I have come to acknowledge that one of the driving forces behind my flight around the world was anger. I could not bear to think that when the history of the New Aviation was being written – of hang-gliding, micro-lighting and paragliding – the views of aviation nobodies would be the last word on my beautiful and difficult flight to Australia.

In the ten long years between the birth of that 80-day dream in front of Kerry Packer and the acquisition of the means to make it happen, I nursed this anger. I have a reputation as an energetic man, but the anger gave my energy a demonic force. I passed into my 50s, subjected to disparaging remarks from friends about my chances of raising the money to make the world flight, about my age, my obsessions, and they barely concealed their contempt for the negligible chances I had of success. This gave me the strength to try even harder. Some years I spent hundreds of hours sending the project out to possible sponsors. Otherwise I made a living as a financial journalist, as the main source of income for Fiona and our two children. After leaving TV-am to make the Australia flight, I never again had a career in the old-fashioned sense of the word. But some years I was successful – as editor and presenter of the daily half-hour TV programme *European Business Today*, for example – while other years I managed to stay off the dole only by spending all my savings and investments and the £21,000 I had inherited at my mother's death in 1993. By the end of 1996, after a stint as editor of BSkyB's *Business Sunday*, I had found my way on to Clive Wolman's *London Financial News*, my first real job as a freelance print journalist after ten years in BBC Radio and 15 years in independent television.

For years, all I got was a straight no to ATWIED (the acronym for Around the World in Eighty Days). I tried packaging the idea in different ways, but without fail the mail would bring back letters with such soulless phrases as, 'not suitable', 'does not fit our current plans', 'interesting but not for us'. When I tried the Virgin Group I had a short, if more human, reply from Richard Branson himself, but again saying no. No one was interested. Working alone, month after long fruitless month, looking for a response, I needed the anger to keep going. Otherwise, I would have given up years ago.

The original plan was to do a solo world flight, possibly on another Shadow, with a bigger engine than the puny Rotax 447 on which I had flown to Australia. But, in the winter of 1995, I was on holiday with a friend called Keith Reynolds and we talked over the world flight. Later, he wrote me a letter saying he had become obsessed with the idea. Why not go together? he asked, and why not do it on a two-seater weight-shift trike instead of a three-axis microlight? I did not think it was possible to make the flight solo, 24,000 statute miles in 80 days in a trike. Or if it was, I did not think I was the man to do it. But Keith's suggestion struck a deep chord, and I was taken with the idea.

I had met Keith Reynolds in 1977 when he won a hang-gliding glide-angle competition I was running at Mere – the only British success in a sea of triumphs by the visiting Australian Moyes Boys. A year later, Keith won the British hang-gliding league in his first year, an amazing feat. He was a member of teams I took to the USA in 1978–79 for the first American Cups, where we beat the Americans twice and scored victories over the Canadians and the Australians, then the giants of the sport.

Keith was a member of the Rat Pack, a laddish group based around the Southern Hang-Gliding Club. Others included Mick Maher, Brian Wood, Mick Evans and Lester Cruise, all great pilots, but men who could sink a pint or three as well. When I moved into microlights, Keith made a similar transition, first as a test pilot, later as a manufacturer and then instructor. After a difficult childhood he had made his own way in life and, at 45, seemed to have settled into a comfortable life with his third wife, Becky, a dog called Pan and a good living from his own school on the Medway Estuary.

Yet, whenever I called him up about an adventure, he always joined in. I remember once leaving a message on his answerphone, asking him to call me, and finding a message on my answerphone: 'Just returning your call, Brian. Whatever it is you're planning, the answer is yes.' He was on the Bleriot flights of 1989 and 1992, and the epic flight from Heathrow to Le Bourget in Paris in 1994, characterised by low clouds, lashing rain, high winds and the fact that we carried eight cases of Famous Grouse whisky between us; the nights were brilliant and the mornings stricken.

Keith said to me once: 'I always knew you would pull off a big flight sooner or later, and I stayed in touch to make sure I would be on it.' Despite doing all my previous adventures solo, I wanted to make this huge flight with a companion, so I increased the projected operating budget to more than £300,000 to cope with the extra expense of flying with Keith, and wrote him into the project.

I do not know how others go about getting sponsorship; my basic premise is that one swaps publicity for money and from time to time this has worked. Publicity is not an end in itself, just a tool to give a sponsor something tangible for their hard-earned cash; it can be measured and a value put on it. I think a lot about publicity: where to target it, how to generate it and how much it is a monster which one tries to ride. It helps that I am a professional journalist with considerable experience in radio, television and newspapers. But anyone who does not understand the basic premise has probably never gone out to get sponsorship and has all the useless confidence of the irredeemably ignorant.

The first glimmer of hope came not long after joining *LFN*, when I wrote a story on a successful entrepreneur called Rory McCarthy. I knew Rory from hang-gliding, and the time when I was on the governing council and he went backwards one day over Dunstable Hill in 50 mph winds. The hacks who galloped after him and his runaway hang-glider had no concern for Rory, but they were hugely worried about his passenger that day, Jimmy Greaves, the legendary footballer and reformed drinker who is a public icon. Though Rory did not damage Greaves on that Dunstable flight, there was some public indignation, and Rory acquired a reputation as a wild man. He then dropped out of a balloon in a hang-glider at 34,000 feet to establish a world record, went into the City as an options trader, bought into a business and wheeled and dealed until, by the age of 35 when I met him, *The Times* estimated his worth at £90m. Among other acquisitions, he owned the major share of the company run by Per Lindstrand that built Richard Branson's balloon, and he was a business partner with Branson, launching a new brand of products. Branson was then planning his world balloon flight, and Rory was to go with him, but when I mentioned ATWIED, Rory got quite excited. He saw it as a perfect vehicle for launching V2 jeans and promised to put it to Branson. I looked the Atwied proposal over, updated it, sent it off and waited. And waited. And waited. It took a while to discover that when the answer with Rory is no, he does not come back and tell you cleanly. Maybe he was still hopeful, but after months I lost hope. I was eventually given to understand that Branson had turned it down as it would interfere with his world balloon flight.

Newspapers are a different form of journalism to radio or TV, and the relationships established with those we interview in print relies much more on trust. With television, every time you talk to someone, they are on their best behaviour, adopting a Sunday-

School voice, straightening their ties and acting. You rarely get close. There's a sort of false matiness about it, tinged with fear on both sides, on the one that the interview will be poor and reflect badly on the reporter, on the other that the subsequent report will make the interviewee look a fool. But on the *London Financial News*, a specialist weekly City newspaper, I learned something of the classic role of a print journalist, the building of trust between interviewee and reporter, and the distillation of thousands of words into just 600, which would still tell the truth. The relationships were different, the more so in that my beat was the City of London, the greatest men's club in the world. One could get close to powerful men with money to spend on ideas; that, after all, was how they had made their living for centuries.

In October 1996, I nearly had a bite. On the *LFN* I wrote a weekly column called 'Ruling Passions', about hobbies and obsessions City people had outside their jobs. I was always looking for the off-beat, chasing people who collected pre-war wireless sets, or spoke nine languages, or made their own wine – one very senior City executive had 56 pictures and artefacts in his office, all on the theme of Adam and Eve. I was attracted to such unusual people. One day I heard about Malcolm Callaghan, in charge of new business at Henderson Investors and connected with the Queen's brokers, Cazenove. Malcolm, who had raced motorcars in his youth under the title 'Mad, Mad Malc', owned a 1934 Lea Francis and had a home in France to which he commuted every weekend. He had set out to buy a barn to house his car and ended up buying a complete village, which he rebuilt as a private house. This was a natural 'Ruling Passions' story, so I phoned him up, did the interview, and we were talking afterwards when the subject of flying came up. Malcolm was also a pilot, and when I mentioned Rory McCarthy and the world flight, Malcolm said: 'We'd be interested in that!'

In putting together the proposal for Henderson I had to focus for the first time on how to really make it work. The dialogue with Malcolm was essential to later success, because, just by the questions he asked, he taught me how to deal with every possible query in the right order to calm a genuine sponsor's fears. The decision rested with three people to make a recommendation to the Henderson board, but their choice went to buying nine inches of space on either side of the helmets on that year's Rothman's-Williams GT racing team instead of ATWIED. Malcolm and I thought it was the wrong decision, but it was no less heart-breaking for that. The up side was, if I ever got another bite, I had a complete argument ready to use immediately.

Early in 1997, chasing another 'Ruling Passions' story, a colleague, Mike Foster, suggested I try a little-known fund management company called LGT – Liechtenstein Global Trust – which had produced its annual report featuring the hobbies of some of its employees. One man, based in London, was Dallas McGillivray, LGT's compliance director – a sort of company policeman responsible for the propriety of all deals – who listed scuba diving as a hobby. I phoned Dallas, arranged a meeting, interviewed him, and again, chatting afterwards, he began telling me about LGT. It was based in Liechtenstein and owned by the royal family of the Principality. LGT had a number of elements, including a private bank and an asset-management company called GT Global, which handled about $16 billion. As Dallas began reciting the cities where LGT had offices – London, Hong Kong, Tokyo, San Francisco, New York – I could hear echoes of my ATWIED route. I asked him if LGT would be interested in looking at my proposal.

What prompted this? It was mainly Dallas's bluff personality. He is an Australian and had been interesting when talking about his scuba diving experiences. I also felt my story of the Dalgety Flight to Australia might strike a chord. I had – I always had – a copy of the ATWIED proposal with me.

'I only want the chance to put it in front of a powerful person, one who can say yes or no,' I said.

Dallas said he knew just the man, and I left no more hopeful than after meeting half a dozen other City people who had said the same thing.

The proposal I made to LGT made the potent link with Jules Verne's great classic *Around the World in 80 Days*, a journey buried deep in the global imagination and which crossed almost all national borders. The book had been published in 1873, so 1998 was its 125th anniversary. Its two main characters, the Englishman Phileas Fogg and his French manservant Passepartout, used public transport to race around the world to win a £20,000 bet made by Fogg with his card-playing companions in the Reform Club in Pall Mall. Everyone in the Western world knew of the story, even if they associated it with the David Niven film and ballooning across the Alps. It gave an extra dimension to the first microlight flight around the world.

A couple of weeks after I interviewed him, Dallas suggested I make a formal proposal to Paul Loach, chief executive of LGT Asset Management. On Tuesday, 25 February, I turned up at their offices in London Wall, full of nerves but prepared to argue my case passionately. In the presentation I had slides of the Dalgety Flight, and a half-hour video compiled by Barry Bayes of ITN and George Davies of BSkyB, about the Heathrow–Paris flight. The first ten minutes of this video, covering the tensions in the rain-soaked take-off by 22 microlights from the world's busiest international airport, make it the best marketing vehicle I have ever used for microlighting.

The presentation began well when I asked Paul, a powerful man in his mid 40s, if he had read the 12-page ATWIED proposal.

'Every word,' he replied.

As these were just words and there were no pictures or PR hoopla, this was good news. I had poured my soul into those words, but they needed to be read. Rattling away with the proposal, it gradually dawned on me that Paul was completely captivated by the idea.

He asked, when it was over, 'Are we in a bidding war?'

I resisted the temptation to lie, and said no.

'We've got to show this to the Prince,' said Paul, 'with a strong recommendation from the London office.'

The Prince was HSH Prince Philipp von und zu Liechtenstein, younger brother of Prince Hans-Adam, who runs the Principality, 61 square miles on the east bank of the Rhine between Austria and Switzerland. The elder brother runs the country, while Prince Philipp was chairman of LGT. They were among the few remaining powerful princes left over from the Austro-Hungarian Empire. The ancient idea of making a plea to a real prince to back an adventure – as Raleigh must have done to Queen Elizabeth I, or the merchant adventurers with the East India or Hudson Bay Companies – was especially appealing.

I left LGT on cloud nine, but weeks went by with nothing happening, except the occasional phone call from Dallas saying they were trying to tie together three separate diaries – his own, Paul's and Prince Philipp's – so we could meet together. Finally, a day was set, 6 May, and I flew to Zurich with Dallas, met Paul and the Prince and went though my song and dance act. The Prince, full of charm, put me at my ease and spent two hours listening to the idea. I took him through the projected route, sketched out how the company could benefit from it and was warmed every time he murmured, 'it's brilliant'.

Halfway through the presentation, as I suggested that we would leave England in the company of 30 microlights, each with a journalist or a VIP on board, Prince Philipp suddenly said: 'I have to be on one of those microlights!'

It was an odd feeling, atavistic, reeking of history, four men sitting around a table pitching a wild and beautiful idea into the ether, weaving together aspirations, doing what I once described as a 'fan dance'. Illusions were spun as I talked and talked, endeavouring to leave creative silences to allow them to make a solid connection between my dreams and the company's view of itself. There were no gimlet-eyed men in glasses, adding and subtracting risks, always more prepared to say no than yes. If a woman had been there she would have asked more rational questions. Because I was talking to a prince, I could make a human plea; I did not have to twist and pervert the idea to suit the political urges of a committee. Those two hours were, for me, the defining moment, however the adventure turned out. I formed in my own mind a private pact with Prince Philipp and Paul Loach that I would never let them down, no matter what hardship I suffered.

On the flight back to London, Dallas poured champagne down my throat and told me it was a 'done deal', but I was more cautious. How often had I thought I had landed a sponsor and failed? I particularly remembered the dreadful individual blood-letting that followed my failure to land the Newton Aycliffe sponsorship for British hang-gliding back in 1981, and the personal loss of £35,000 trying to support the hang-gliding Superleague in 1989–91, a factor in the break-up of my marriage. I would not face motions of no confidence from aviation luminaries like Roy Hill or Colin Lark – as I had with Newton Aycliffe – if I failed LGT, but I would be heart-broken. When would I ever get such a chance again?

Dallas phoned next day, 12.50 p.m. on 7 May 1997, to tell me the Prince had said yes. Dallas said that LGT knew very little about sponsoring such an event and would need me to outline exactly what was involved. LGT had bought the idea with its heart; I needed to make the case in brutal financial and marketing terms to win over the head. I resigned from *LFN* and spent six weeks learning about the three and a half companies that made up the Liechtenstein Global Trust. This ended with ten days in France alone with my computer, drafting a 30-page outline on how to handle the event. Aside from my own operating budget, covering a year's work – full time for me and part time for Keith plus a full-time organiser and all equipment and expenses, there had to be a second budget for marketing. I estimated this at £600,000, to ensure the ideas behind the flight were put over to the media.

I was aware, as I planned this enormous event, that the Batterseas, Burrs and Cosgroves of this world could have the last laugh. Were Keith and I up to the world flight? Had we within us the stoicism, the experience, the right approach to courage and to caution, required to succeed? Would all the distractions that we would have to endure to make the flight work, taking photos, writing journals, operating TV cameras, dealing with media demands, get in our way and bring us down? Armchair critics could afford to watch and wait, I expected them to be shrill in condemnation whenever things went wrong, with a pained silence at any success.

I had no illusions.

2. PREPARATIONS AND RESIGNATIONS

Almost the first thing that happened when I told Keith I had got the sponsorship, was that Becky told him their marriage was over and he had to leave. Keith spent days, guilt-ridden and shell-shocked, making financial arrangements to look after her and resisting her demands for his dog, Pan, as well. Then he found out Becky was sleeping with his best friend, threw her out and set about divorce proceedings. The only thing that held his mind together during those awful months was the prospect of flying around the world.

My own marriage had sadly ended three years earlier when my wife asked me to leave. We had drifted on without getting divorced while she put her life together again and looked for another partner. Our marriage had lasted 24 years with all the usual ups and downs, and I was very reluctant to end it, or even, at times, to believe it was over. I had moved into a house we had bought in London's East End, which we had seen as our pension, while our children lived with Fiona in our much bigger house in Tufnell Park. At the time, James was 19 and at St Andrews University and Jade was 16 and at South Hampstead School for Girls. When I landed the sponsorship, I resolved to tidy up my life so that, when I got back, I could start anew. It was a theme of the flight.

Fiona had been with me in my darkest and also most exciting moments, and without her it was far more difficult to work through the logistics of this huge enterprise. I had close friends who were interested, but they were no substitute for a wife. So Keith and I entered the adventure alone, he with fewer ties than me – I had my children – and we drew solace from each other.

I also had a secret which I made light of in public, but which was much more serious in private: I was afraid of heights. Everyone used to laugh when I admitted it, but that did not stop it happening. Its origins were an accident on 13 November 1978, in an early version of a microlight – a hang-glider with an engine attached. I had turned one upside down at 250 feet, fell into the sail, the wing broke up and I tumbled into a field near Mere in Wiltshire. Because the farmer, Rodney Coward, had ploughed his field the previous day and it had rained overnight, I had not been killed. The accident had been caught on film by a BBC cameraman. Millions of people in the world have seen me falling out of the sky.

Unsurprisingly, it put me off microlights for six years. But, in 1985, I found the courage to fly once more with an engine, and in 1987–88 piloted a CFM Shadow microlight to Australia. On that flight I went insane for three days in India because of long, long hours alone, a condition lone yachtsmen are more prone to than pilots. At 5,000 feet in January 1988, on a still foggy day between Bhopal and Allalhabad, a disgusting creature that I called a Djinn stood on the nose of my Dalgety Flyer and told me to jump. I had no parachute, and was petrified.

'No, no,' I cried out loud, 'I'll die, I'll die!'

'Go on, jump! Jump! Jump!' it said.

I was sorely tempted and within a fraction of a second of complying. Whenever I could do something, call on the radio, find a landmark, study a map, the Djinn faded away. But when my mind had nothing else to do, he jumped in again, shouting for me to jump. I knew it was madness, I knew it was in my head, but it was the only head I had.

I wrestled with this dreadful creature for three days over India and Bangladesh, and finally discovered a bizarre way to beat him. If, in my mind and in the cramped cockpit of the Dalgety Flyer, I made love to a girl I knew – it could be virtually any girl, but it had to be credible – then the Djinn stopped shouting. When I discovered this, I lined up half-a-dozen girls in my mind and thought of them when I felt him close. In this way I was able to drive him back down the corridors of my mind until he was locked away, and I had the means to beat him when he did appear.

But the Djinn never died, and in the flying I had done since, his memory haunted me. Lining up women for carnal relations lost its power to divert him and over the years I had fallen into a state of mind where I could not go above 1,000 feet without breaking into a cold sweat. Below that height I was as other pilots, happy in the air. Above it, and I would feel unmanned. I could see every foot of air between me, the seat, the keel and trike skirt, all the way to the ground, and feel myself falling through it. I would be on the edge of madness, helpless with fear. The rational argument, that one dies as easily falling from 1,000 feet as from 10,000 feet, did nothing to my nervous mind. But the condition eased a great deal if I carried a passenger, because I would be responsible for them, and that responsibility overcame the mad, insistent urge to jump. Looking at my log-book, I can see how often I sought out passengers whenever I wanted to fly. I thought, in an old-fashioned way, that it was a weakness in my character.

There were two other manifestations of this fear: I always chewed gum in flight, all the time, from take-off to landing, because without it things got worse. And I often welcomed turbulence which would make other pilots fearful, because it was in still air that the Djinn was most likely to strike. When being slung around the sky, I was too busy to admit him to my mind.

Was it irresponsible of me to seek backing to fly around the world, when I harboured such fears? I did not think so. It just meant I had more to overcome than other pilots. And if Keith came with me, I could not possibly wimp out in the air in front of him, so he was my real defence. But, as we made test flights, I found he was not quite enough.

I signed the contract with GT Global, Dallas McGillivray as the counter-signatory, on 11 August 1997, and received two-thirds of my operating budget the same day. It was, sadly, the high point of my relationship with Dallas. The terms of the contract meant all operating costs were down to me, including landing fees and delays. I did not expect to go back to GT Global for more money, as staying in budget was an obsession with me, an article of faith with a sponsor. I was contracted to get a microlight around the world with Keith Reynolds (or any other person of my choosing) as co-pilot. No time-limit was set – the 80 days were a target, but GT Global were rightly fearful I would take extra risks if the 80 days assumed too much importance. I had a statutory responsibility to ensure that the aircraft was in a suitable condition to make the flight and to keep it that way.

I immediately ordered the latest and most well-proven microlight, a Pegasus Quantum 912. It had a lovely flying wing, with which I was comfortable, and its engine – a Rotax 912 – was four-stroke, four-cylinder, and much more reliable than the two-stroke, two-cylinder engines I had flown until then. It also had dual ignition, two sparking-plugs in each cylinder, a comfort on sea crossings. Even though Keith flew as a test pilot for the rival Medway Microlights, which had a lovely wing too, but a less advanced trike, he was in favour of the choice of a Pegasus 912.

In the budget I allocated a year's work to me and paid Keith, who wanted to keep his flying school going as long as possible, 25 weeks salary at £800 a week, plus all expenses, as a freelance employee; this also included two weeks' pay beyond the projected 80 days. I also found an extra £5,000, plus expenses, in the marketing budget, to compensate him for test flights, filming and press interviews, all of which were not strictly part of the world flight. This did not stop him teaching at his school when nothing else was being done, though winter is a slack season.

One principle was established at the start: we were not taking anything new with us. Every piece of equipment had to have been proved elsewhere. If someone came to us with a new engine and extolled its virtues, we were not interested. If the technology was proven, then the only thing in question was our personal qualities. We knew our courage was going to be deeply tested anyway, and we did not want to be wrestling with unproven technology.

I had problems finding an organiser for the flight, another charge on my operating budget, and settled on a 23-year-old American called Charles Heil, who had been at university with my son James, and had produced a play which James directed. Charles had experience holding together chaotic productions and handling money, he saw a future for himself in Hollywood. He was confident that he could cope, and I saw him as a clone for Neil Hardiman, the brilliant 24-year-old organiser of the Dalgety flight. But the Charles I hired, tall, red-haired, friendly and charming to everyone, bore little resemblance to the gaunt, harassed figure I was to meet when the flight was over.

The link man between GT Global and my little unit was written into the original proposal. Simon Newlyn had made a good impression when he worked for Shandwick and had been taken on, at my recommendation, by Dalgety to organise coverage of the Australia flight. But his then boss at Dalgety was Tony Spalding, one of the best PR men in Europe, so the buck never stopped with Newlyn. I had stayed in contact with Newlyn over the years, first, during his continued rise inside Shandwick, then later when he worked as a freelance, without inquiring into why he had left one of the most vibrant PR companies in the UK. Before introducing him to GT Global, I went to see him to settle two matters that I thought vital.

On the Dalgety flight I had carried a video camera for ITN, who used virtually everything I shot. They made 20 news bulletins totalling half an hour with my material, and later put together a half-hour programme which they sold to 25 countries around the world. I did not see a penny from these transactions, and resolved it would not happen like that again. I wanted copyright established on all moving pictures of the flight; news organisations would pay for these pictures, the price would be what the market would bear. The second lesson I had learned was in handling the photographs. I still do not know where most of the hundreds of pictures I took on the Dalgety flight, and sent back to London, are now. On the world flight, I wanted all pictures to be handled by Rex Features, a tough London-based family-owned news picture agency that lived or died on its judgement. If the pictures were no good, then Rex would not put them out. Newspapers would not use poor pictures anyway, just because they were given away free. I also wanted copyright established for them and for newspapers to pay the market price, which Rex could determine.

I secured, or thought I had secured, agreement from Newlyn that this was the way to handle this side of the story. It was not in writing; why would I need to do that? I saw direct benefits to GT Global, who would be saved tens of thousands of pounds it would otherwise have to spend getting pictures out to the media. The marketing budget, created separately from the operating budget, was supposed to be devoted almost entirely to getting pictures in front of editors. This would allow TV stations and newspapers, on the strength of the story and picture together, to choose whether or not to run with it.

At the time, before I signed a contract with GT Global, there seemed to be a meeting of minds between Newlyn and me. We apparently had the same enthusiasms, and he was full of praise for the detailed marketing outline I had produced. The only rueful comment he made was that I had left very little for him to do, because all my ideas looked workable. It only struck me later that he saw himself primarily as an ideas man – which other people would implement – and not as someone to implement my ideas. What I needed was a doer, rather than someone who saw himself as a creative thinker. It was a fatal mistake on my part. The whole project would have had a different conclusion had I not made the regrettable mistake of bringing him in.

Newlyn's first two resignations came within a week of each other, and seemed to be designed to gain control of the £600,000 marketing budget. Dallas had suggested we use a woman who had applied to him for a job, Alison Harper, on the media team, and I had brought in a woman from *London Financial News*, Taran Spiro. When this little team met to decide how it was going to operate weekly, Newlyn said nothing for a while, and then on some minuscule issue, I think it was how detailed the minutes should be, he resigned. He picked up his papers and walked out. I raced after him and spent 90 minutes convincing him to stay. He listened with a little smile on his face and, for a week, he stayed. At the next such meeting, again on a similar trivial issue, he resigned again. This time I did not race after him.

But, in fact, he was being paid as a freelance adviser by GT Global, working directly for Dallas. I found him the following Monday, with Dallas, proposing to change the name of my Flyer from 'The LGT Flyer' to the 'LGT Global Flyer', to the one person most likely to reject it, a chap called Hans-Martin Uehlinger. It is not worth going into the politics of the three and a half companies that made up the Liechtenstein Global Trust at that time, but each camp was preoccupied with its own identity, normal in any company. Uehlinger represented the private bank in Liechtenstein, BiL, and would naturally resist 'GT Global' being favoured over others. Newlyn, having no idea of the hornets' nest he could stir up, was trying to stamp his own identity on the flight.

It was not just that he was trying to make this change, it was the sneaky way he did it that made me angry. I wrote a long letter to Dallas, full of passion, outlining my fears about such behaviour, and saying Newlyn's resignation should be accepted. I followed this up by going to Dallas's house and appealing to him personally. This had exactly the opposite effect to that intended. Asked to choose between the two of us, Dallas chose Newlyn. As the project developed, Dallas came to rely more and more on Newlyn and less and less on me. I thought my 25 years in national television, radio and newspapers were better qualifications to measure up to Newlyn's judgement forged in a single year as a clerk with BBC News Information before he went into public relations. Dallas came to a different conclusion. In the months before Christmas, I twice tried to say I thought we were handling the marketing wrongly. Each time he cut in quickly: 'Without Simon, we are out of this project.' It meant that after the early days I never went to Dallas to talk things over, despite his position as GT Global's official co-ordinator for the flight. We drifted apart. In so small a team, he became Newlyn's man. Those two made the decisions about the marketing budget, and thousands of pounds were spent on items that had nothing to do with its principal object: getting pictures back. It was obviously Dallas's right to agree that, but it had a disruptive effect on how the flight developed.

During the autumn of 1997, Newlyn and I tried to work together. Charles set about learning how to get permission for us to fly through 25 countries, while Taran Spiro did not do my reputation as a people-picker any good by working an average of only three days a week, a situation that lasted until near Christmas when Dallas fired her. Newlyn brought in a protégé, a Ms Sarah Browse, a woman in her mid-30s with experience of working in PR, who promptly got up the noses of Charles and Alison with her condescending attitude to them. It was not a happy office, and at the sharp end I felt the wear and tear more than anyone. That got in the way of physical preparation for the flight.

There was another distraction around this time, the resignation of my financial adviser, David Patterson. I had known him for years and deeply admired him. He had been a moving force behind the success of Newton Investment Management, and I vividly remember a long letter he sent me from Shanghai, where he had fallen in love with Chinese culture. He was retired, but very shrewd, and I placed a high value on his opinion and advice. He knew as much about ATWIED as anyone in the world and was, I thought, very committed to it. But one day at lunch, just after the Countryside March on London, I said I would love to ride to hounds and he cut all ties with me that day. There was no possibility of discussion on the matter. I was beyond the pale.

I spent half my time in the office working on marketing ideas, or writing all I knew about the history of flight for brochures Newlyn was preparing. The other half of my time was spent at Keith's airfield on the Medway, discussing the equipment we needed to buy. To stay fit, I swam half a mile a day, Monday to Saturday. Andy Webb of Figaro Films produced a VNR – a video news release – to sell the story to production companies in the autumn international TV festivals, but we did not succeed in raising front money to film the flight as a documentary series, which I was determined to have made.

The Flyer itself was delivered at the end of September, and Keith and I planned a test flight to Iceland. But the weather in northern Scotland was so bad – a fishing boat was sunk by storms – that we headed south instead and had eight days' brilliant flying in early October through France and over the Mediterranean to Corsica, Elba and the north-west coast of Italy. We tested an in-flight fuel system and flew over the Alpes-Maritimes in the middle of the day, fully loaded and whacked around by thermals, which gave us confidence in the integrity of the aircraft.

In Corsica the thin tyres the aircraft was sold with were so poor they punctured seven times, and landing at Elba later in the day one of the tyres just blew out. Heading north to Albenga in Italy, we had an early taste of how bad bureaucrats can be when we were allowed to land and then banned, because we were a microlight, from taking off again. It needed an official letter from England confirming we were a registered aircraft before we got away three hours later. Down at 500 feet, crossing the big bay in which Nice is situated, Keith shouted: 'Whales!' And sure enough, a school was wallowing around beneath us, a wonderful sight. That evening I developed a crush on the small, tough and stylish proprietor of the Malaga Hotel in Carpentras, Marie-Joseph Bravo, and took her flying early in the morning to impress her. But she drove her car like a cowboy and was not easily impressed.

Heading up the Rhône Valley, in high winds and low clouds, we were at 500 feet above the ground when Keith, at the control bar, shouted again: 'Jesus! Jets!' I just saw a French fighter aircraft pass right under us at about 200 feet. We landed very quickly after that and, with bad weather forecast for days ahead, Alison Harper drove 300 miles to pick us up and trailer the Flyer home.

Interestingly, even on that short flight Keith and I had different attitudes to flying in poor weather. I was more 'go for it' than he was, but we felt good as a team. We were pleased to discover that our daily target of 300 miles was quite possible: in eight days we had exceeded it twice and in five of the six other days we could have exceeded it. As for my fear of heights, it had come and gone, especially in the mountains, but I had climbed to 4,000 feet without going into a fit of the gibbers. I used distractions, like the video or the stills camera, or played with the GPS [global positioning system], whenever the fear threatened to engulf me. Sometimes Keith must have wondered at the inconsequential conversations I started, which were really to divert the Djinn. I still liked turbulence better than still air.

Two friends in the City, Stephen Lewis and Roger Nightingale, put me up as a member of the Reform Club, as Phileas Fogg had been. Stephen hosted a reception at the Club on 21 October for ambassadors and air attachés from the countries through which we would fly. The Chinese air attaché, Colonel Li, was taken with the flight, but the most influential guest – we thought – was the Russian Ambassador Anatoly Adamishin, who looked over the route with me through Siberia and the Kamchatka Peninsula, and promised every help. It was a meeting I referred back to time and again on the flight, but we found no power in his promises. It did not help that Yuri Fokini took his place at the end of the year and we had not wined and dined him.

A week later we set off on our second big test-flight to Liechtenstein, to show Prince Philipp the aircraft. I flew the first day, via Headcorn and Le Touquet, to land just before dark in St Die, close to the French border with Germany. Our route took us along the Western Front of the First World War: Arras, Beaumont, Albert, Rheims, Verdun – names which were deeply moving to me. On the second day, we arrived at the airfield to find everything covered in frost. Keith took us over the mountains at 5,500 feet and into a giant valley, which we had to cross to reach the German mountains on the other side.

Until then I had coped with the height, but something about the day, the evocation of war and death, the cold, the clear blue sky, the huge distance we had to cover to the next mountains, all combined to put me into a dreadful state. I concealed my fear from Keith, but every second was madness, pure terror. I wanted to go down, but was so ashamed of the feelings that I could not ask Keith if he would reduce power. I did not know how I would endure it, when into my head popped the image of a young woman called Helen Dudley, and the fears went away.

I had written about Helen Dudley in the last of my 'Ruling Passions' pieces for the *London Financial News*. Helen worked for City Index, a spread-betting house, but her ruling passion was acting, and I had seen her in a musical which I had reviewed. Who knows why I chose to write about her rather than a dozen other characters in the Stock Exchange Dramatic and Operatic Society? The quality that I most admired, aside from her obvious beauty, was her courage: she had been rejected by acting schools five times, but had persisted until she was now playing leading parts. Once, at 21, playing Cinderella, a piece of furniture had hit her in the face five minutes before she was due on stage, leaving her with an enormous black eye. She saw herself in the mirror, laughed, burst into tears, then put make-up on and went out to play her part, and carried on playing it for the next two weeks under heaps of make-up. In an interview, in which I thought we might drink a glass of wine together, we ended up sharing three bottles and talking our heads off. She was young enough to be my daughter, and we both knew all about men of a certain age and actresses, but we became friends. The combination of beauty and courage was extremely attractive. I had other girls as friends at the time and I did not know why it was Helen that popped up to rescue me. What is more, I did not want to know. If she worked, I was deeply grateful.

It was not like the Dalgety flight. I did not need, in my mind, to make love to Helen. It was the memory of little things that soothed my fear, the way she put her hand through her hair, walked through a doorway, handed me a glass of wine, disagreed with something I said, innocent things. She was cross-grained, but all interesting people are cross-grained; you are never sure how they will react. I saw her as classical woman and I brought her image into my own personal battlefield, the way bomber pilots used to paint ladies on their fuselages or, even earlier, sailors carved the images of women on the bows of their ships. It was an historical throwback – like those early films about good and evil, where people put a cross in front of Satan. Over that high valley leading into Germany, I first used the image of Helen and she banished the Djinn.

Keith flew brilliantly into Liechtenstein in appalling weather, low cloud and fog, and we followed a river to stay over low ground between mountains. We flew every day for eight days, a minor miracle in late October. I used Helen's image on all the high flights, including one to 9,000 feet in which I was at the control bar and she was the only force between me and madness. The Prince came flying and was a model passenger, and we stocked up on photos and video of the Flyer to use for publicity, all, as it turned out, uselessly. When we found out microlights were technically banned in Liechtenstein, which is legally part of Switzerland, the Prince laughed and said that if I went to prison, he would come with me.

On the way back to England with a terrific following wind, I elected to land again at St Die and we were trashed out of the sky by turbulence, having forgotten our injunction: never fly in mountains in wind. When I took off again, I climbed to 5,000 feet in washing-machine conditions until I broke through to smooth air again, and I refused to come down from that height for the rest of the day. The trashing had the effect of allowing me to live with heights, though Helen was always first reserve.

I told Helen when I got home about the odd way she had saved my life. It is hard to say if she was complimented. She did not sling me out the door. I later gave her a Blue Peter badge as a token of innocence. She gave me a little plastic teddy bear.

I did not see much of Paul Loach, but one day he called me into his office and asked me if he wanted to change anything on the Flyer, when would it get expensive? I said that we started filming in Malaga for the main video news release in the middle of November, and that would cost £25,000. He just smiled. The mystery was solved on 15 November when he told me Prince Philipp had put the asset management side of the business up for sale and was looking for a buyer.

'This does not affect our sponsorship of you,' said Paul, 'except it's no longer the LGT Flyer, but the GT Global Flyer, so get a new sail and change the markings on the trike.'

That meant we were now attached to one of the companies inside the Liechtenstein Global Trust, GT Global, whose manager in London was Mike Webb. He and Dallas became the main decision-makers, under Paul, who threw himself into handling the sale. An eventual buyer did emerge, an American company called Amvesco, and the price tag was $1.3 billion.

I did not care how I got the backing from a sponsor, so long as I did.

We changed logos, fitted a new sail and spent two weeks in Spain doing all the work again that we had done in Liechtenstein, providing pictures for Andy Webb to make the definitive VNR2 to market the flight worldwide. This we produced in English, Japanese, Mandarin, Cantonese and German, and in the various broadcasting formats used across the world. I had written the blueprint of a plan to supply television stations on our route with a library of moving pictures, free for the period of the flight, so they could cover the story without having to send their own cameramen out.

Keith and I had our first incident on the Malaga shoot; we were climbing away at 200 feet when a water pipe blew off and showered the engine with anti-freeze, but I landed the Flyer safely. We flew at

8,000 feet in the Sierra Nevadas – Helen worked very hard that day – and collected stunning shots low over the sea, or chased across lakes in the mountains. The camera team on a second trike, Graham Slater as pilot and Barrie Bayes on camera, worked very well together, though Bayes was a prickly character. He spent one evening at dinner contradicting everything I said, maintaining that 'someone has to keep you in line'. Oddly, he thought it should be him.

That was the period when I first came to know Sarah Browse, sent out by Newlyn specifically to get still shots of Keith and me wearing GT Global logos, who ruined two flying suits by insisting on super-gluing the badges to us so we flew with them. Keith took a shine to her and she to him. I felt differently.

She was, inadvertently, the cause of Newlyn's third resignation. I was in the office after the Malaga shoot, doing my expenses, when Sarah came down from accounts, moaning that she had run up expenses in Spain and she could not get them paid. At this time Newlyn arrived for work. Christmas was coming, and even if I did not like her I did not see why she should suffer because she could not get paid; she and Newlyn had made their own freelance arrangements with GT Global over pay.

'How much is it?' I asked.

'It's £200,' she said.

'Well, I'll pay it to you now, if you like, and when you get it you can pay me back,' I said.

'That's not the fucking point!' screamed Newlyn suddenly, startling the rest of us. 'That's not the fucking point!' And for the next five minutes, still in his overcoat, he shrieked about how he had not been paid for six weeks, gibbering that he was supporting the project, that it was unfair and I had betrayed him (I never worked out why). He was beside himself with rage. He seemed completely out of control.

Then, with one final shriek, 'I resign!', he picked up his bag and rushed out, slamming the door.

Sarah looked shocked.

The door opened again and Paul Loach came in.

'What's going on?' he asked.

I was embarrassed. How does one explain such behaviour? I tried not to put any blame on Newlyn. Paul told me it was making a very bad impression with the rest of the company. But how did my offering to loan Sarah Browse £200 precipitate Newlyn's resignation?

Later that day, I had a furious note from Dallas, demanding that we instantly show him the accounts and a detailed explanation, chapter and verse, of where we were with permission to enter every single country we were to fly through. Alison had the full accounts in a few minutes, while Charles sighed and set about spending an extra half day answering this note. I wrote to Dallas, explaining how Newlyn's third resignation had come about. I had no reply. I understand the delay in Newlyn's pay was rectified. He turned up at the office only once in the next 15 days over the Christmas period. This is not to say he was not working, because he was, morning, noon and night. He lived the project. It was, I thought, his way back into the big time if he could ingratiate himself with GT Global. He was just not working with me, the originator of the idea and the main pilot.

The public launch date was to be 7 January 1998, and Keith and I were to bring the Flyer to the Tower Hotel, next to Tower Bridge, for a photo shoot. When I saw where the Flyer was to be rigged, outdoors next to the bridge, Keith and I both felt it was too exposed to the elements. I wrote a careful note to Newlyn at his home, saying I thought we needed someone to look after the aircraft when we were not standing by it, because she could easily get blown over by the wind. I suggested a friend of Keith's as a guard, Jim Hill, and thought he should be paid from the marketing budget as it was a press conference. I felt I was treading on eggs, desperate not to provoke another resignation.

Newlyn wrote an extremely rude note back, telling me that if I thought a guard was necessary then I should pay, but he was not authorising GT Global's money to pay for one.

I was rude in return, telling him I had a duty under the contract not to risk the Flyer needlessly and he wasn't getting her unless he provided a guard.

I went in the office on 30 December and found an e-mail message from Dallas. It was a sort of New Year's present.

The note said that because of my arrogant behaviour, he had talked things over with Paul Loach and Mike Webb: GT Global was pulling the sponsorship.

3. THE VIRGIN CHALLENGE AND

THE LILIENTHAL DREAM

The nine days between receiving that message from Dallas and sitting down with him and Mike Webb were as bleak as any I have ever spent. The period covered the public launch of the project, which lost its impact because of *faux*-sophisticated arguments put forward by Newlyn that journalists do not respect embargoes. Stories for general releases often go out under an embargo – not to be used before a certain time – to allow every part of the media a fair crack at them. Sometimes embargoes are broken, but never when they are imposed by the main source of news, because we would starve that part of the media of future news. So, when Newlyn allowed the story to break without an embargo, it dribbled out in a messy way. It broke six days ahead of launch on a local TV station, Meridien TV, and then featured two days later on Sky TV and the *Sunday Telegraph*, both contacts of mine who had been prepared to accept an embargo. But if there was none, why should they wait for the official launch?

I went through this period in a daze, continually calculating whether or not I could make the journey with the money I already had. I had been spending it for the past five months as if the remaining third would be paid. What if I had not enough money? I had, in the budget, a 10 per cent contingency but, based on past experience, I knew I was going to overspend that. Could we pull our belts in and go it alone? The way the contract was written and the frivolous way Dallas had proposed to remove the sponsorship, made it unlikely there was any legal case for me to hand the money back.

I told Keith we had problems, but that the flight was going ahead anyway. It would not have affected him, unless I cut his wages along with my own. He said repeatedly that money was not a factor for him.

We were very busy preparing for the launch. It was a weird form of limbo, going on as if the event had momentum and could not be stopped. Newlyn did, in fact, spend money to bring Jim Hill up to London to look after the Flyer, and weather conditions were so bad we really needed him. From then on, Jim was hired as watchdog wherever we took the aircraft. It was a sensible precaution, even if it had precipitated Dallas's ultimatum. I saw Dallas at the press conference at the Tower Hotel, in the company of Paul Loach. It all went slickly and Dallas was full of compliments, but no word about pulling the sponsorship. I could not understand it.

Our story was in competition that day with the roofs of some houses being blown off by a hurricane in Lewes, and our challenge was deemed less important. Sky TV, which had featured us the previous Sunday and run it hourly at least five times, because of Barrie Bayes' beautiful pictures, came back live to cover the launch. BBC network TV News did not think we were a story, and nor did ITN.

But an event occurred two days before the launch that changed everything; it may even have affected Dallas. I heard from Sky TV on Monday, 5 January, that Will Whitehorn, head of corporate affairs for Richard Branson, was chasing me. One of Virgin's press officers, Alison Bonny, arranged for me to see him the following day, without a reason being given. I phoned Whitehorn to find out what he wanted. He had seen stunning pictures of the Flyer on Sky TV and made me an offer that once upon a time I would have nearly died for.

'We want to sponsor you,' he said.

'You can't,' I said. 'I am already sponsored.' (Why should he need to know about Dallas's threat?)

'Who's that? We didn't see any sponsor mentioned,' said White-horn, sharply.

'They're called GT Global, and they are a rival of Virgin Direct in the financial products business. It's on the top of our wing.' (Upside down, because of another of Newlyn's wilful decisions.)

'Anyway,' I said, 'you turned me down twice.'

A longish pause.

'I remember you. If you had come back again, we would have sponsored you.'

I thought that highly unlikely. Who ever went back to a potential sponsor when they had been turned down twice?

'Right,' he said, 'We'll take you on. We'll race you.'

I did not think he was serious, but told him we were leaving in ten weeks. I wanted to work with him, though, because at the time we were looking for a Boeing 747 from whose wing I wished to take off with the Flyer, and I had seen a Virgin Jumbo at Gatwick which would have been perfect. I put the suggestion to White-horn.

'We might consider it if you began the whole flight around the world from our wing.'

Not bloody likely! I thought. The wing flight had got to be done solo, with a light load, not with two pilots and all the gear of a world flight. It would also look on television as if we were doing the flight with Virgin's permission. We tussled amicably over this matter. And over the next two weeks, while Richard Branson was winning his libel action over the National Lottery bribe offer, I sent letters to Whitehorn making the case for a wing take-off. Two letters were faxed on 9 January and another on 15 January; Whitehorn was not interested. I thought his threat was just one of those things, the way any powerful person reacted to being thwarted, and nothing to worry about.

Richard Branson had, by then, seen his latest attempt at balloon-ing around the world come to nothing when his envelope was blown away in Morocco by a gust of wind, and though he had ordered a new envelope, weather conditions were not right for another attempt. The press had been teasing him, in the cruel thoughtless way it does, about these matters. In a lot of the interviews I did about my own flight, I defended Branson at every opportunity. I admire him and sympathise with what drives him. He had once said that if you look at *Top of the Pops* on TV, and turn down the sound, the dancers all look like loonies, but that is because you can't hear the music. He could hear the music, as I could, and as others could not. The fact that he was rich did not detract from the dangers he ran, and his life was no less at risk than if he was as poor as me.

I told Paul Loach about the Virgin threat to race us. He asked for an honest assessment of their chances. I thought they would pick a three-axis aircraft with a big engine, much faster than my Pegasus 912. Virgin would not be restricted to the long route I had chosen around the world, influenced by Phileas Fogg; they could go straight across Russia, miss out San Francisco, and knock thousands of miles off the route I was committed to take. But, despite their vast experience of mainstream aviation, they knew little about the New

Aviation of microlighting, and if they built a CFM Shadow, for example, it took much longer to be completed than a weight-shift trike. The obvious people for them to involve were Richard Meredith-Hardy, who had flown a microlight from London to Cape Town and later become world champion, or Colin Bodill, who had just returned to England after taking my London–Sydney record, doing the flight in 49 days whereas I had taken 59. Ours is a small community, the entry of a giant like Branson would set tongues wagging somewhere. We checked and found none of the obvious moves had been made. I told Paul there was, at most, a 30 per cent chance of being beaten and if any threat emerged, I was prepared to leave within a couple of days.

'So, carry on as normal, then,' he said.

On 9 January I met Dallas and Mike Webb. They said they wanted to sort out my appalling relations with Newlyn, and claimed they would have a similar meeting with him, separately. I said I had no confidence in him and had told Dallas that last September. Dallas and I had an argument. The Virgin offer hung mutely between us. I asked him what had happened to his threat to pull the sponsorship?

'It was to teach you a lesson,' he said.

The lesson, apparently, was that I had to accept that if Newlyn wanted the Flyer at press conferences, the expense of guarding the aircraft was mine. I did learn a lesson from the experience. In passing, he revealed that Newlyn had resigned, a fourth time, on this issue, but when Dallas asked if he was really suggesting we look for another media adviser, the resignation was hurriedly withdrawn.

I look back on the whole period, which should have been exciting and full of expectation, as a dreadful nightmare, and could not wait to be rid of it and out in free air. There, Keith and I would be tested, and the only thing I could lose was my life.

By now we were traipsing around studios and giving interviews, an experience that gave Keith a deep distaste for the media. Every day that I could, I got away from the London office, with its serial resignations and threats, and joined Keith in his contemplation. We hired a four-man dinghy, bought survival suits, two Skyforce GPS's, fixed cameras to the wings, lights to the front, and Keith checked everything from top to bottom. We were ready to go long before the window opened on 15 March. The absolute deadline for leaving was 3 April, to avoid the monsoon season in Bangladesh.

During this period there were dozens of initiatives taken that led nowhere. Aside from flying off the wing of a Jumbo, we wanted to land and take off from two barges on the Thames, Newlyn's one original contribution to the flight. It would graphically illustrate the short take-off and landing capabilities of the Flyer. We approached Amtrak in the US about getting a special train to follow us across the US on Fogg's route. We tried to see if the American soaps, like *Frasier* or *Seinfeld*, would write us into their script. All were no-gos.

There was a time-consuming search for an imaginative place to take off from in London. We identified four candidates: The Mall, Horseguards Parade, Hyde Park and the Millennium site. Televisually, we wanted to leave from somewhere that was instantly London, rather than an airfield on the edge of the city. The obvious place was The Mall, right behind the Reform Club, so, in effect, Keith and I could stroll down Duke of York steps into our already-rigged aircraft, stop the traffic for two minutes and be airborne, leaving London by the helicopter route down the Thames. For a while Horseguards Parade was a goer with the Royal Parks Authority, but then they said no. We actually got down to detailed planning on a Hyde Park take-off, with agreement everywhere except within the aviation bureaucracy, the Special Rules Group, the SRG.

In the search for political backing to overcome this resistance, I found support from MPs like Home Office Minister Mike O'Brien and Fiona McTaggart. We had an enthusiastic champion in Richard Threlfall, a personal assistant to the Deputy Prime Minister, John Prescott, who was also Minister of Transport. But none of them had the power to overcome the earnest refusals of the SRG's Robb Metcalfe, who was able successfully to defend the capital against the dire risks poised by our early-morning take-off within central London. A last-minute attempt at getting off the Millennium site, where we could look down the river and actually see the edge of the London Control Zone, marked by the Thames Barrier, was also successfully blocked by Metcalfe.

We ended up with the best we could get, Brooklands, once a famous motor-racing course, now an aviation museum.

There was a great deal of idealism in the way I planned the flight, which had appealed to Paul Loach and Prince Philipp at my original presentation, but which in all the in-fighting that was going on had been submerged. Keith and I felt we were striving for something pure in the adventure, without compromise, a throwback to the 1920s and before. We want to be on our own when we set off, without a chase aeroplane. Aesthetically, a trike is a very physical aircraft, much more so than a three-axis aircraft with aerilons, elevators and a rudder. As pilots, we were the aircraft. We were attracted by the physicality of flight. There was a wimpishness about the 1990s that we rejected, where the perception of the risk we were taking was so enormous that it took a clear-sighted man, like Paul Loach, to see the risk for what it was. It was far smaller, so long as we kept our nerve, than it appeared. Paul saw the flight as an allegory for investing in emerging markets. For many, it was too dangerous to even contemplate. But make the right decisions and the rewards would be large. Backing my flight took a lot more money than any other microlight flight had won from a single sponsor, but in the sponsorship game it was small potatoes. Yet the rewards, in publicity, in association with aspirations of courage, could be high. Even the PR 'pair from hell', when they were not making mischief, seemed affected by this purity of intention.

There was one big test-flight we had left to do, linking the two great nineteenth-century aviation pioneers together, Yorkshire's Sir George Caley and Berlin's Otto Lilienthal. Our form of aviation, the New Aviation, went back to these pioneers, rather than the Wright Brothers. We knew where the Wright Brothers led to, jumbo jets, Concorde and space flight and all the stifling safety regulations that now burden mainstream aviation. When hang-gliding started on 23 May 1971, in southern California, the 14 flyers there that day were celebrating what would have been the hundred and twenty-third birthday of Otto Lilienthal. The longest distance they flew was 196 feet, the longest time in the air was 11 seconds. Now, in a direct ancestor to the rogallo at the First Lilienthal Meet, we were proposing to fly around the world.

Otto Lilienthal had died at the age of 48 on a wing he was testing near Berlin. He had made more than 2,000 flights on his foldable wings in the five years between 1891 and 1896 and covered distances of up to a quarter of a mile. His achievements broke the mind-set of the world; before Lilienthal, people said, *if* man could fly, after him they said, *when*. It was his death that set off Wilbur and Orville Wright, bicycle makers in Dayton, Ohio, on their own aerial experiments which led to the first powered flight. But Lilienthal was the true father of flight.

Lilienthal had paid tribute to the work done by an English pioneer, the baronet Sir George Caley, in the 1840s. Caley thought the 'vaulted arch', the cambered wing, was the key to flight – as was subsequently proved with the aircraft we fly today. Keith and I planned to carry out a pilgrimage from Caley's home in Brompton, North Yorkshire, to Berlin, in February, a month before leaving on the world flight. It entailed flying over the North Sea in the middle of winter, the bomber's route to Berlin over northern Holland. It was, in our eyes, a Wagnerian gesture, washing our shields and cleaning our spears, a dedication to the original warrior-king, before setting off on our own adventure.

With Jim Hill acting as sweeper, we towed the Flyer to Yorkshire on 6 February, staying overnight in Nottingham to hear about the experiences of Colin Bodill, newly returned to England after setting the London–Sydney record. Listening to the nuances of Colin's conversation, I did not feel he was satisfied and that he would be following our progress restlessly.

At dinner the following night, I listened to Newlyn and Browse trying to corrupt Keith with the idea that they could make him famous, and that this was as much his project as mine. All he needed to do, they said, was put himself in their hands. Keith said he was not interested and stonewalled his way through. But looking back now, I wonder if the machinations of that dreadful pair had some effect on his mind.

We stayed at Brompton Hall, Sir George Caley's original mansion, now a home for disturbed boys, and set off in blustery weather on 9 February, to make the much-feared crossing of the North Sea. We were expecting dark thunderous clouds and that we would have to hang on for grim death – 'gorilla-grip' conditions. What we got was smooth easy air, the cloud below us fading away, a ground speed of over 80 mph and we landed in eastern Holland after four hours in the air. Keith flew us to Berlin the following day, and we hung around a satellite airfield called Schonhagen for a couple of days before flying into Templehof Airport on Friday, 13 February, in rain and mist.

Visiting Lilienthal's man-made hill in Lichterfelte, a suburb to the south-west of Berlin, was a moving experience. Here was the grass he had walked on, there was an imaginary landing place. We rigged the Flyer and climbed to the top, now a shrine to his memory, and looked west. I dearly wished I could show him the aircraft we proposed to take around the world. Had he come back, on this the 150th anniversary of his birth, he would have looked at a jumbo jet in awe and wonderment, but he would smile with familiarity at our own craft and see us for what we were, his children.

Later, putting flowers on his grave, touching the bronze cover, I felt close to the spirits of two unusual men, giants of aviation, without whom the history of the twentieth century would have been different. Flight would have come, but without these two men it would have progressed at a later time and in a different way.

Back in England, I was paid the second tranche of GT Global money, and, tidying up our affairs, I was driving home from Keith's airfield on Thursday evening, 12 March, when my mobile phone rang, and I heard a smooth, charming voice which I vaguely recognised.

'It's Rory McCarthy, and I have a proposition to put to you. Would you delay your flight until May? Richard Branson wants to make a race of it. It would be a much bigger story if he is involved than if you do it on your own. If you agree the delay, we will offer a million-pound prize for the first microlight to fly around the world.'

We had two initial phone conversations, that evening and on Saturday morning. Rory told me that Branson had suddenly been taken with the idea of a microlight flight around the world, having felt 'humiliated' by the reaction to the failure of his world balloon flight. Wherever he was in the world, he phoned McCarthy 'six times a day', urging him to make things happen. McCarthy had taken full charge of the project three weeks before he called me, and ordered three Shadow microlights, the same type of aircraft as I had flown to Australia, but with clipped wings – to go faster – and special dispensation for Rotax 912 engines. They would be capable of cruising at more than 100 mph, compared to the 60 mph our own Flyer did. One pilot was to be Rory himself – he owned five aircraft and was very experienced – while the other was to be a hotshot US female fighter pilot called Jackie Parker. A third aircraft was to be spare, in case they smashed one up (Rory wiped the undercarriage off his Shadow on his first flight).

Richard Branson would not make the whole microlight flight around the world, but hop in and out in high-profile places like London, Hong Kong, San Francisco and New York. Otherwise, the pilots would fly alone, or perhaps have other celebrities – Ruby Wax was mentioned – to give the media something new to write about. The million-pound prize was to be put up in the name of the race co-ordinator, a man called Mike Kendrick.

'But I should tell you, Brian,' said Rory. 'We have no intention of losing. Our aircraft are capable of going around the world in 30 days.'

McCarthy told me to keep the offer secret, which I rejected, but I did not spread the news far. I wrote a note to Paul, Dallas and Newlyn, and kept Keith fully appraised of what was happening. Dallas wanted to reject them out of hand, but I argued that you could not do that to someone as rich as Branson. I thought Rory wanted a delay because they were having problems getting their aircraft ready in time – in fact they had over-heating difficulties with the big engine – and there was an implied threat anyway. Rory had said: 'If you break this news, Richard will get really angry and throw money at the project. He'll stamp all over you.'

They were not bound to take the route we were taking and they had lots of clout within mainstream aviation, so getting permission to fly through various countries would be easier for them than for us. Being in the professional aviation business, they would know better than us the right man to go to in Russia to get permission to fly across the country.

The initiative to make the two phone calls came from Rory alone. But the meeting I had with Rory at his offices in West Kensington on Monday, 16 March, was – said Rory – sanctioned by Branson. I took Dallas with me and Andy Webb, who wanted to make a film of my flight but had not raised the front money from either BBC, ITV or Channel 4, or any of the foreign media – no one wanted to take the risk. Andy, whose recent programmes about the Grimaldi and Gucci families had attracted widespread praise, thought that a documentary about a race with Branson would attract a lot of production money. If a deal could be struck with Branson, he was in favour of it.

In the discussions, Kendrick's prize of a million *pounds* changed to a million *dollars*. Rory said that if we delayed until the middle of May, we could have a ten-day start on Branson's flight. I asked what he proposed doing about the monsoons in Bangladesh, and he cited – absurdly – El Niño. We agreed not to play any dirty tricks on each other, such as Branson using his influence with the aviation authorities to refuse me permission. Rory asked, in return, for me not to portray the race as the big rich giant trampling over two ordinary chaps, but I said that was the truth about what was happening and not a dirty trick.

Rory was someone I warmed to, an engaging character who did not seem to be able to stop himself admitting the truth. He said that the world microlight flight was just a game for Branson, 'whereas for you, it's blood!'. He also worried out loud that he might be 'past it for this sort of thing. I'm 37, you know', which caused suppressed titters from Dallas (39), Andy (49) and me (55).

I told Rory there was a factor in this 'race' he had not considered, that was Colin Bodill, who still had his aircraft in Australia. There was nothing to stop Colin leaping into his microlight and flying back up Indonesia and on to the northern hemisphere route around the world. He had been offered £70,000 in sponsorship to continue around the world. Flying for a million-dollar prize would galvanise him.

We told Rory at the end of the meeting that we could consider his proposition, but it was never on. Dallas was obviously against it, but I would not have delayed for the chance to win a prize of ten million dollars, never mind one million. When Rory phoned, three days later, to ask if we had made a decision, I told him the answer was no.

'Tell me one thing,' he said. 'You don't have to, but tell me. When do you propose going?'

'In five days' time,' I said.

He swore, and said he would not be able to catch us. But I did not believe that, either. One slip by us and the Branson challenge could come roaring into life. Sadly, it corrupted my whole flight and returned to haunt me at least three times in the subsequent months.

That week there was also a crucial meeting with Paul Loach, Dallas and Newlyn. Having watched the videotape be handled by Newlyn in a different way to our agreement, I was beside myself with rage at the casual way he shafted the agreement to handle photographs through Rex Features. Newlyn wanted to give the pictures away.

Paul Loach said: 'Never mind. You should really concentrate on the flight itself,' and I resolved to do so. My enthusiasm for taking photographs, and getting them back, waned. From that day to this, except when absolutely necessary, I shunned Newlyn. I cannot think of anyone I detest more.

I was also fearful about the conflicting demands for videotape between Newlyn and the news organisation, and Andy Webb and his documentary. Dallas said that the newsworthiness of the adventure had more value to GT Global than the documentary and would therefore take priority. There was no discussion.

A television documentary might not get made anyway. While I bought cameras and video stock for use in flight, a vital element was shots from an outside source. Andy Webb wanted to visit a number of cities on our flight – Muscat, Calcutta, Hong Kong, for example – and conduct interviews, but he had not the money to fund this. I asked GT Global if they would be interested. They said no. I asked Andy how much money he needed to ensure that we at least had a story, if there really was a story in the flight, at the end of it.

'We could do it for £40,000,' he said.

I tried to interest some of the rich and powerful men I knew in the City in putting up this money for a share in the equity, but they said it was an area they knew nothing about, so no thanks. So I talked it over with my daughter and with Keith, emphasising the risk that was being taken, then put the money up myself. Keith knew what was at stake for me, because I was risking everything, including my children's inheritance. I told Andy I wanted no editorial interference with the documentary, and he would get none from me. But I could see no other way to get it made.

Our original choice to open the window on departure was 15 March, and we wanted a good day with a west wind blowing. But the project had become so big, with so many people involved, that the purity of making an aviation choice went out the window. The first seven days after 15 March were vetoed because of the media attention around Gordon Brown's UK Budget speech, so Keith and I spent days looking at good weather conditions – at least in England – when we might have gone and done a big first day. The key was getting over the Alps. After the second day on the flight, we knew that we would be at the mercy of the weather anyway.

The choice of 24 March emerged from all the competing days, essentially selected by Newlyn, whose PR genius had not realised that it was also the day of the Oscar results for breakfast TV, so our story was competing with Hollywood. My friend Kay Burley of Sky TV's *Sunrise* programme put up a spirited fight against that departure date, but lost because of the momentum that built up around it. A key factor was that it suited our backers, Paul Loach and Prince Philipp, who had built their diaries around Newlyn's suggested date.

On Monday, 23 March, having said goodbye to friends, Keith and I loaded everything into the GT Global Flyer and flew her to Brooklands. We rendezvoused with our cameraship pilot, Graham Slater, exactly on time, 12.55 p.m., south of our destination, and landed at Brooklands. We were overloaded with video cameras, stills cameras, video tape and stills stock, a computer, clothes for all climates – despite paring everything to the bone. That afternoon we did a number of media interviews, and in the evening, dressed in black tie and dinner jackets, took a car to Pall Mall and the Reform Club where Phileas Fogg had started his own journey around the world in 80 days.

Among my guests – I had recently been made a member – were Prince Philipp, Paul Loach, Dallas McGillivray and friends including Kay Burley, Moira Thomson, Graham Slater, our cameraman Barrie Bayes, Brian Winterflood (from the charity, Remedi, which benefits from the flight), my son James and Stephen Lewis, who had put me up for club membership and to whom I entrusted my last will and testament. Afterwards, not wisely, Kay took the Prince, Keith and me off to Langan's Brasserie for dinner, and it was late when we made the long taxi ride back to the Oatlands Hotel in Weybridge to be close to our take-off point. It was hardly the sort of thing men in training should do before a long flight, but there were lots of precedents, including Charles Lindbergh's sleepless night before the Atlantic crossing in 1927.

We could hardly wait to get away.

4. RACING ACROSS EUROPE TO CYPRUS

In media terms, the departure was a gang-bang. There were a lot of TV crews, and friends turned up as well, for whom we had less time than we wanted to say goodbye. They included Moira Thomson and her sister Julie, neither of them renowned as early birds, James and my ex-wife, my sister-in-law, Jeannie, Peter MacNamara from France, Mike Foster, Helen Dudley and her friend Sue. There were two surprises: Flossie Waite, aged eight, eldest daughter of BBC presenter John Waite, made a pretty speech thanking me for introducing her father to her mother ('otherwise I would not be here'); and the band of the RAF Regiment marched around and their leader said some nice things about us.

It was a good day to fly; blue skies, little wind, good visibility, but what wind there was blew from the east, the direction we had to travel. Paul Loach, Prince Philipp, Mike Webb and Dallas McGillivray saw us off, then tore across to Fairoaks Airport to pick up a helicopter. They set off for Headcorn airfield, where 30 microlights carrying journalists, GT Global VIPs and also my daughter Jade were waiting to accompany us across the Channel. I knew most of the pilots, but not Phil Good, who was later to be involved in an accident at Le Touquet. Keith and I circled above Headcorn, with Graham Slater and Barrie Bayes in tow, filming us, while those below took off. The last to go were the GT Global bosses newly arrived by helicopter – Dave Simpson took the Prince and John Hunt took Paul Loach – and then we punted off to Le Touquet, our first airfield landing in France.

It was a fantastic sight, dozens of microlights arriving by different routes across the water to Cap Gris Nez, the nearest point in France to England. Keith and I felt slightly harassed as faster microlights, with cameramen on board zoomed in to get their photos. We were three hours on the ground at Le Touquet, instead of 30 minutes, saying hello to the media, goodbye to my daughter and my friends and taxiing to the threshhold, still accompanied by our film crew. It was here we had a puncture, and while mending it, Phil Good had his accident, which we vaguely heard about. Good had started his engine for the return leg to England but hadn't realised that the throttle was open. He crashed into a plate-glass window and had suffered severe injuries. We sweated to get the repair done quickly, took off, and spent the next five hours in the air, fighting another headwind, trying to get to Frederichshaven in Germany. It was not possible, with a ground speed often below 50 mph.

It was thermic for much of the afternoon, but not vicious. I had to work for a living, gorilla-gripping the bar. We had a close encounter with two jet aircraft, as startled to see us as we were to see them. It got very cold as we flew into the dusk, and we set our sights on St Die as the day's goal. We were 1,100 feet up, surrounded by small mountains, and we finally landed a few minutes before total darkness. Despite punctures and other delays, we had spent eight hours in the air, averaging 50 mph, we were tired but not exhausted as we put our aircraft in the hangar. After all, we had flown the same distance – 400 miles – as Richard Branson did on his attempt to go around the world in a balloon the previous year, and we were still in the game with 80 days left to fly.

On day two, 25 March, we were again looking at fantastic weather, clear skies and high pressure, the perfect day to cross the Alps into Italy. It was Keith's turn to fly, so I was crammed in the back with a video camera on one knee, a GPS on the other, wearing moon boots and full kit against the cold. The temperature on the ground was - 3°C; we knew it would be very cold at 6,000 feet, where Graham Slater's hands became so cold he couldn't feel them and had to land on a road just to get the feeling back. We flew to Constance and landed, but it was not microlight-friendly, and nor was Frederichshaven, so Keith followed Slater to Kempten, 155 miles from St Die. It proved difficult to find the actual field under all the snow, Graham went in first (Barrie knew the area) and we followed in.

'I'm not sure we can get off this,' said Keith.

We refuelled, filed a flight plan to Trento in Italy on the advice of locals and taxied out to take off. It proved difficult and dangerous. The snow constantly slowed up the Flyer, just below flying speed, and though Keith virtually stood on the foot throttle, we covered more than three-quarters of the grass runway before we were in the air, and then only a few feet up and just off the stall. Keith managed to gather flying speed and had to turn right to avoid a hill and fly under tree height around trees to get us to safety.

We were accompanied into the Alps by Graham and Barrie and a local German pilot who showed us the way. Keith took the Flyer up steadily to 9,000 feet, while I sat in the back and marvelled about how my fear of heights was missing. Conditions were smooth, but we crawled along at 45 mph. After an hour we said goodbye to our companions and they turned away to go back to Kempten. We were truly on our own. It was a moment we had looked forward to.

Keith opted to dodge around the higher peaks, rather than fly over them, and the highest we climbed was to 9,500 feet, picking our way through terrific country. After crossing one peak, the air became very unstable and, despite the lack of clouds, it got frightening. Keith muttered every now and again from the front, battling against a live control bar and trying to keep the Flyer on course. I became detached, not allowing myself the thought that I was suffering too. It was not too bad north of Innsbrook, but heading south over the Brenner Pass, Keith used the term 'gorilla-grip country', the first time I had ever heard him use this term. We endured, heartened by noting that we finally had a tail wind, and our ground speed shot up to 80 mph, while indicated air speed was just 62 mph.

Having covered 150 miles, we arrived at Trento to be told we were not welcome. Microlights seemed to have the same position in the aviation world that black people once had in European society. Some firemen arranged hangarage, while I battled away with the aviation authorities. I woke in the night to write my journal and heard a couple nearby making love, and I thought idly that the noises women make seemed to be the same in any language.

On day three, 26 March, I had my usual call from Kay Burley of Sky TV, who was now featuring the flight daily on her *Sunrise* programme. We got away at 8.40 a.m., climbing into clear, cold, beautiful air, between mountains, heading south-east for Forli, our first legal stop in Italy. It took us two and a half hours to fly 130 miles. We had to make a number of dog legs to avoid air-space around large airfields, but we noticed to our delight that our ground speed was improving. At Forli, a huge runway with little traffic near the Adriatic Sea, they were kind, quick and efficient. We took on a full load of petrol for the next long run, 310 miles to Bari in southern Italy, and climbed away at 1.30 p.m. local time. The Flyer was reluctant to leave the ground because of the heavy load. I settled in at 1,500 feet, made it to the coast and sped south with a following wind, at speeds up to 80 knots.

After three and a half hours' flying, I took the Flyer inland, in contact with an excitable air-traffic controller at a military base, demanding constant news of my bearing and height. Keith thought the big lumps of rock, up to 3,500 feet, that made up the spur on the heel of Italy, were likely to produce dreadful turbulence. The rotor felt like a washing-machine when I flew into it, and we had ten minutes of extremely difficult flying, while Keith kept saying 'Christ!' every ten seconds, barely able to keep his hands off the back wires to give me help.

We landed at Bari in a crosswind of 16 knots, with gusts up to 25 knots. I wrestled the Flyer out of the sky and was very relieved when we got down. Taxiing to the airport terminal, we were told to wait until the following day to refuel and that there was no hangarage available. When we stopped it was shocking to discover how strong and violent the wind was. As I was struggling to get out of the Flyer past all the wires and cameras, she was hit by a huge gust of wind and the left wing lifted. Keith was distracted, I shouted, he grabbed the wires and for ten frightening seconds we fought against being overturned and cartwheeling across the grass. It was touch and go: nothing seemed to have an effect. But we were successful, we removed ourselves carefully from the aircraft, all the while holding the wing into wind and grabbing it whenever it lifted wildly. If we had gone over, it would have been a repeat of what had happened to me on the Dalgety flight to Australia, ten years previously.

Getting the Flyer safely into a hangar, after a lot of argument, without wrecking her, was a particular relief. We heard reports of a great storm in Greece and a squall front between us and Corfu, our next destination.

On day four, we had our first emergency: we were going out over open sea when all our communications equipment shut down. We shouldn't really have been in the air anyway. What was described as the worst storm in living memory had struck Greece, with winds uprooting 5,000 trees in the Athens area. There was flooding at Marathon, one of our target airfields, and the computer system at the Met Office was knocked out. Forecasters said we would run into squall lines in the Adriatic, rain was forecast and the winds we had already suffered made us fearful we were going to get behind schedule so early into the flight.

In the air it was bumpy and fresh, but we rejoiced that we were leaving Italy after a number of mindless bureaucratic delays which left us irritable. It was a big factor in the way Keith reacted to the communications failure.

One minute we were talking to each other, next everything shut down, like we were riding on muffled air, each cut off from the other. Sound came back from time to time: 'What's going on?'

'I can't hear you!'

'Can you hear me?'

It reflected our confusion and alarm. Then the sound went completely. At the time we were coasting out on the first long sea journey, about 100 miles across the Adriatic, and the dangers were obvious. Keith fiddled about in the front, changing this or that lead to see if sound came back. It didn't. His obvious choice was to land and discover what was wrong, but he (and I, silent in the back) was not keen on being involved with the Italian aviation authorities again. I smiled at the small gesture Keith made, indicating he intended to cross the Adriatic anyway. Better to blag our way into Corfu without a radio, still making distance, rather than land back at Bari.

Keith soon had the emergency link out of the lady's handbag (our name for the map box on the pilot's knees), which enabled him to at least use the radio again. Whenever he took his hands off the control bar I steered on the back wires, following the course on the GPS. Soon he had stuffed an earphone into his already crowded ear, rigged up the mike to work and sent out a 'Pan' call (one level below a 'mayday') on the emergency frequency, 121.5. It was the first time he had ever done this for real, and he enjoyed it. A Jordanian airliner picked up the call and relayed it on to Corfu, warning them of our communications difficulties. Keith settled down for the 90-minute hack across the sea, with a ground speed around 60 mph, while I daydreamed in the back.

It was lovely to fly in over the first Greek islands, to pass over a highly populated Corfu and see Albania brooding in the close distance. On landing we were greeted by a man called Paris and the airfield controller, Sophie. I had met Sophie ten years earlier when she first took up the job and I was flying to Australia, and had described her then as 'forceful'. They were both charming and allowed us hangarage next to the local police helicopter. We resolved to charge the batteries in the earphones every second day to avoid another breakdown in communication.

I spent some time quietly investigating the absence of my

dreadful fears about heights and thought I had one answer. It was when I was forced to fly high on the way back from Liechtenstein the previous October, because of turbulence, and had got used to it. A second factor was that I was falling in love with the GT Global Flyer in a way I never did with my Australia aircraft, the Dalgety Flyer. When I gingerly tried to discover why I was not frightened, I could not find the fear. Perhaps if I looked very hard, I could. So I didn't.

On day five, we had another emergency, after discovering Keith had left the transponder running the previous day, which drained the battery. He hand-started the Flyer, but we loaded the still-uncharged battery with too much equipment and after I took off the charging light glowed red and all the electrical systems started dying. I had reached the south of the island when I discovered this and I elected to go back, rather than fly on as Keith had done the previous day. Neither of us were electricians, but we finally discovered that a major fuse had blown, which we replaced, and then spent half an hour recharging the battery before flying away.

I was not to know it then, but it was a harbinger of much more serious things to come in Russia. But then, just fixing the fault made us smile for half an hour.

The weather still looked okay to fly to Marathon, despite sombre warnings about storms and turbulence. Just before 1 p.m., late but happy, we took off again. The air was smooth and we were entranced with the misty Greek islands which passed slowly under our wings. Gradually, the sweat dried and we began to feel the cold again, but it didn't matter much because we were flying. Our ground speed was above 70 mph and we tramped 120 miles south to Araxos, then turned left into the strip of water with a venturi in the middle, created by mountains, that is the Corinth Canal.

'I know the winds are going to increase here and be against us,' I said.

We made time slowly, hacking eastwards, thankful to see our airspeed climb again. At the end of three and a half hours we were in radio-contact with Athens and I was looking at the map and calculating a better course to Marathon, north-east through a valley between Thisyi and Vayia. I reasoned that by going this way we would emerge over low ground and avoid mountains which were covered in cloud and mist.

Severe turbulence is particularly frightening in soft-wing trikes, because of the physical effort required to keep flying. It soon became apparent, as we passed Thisyi, that we were in serious trouble. The Flyer was wrenched and slung all over the sky, with me hanging on for grim death, and the occasional strained comment from Keith, suggesting I get into the middle of the valley. It was so bad that neither of us swore. I was reluctant to take Keith's advice because I looked left and saw a huge mountain, covered almost to its base with snow, and I knew instinctively that this was causing the problem, tons of cold air rushing down its sides and swirling around the valley we were flying in. There was nothing to do in such situations except endure. You cannot pretend you are not there. You could land, but it did not look inviting, and, anyway, we had to get through, it might as well be then as ever. Keith twice was bumped out of his seat against his lap-strap. For 15 minutes I fought my own little battle for our lives. There was a dispassionate steeliness to the trashing that was entirely missing in thermal flying.

'Rotor is bad news,' Keith said later. 'Rotor is what can kill you.'

We eventually emerged on the north side of the mountains into smooth air below misty clouds, typical English conditions, and flew eastwards, looking in wonder at the severely flooded valleys. We were happy we had not arrived two days earlier. There were problems communicating with Athens ATC (air-traffic control) but passing airline pilots thousands of feet above us were kind and relayed our messages.

Marathon airfield, to the east of Athens, was full of small aircraft and surrounded by flooded fields, but a welcome sight after 280 miles in the air. We were met by a small group of people, but found no hangarage; we left the Flyer half-rigged and tied down, hobbled, with two fresh cans of fuel next to her.

I remember thinking about half a dozen times that day how happy I was to be there. There was nowhere else in the world, even when fighting the horror conditions in the 'Valley of Death' near Thisyi, that I would rather have been. It was as life should be, on the edge and going somewhere. My usually restless mind was at ease with itself.

On our sixth day, we were greeted at Marathon Airport by four dogs, one of them with only one eye, who were once stray and were now a feature of the airport. It was a calm day. Keith bustled around the Flyer, while I set off to buy fuel – the avgas man was due to arrive after our take-off. Keith warmed the Flyer up; she had started easily, with the battery now fully charged again, and we set off for Rhodes. It was clean and beautiful in the morning air, the islands looming out of the mist, and Keith was obviously cheerful in the front, while I struggled to use the Sony camera, which was suffering from the daily attrition of our flight. The continuing cold, below freezing at all times, made it difficult to get enthusiastic about taking pictures, but how else could I show what was happening? After a while it started to rain.

In an open microlight most pilots dislike rain; it was not just the getting wet, but the fear that the rain will get into the flying instruments and stop them working. Keith was irritated, but in the back I felt oddly buoyant. This is the life. *The lonely sea and the sky.* It was clear either side of the rain clouds, on the left Turkey, on the right more sea and fewer islands as we tramped east. I watched the ground speed touch 90 mph and calculated we could easily make Cyprus that day if we did a quick turnaround at Rhodes. But Keith wanted a better weather forecast than just peering into ten miles of sky. Cyprus was 300 miles on from Rhodes, with no islands in between. After an hour of rain, Rhodes loomed out of the mist and, using the map because the GPS wasn't too good on detail, we found our way to Paradisi Airport, and Keith turned to land. It felt like he had walked into a brick wall, the wind was so strong, and Keith brought the Flyer in carefully. He was right to be cautious, because the last 50 feet were very difficult, the bar being torn either way in his hands and he had to force the aircraft to the ground. We both hung on while taxiing, fearful of being turned over.

We refuelled but decided not to fly on, because we were still chasing a huge storm and we did not wish to catch it. It was too early to take such risks.

The airport fire department removed one of their vehicles from a tall garage, and we snuggled the Flyer inside and worked over her. Two local pilots, Bangelis Pappas and Costas Tsapis, turned up to watch us work, and took us out to dinner that evening. We visited an Internet café to look at the gossip generated by the flight.

On day seven, 30 March, we woke up, secretly terrified by the wind. It had roared past our window all night and the trees thrashed more then ever. Any self-respecting microlight pilot would have taken one look at conditions and gone back to sleep. Flying was daft. Yet when I walked outside and looked at the waves crashing on the beach at Rhodes, I could see seagulls were up and enjoying themselves. We learned later that the RAF Flying Club at Akrotiri was laying money that we would not fly. It was not a bet we would have taken ourselves.

Bangelis and Costas drove us to the airport at Paradisi, and we walked over to the fire station where our Flyer was safe behind closed doors. Keith and I said little to each other. Neither of us wanted to be the one to say, 'Let's go back to the hotel and get the laundry done.' So we maintained what we each thought was a fiction that we would fly. The wind was almost directly across the runway, between force six and seven, and fully loaded, it was impossible to imagine how we would get into the air without being trashed.

When we began to think rationally, we saw the wind was at least blowing in the direction we wanted to go. Once in the air there was no reason for us to be terrified. I asked ATC if they would let me take off across, rather than along, the runway, so that we would be into wind. I lined up and found I could hold the bar easily, without that violent feeling you get when the wind tears at the wing. This was, I told myself, no more than a fresh day in England and I had often flown in such conditions. Suitably impressed, I pressed the accelerator, Keith rode the hand-throttle, we rushed across the tarmac and rose into the air.

'Yeeeehaaahhhh!' I shouted.

We turned right and climbed to the north, before turning east with a gratifying ground speed of 75 knots, and looked for height. Getting caught by rotor (the turbulent air behind a mountain) to the east of Rhodes was my main fear, so for the next 50 miles I stuck at 4,000 feet, looking down at the blue sea full of white caps and feeling only a little disturbed by being so high. Turkey lurked to the left, shrouded in mist. There was little cloud. It was a perfect flying day.

The air was not as still over the sea as we had imagined. We were hit by pockets of wind which played with us and always added about 5 to 10 mph to our ground speed on the GPS. We speculated about sea thermals, but could not see how they were formed. With such thoughts, we crossed 300 miles of sea, the longest single journey we had yet made over water. I sat and steered and sustained myself with daydreams, happy that the electrically heated gloves were at last working. Keith spent the first three hours content with his own company and was only bored in the last hour. We listened to some amusing conversations on Nicosia ATC.

The RAF base at Akrotiri, on the south side of the island, is said to be the biggest air-force station in the world. We went in under strict control from ATC, but there was some stiff upper lip in the information we were given – the wind was 25–30 knots and across the runway. I did not think this was as alarming as they did on the ground, because trikes could land in places grown-up aircraft would not attempt. We came whistling out of the sky, lined up to land and landed easily, much to the consternation of watching general aviation flyers.

'I didn't know microlights could do that!' one said later.

We were guests of the RAF Flying Club, who refuelled our tanks and saw us down a terrifying taxi journey to the safety of a huge hangar, so big it seemed to have its own weather system. Wing Commander Robert Cunningham, Officer Commanding, Operations, was our host, along with the club president, Hanni Awad. We sat down for a much-welcomed beer. Debbie Davies, helping Andy Webb make the documentary about the flight, was everywhere, asking 'why' when we did anything.

The storm we were chasing across the Mediterranean seemed to have headed north, but more bad weather was due. For the moment, however, conditions were forecast to be perfect to fly to Amman via Beirut and Syria. I called Judy Leden to ask for help with Jordan, but she had already been phoned that day by King Hussein of Jordan. They have been firm friends ever since Judy made her flight for life to Jordan with Ben Ashman, in memory of a beautiful Jordanian girl, Yasmin Saudi, who had died of cancer. The King was in England, but promised Judy we would be welcome in his country. I wear his watch from my only other visit there when I passed through during my flight to Australia. It was gratifying that he should remember me.

Unknown to us, we were heading for a confrontation with the Syrian Air Force.

5. THE MiG-21 INCIDENT IN SYRIA

It was only later that we worked out it must have been one of the dozens of Russian-built MiG-21s flying for the Syrian Air Force. Keith saw it first, as it flew, banked over, from left to right in front of us. We were at 100 feet, 15 miles north of the border between Syria and Jordan, well clear of the controlled air space around Damascus. Neither of us were happy to see such a big, black fighter aircraft so close to our fragile little Flyer. We watched it circle to the left and zoom behind us.

'What's he doing?' asked Keith, as I twisted in the back seat.

I said it was coming up on us again, this time on the right hand side. The MiG passed within 200 yards, banked over right in front of us and almost at our height. We worried about the effect of its wake upon us, a thought that must have occurred to the fighter pilot. When he came by next time he was much closer, so close that, even through our earphones and the noise of the Flyer's own engine, we heard the roar as the fighter jet's afterburner kicked in.

'That was seriously close,' said Keith, by now picking his route over the desert flatland of southern Syria so that we passed over villages instead of avoiding them.

If the MiG shot at us, we wanted him to hesitate at the thought of his bullets hitting other Syrians, while we continued to 'race' at 55 mph into the headwind, making for the nearest point on the Jordanian border. The fighter aircraft must have been going about 350 mph. Again he came by, and again, and again, trying to get closer and obviously frustrated. We waved gaily and pretended we were tourists.

Was he playing with us? What did he want us to do? Why was he winding us up by flying so close? We could think of nothing else to do but to plod towards Jordan, because there was nowhere to land but a road below us. You can imagine how the Syrian authorities would treat us if we did land on the road.

On the eighth day out of London, we had bustled around RAF

Akrotiri in the usual frustration of pulling together too much kit. I had done a big laundry the previous night, but it had not dried completely, so I was distracted. The RAF base was so big that you could not go anywhere except by car. It did not help that the Americans were operating a U2 spy aircraft from the apron right next to where the Flyer was being rigged; there are few microlight pilots who have been number two on take-off to a U2.

Keith spent a lot of time getting our flight plan right with the experienced men in air-traffic control. We wanted a route direct to Beirut and Damascus and then turn right and go directly to Amman. Despite fears that we might be sent 100 miles out into the desert to a 'reporting point', only to come back another 100 miles for a net gain of just 30, we had the plan approved. We climbed away in what was predicted to be perfect weather for the whole flight; no cloud, little wind, a window in the rough violent storm that had hit the area. We thought it would be a doddle, and we were quite wrong.

Trouble started 75 miles out over the sea, still with 100 miles to go to Beirut. It was a characteristic of air-traffic controllers that, when they came across so unusual an aircraft they harried us constantly. We soon grew weary of the phrase 'Golf, Mike, Golf, Tango, Golf,' our call sign, when, on answering, all he wanted to know was exactly where we were and our estimated time to some future reporting point. Our estimates were really guesses within ten minutes or more. All morning we felt harassed by Nicosia ATC, and when we were passed on to Beirut, the same obsessive nannying interest was expressed in us. The bad news soon came: 'the military' objected to our approved route and we had to change it. We could only cross Lebanon if we went to 13,000 feet, which was ridiculous.

'There are big mountains in our country,' said Beirut ATC, 'so go north.'

The corridor south of Beirut, where we wanted to go, had been closed three years previously, though no reason was given. It had been ideal for us to fly south of Beirut and go straight to Damascus between mountains, then south for Amman. We could not, of course, have gone over Israel, direct to Amman. Instead, we were routed further north, entirely the opposite direction to the way we wanted to go. It was obvious we were being sent around the whole country of Lebanon, up into flat countryside, right through Syria. I had memories of Judy Leden's microlight flight to Amman four years earlier. Damascus ATC had insisted she fly at 24,000 feet, another absurdity, and she had done the journey at 50 feet to stay below radar detection. Was the same thing going to happen to us?

We hit the Syrian coast west of Homs and climbed slowly into high flat countryside, dotted with rough-looking villages. Soon we were past the mountains and turning south, still in contact with Latakia ATC, which was thankfully laconic. Controlled air-space came up on the moving map of the GPS, so we talked over how we would fly south and whether to go east or west to avoid Damascus. Below us an unusual number of military camps passed under our wing. It was unsettling to look down at a dozen tanks, especially when one crawls towards you and stops while you wait to see if you are followed by its turret.

Keith took the Flyer up to 6,000 feet above sea-level, but we were always only 500 feet above the ground, open, broken desert that looked like the shells of thousands of oysters, with villages and camps dotted around. As we tramped south, we had a continual discussion about the best route, balancing the high mountains to the west against the much longer journey east to avoid air-space. We decided to go east while still 20 miles north of Damascus, but bumping up against its air-space, because the ground we were flying over was flat and much lower than elsewhere. Keith was worried about our fuel consumption, after hours of using near-maximum revs.

'If they send us out into the desert, we've had it,' he said. 'We just don't have the fuel.'

We continued low and slow, trying to be inconspicuous: we travelled first east and then gradually south, seeing the border of Jordan come up on the GPS, and avoiding towns and camps. The Flyer was battling into a headwind, its speed sometimes down to 45 knots, so we stayed low to avoid going even slower. One delight was to fly over bunches of children and watch them wave and jump up and down – one little group even started to run after us. What other aircraft could inspire that?

We were well south of Damascus and beginning to think about that first beer of the evening, when the MiG buzzed us for the first time.

In all, he made ten passes, each one more menacing than the last. It was like a bullying man harassing a small child. The man could easily whack the child to get it to obey, but anything the MiG did to us would kill us. He could have flown so close over the top of us that his turbulent wake would fall on us and we would be likely to tumble out of the sky. He could not fly below us, a really scary tactic, because we were so low ourselves. Instead, he settled for whooshing across our bow, from right to left, and dropping in the afterburner, in the hope we would do what? We couldn't stop dead in the air and there was no suitable landing place below. We were being intimidated, but to do what?

On the ninth pass he made it obvious what he wanted. He went by, as slow as he could, almost teetering in the air just off the stall, with his undercarriage down. That was the international signal to 'land now'. We could see from our GPS that we were within three miles of Jordan, and we did not want to land. Would he have been in his rights to shoot us down? We did not know, but what we did work out was that, if he did shoot us, we would not be part of the argument afterwards about whether he was right or wrong.

'What shall I do?' asked a clearly distressed Keith.

'We've got to carry on,' I said, just as distressed.

It was a rhetorical question. We continued in rather a detached state of mind and waited to see what the MiG would do next. If he did shoot, I thought, we wouldn't know much about it. If he didn't, we would make it to Jordan. We scanned the horizon for helicopters, but thankfully there were none. I watched the MiG come back for yet another pass in front of us, but this time he was higher.

'He's going away!' said Keith, and two minutes later we recognised the border with Jordan, two huge lorry parks around the customs posts.

Legally, we had done everything right, in our preparations and flight plans, in obeying ATC instructions to route north. But in countries like Syria, we were never certain of the intentions of anyone. We were so small and slow, and so easily bullied, that it happened to us naturally in the pecking order of the air. We might have sought help and issued a 'Pan, Pan' call, as we headed south, to come under ATC control when Latakia faded in our earphones, but we didn't, because of the consternation that was likely to cause.

Arriving at Amman Marka airport was a huge relief. Our fuel was down to ten litres after six and a half hours' flying, which was worrying. On landing, we were directed to the Royal Squadron's hangars, where various air-force officers asked why we were late. We explained we had been sent all around Lebanon. Damascus ATC wanted to know our route and we told Amman to pass on the message that we had avoided all controlled air-space. Our Flyer was refuelled, our flying equipment stacked away and a huge Mercedes was put at our disposal. Major Mohammed Sayen became our guide and we were driven to the Intercontinental, and stayed as guests of King Hussein. By then we were too tired to go out to eat, so Keith and I settled for a hotel meal.

Over beers, we considered ourselves lucky to be alive.

'It was down to time, fuel and hanging in there,' said Keith. 'I don't think we had an option. I'm sure we were right to go on. With so little fuel left we might have had to land out in Syria. That would have been a nightmare.'

We were certain that, as that jet pilot circled us, he discussed opening fire with his air-traffic controller. In the end, thank God, he didn't. We looked so innocent, colourful and harmless, just a kite with an engine, how could we possibly be a spy? The U2 we had seen in Akrotiri that flew away every morning and came back every afternoon, would have seen thousands more things than us.

If the jet had been a helicopter, we would have been toast.

6. DESERT TROUBLES, SIX ROAD
LANDINGS AND AN ENGINE CHANGE

On our ninth day, 1 April, we had heard we would be barred from flying along the oil pipeline that ran from the Arabian Gulf to the Mediterranean, the site of the Gulf War against Iraq in 1991, because it was full of secret installations. When we left Amman we were told to go to Hail, right in the middle of the Saudi desert and well south of the pipeline, a destination we accepted reluctantly. But it was soon evident that a headwind was slowing us down so much that we needed to refuel somewhere, and Saudi ATC, which until that point had been obstructive, suddenly routed us via Turayf, the first of the pipeline towns: I turned the Flyer north, and we looked down on a countryside like the dark side of the moon. The great storm which had ravaged Greece seemed to have had an effect here, too, with pools of dirty water everywhere. At least it cut down the risk of sandstorms.

When we reached Turayf I was deeply impressed with the new airfield, it had fantastic facilities and a huge runway, obviously built by the Americans. Its military potential was obvious, big enough to take large jets for another war, but there were no aircraft on the tarmac. I did not pay enough attention to my landing, flopping in like a pregnant duck from about 50 feet, happily without damage. I was shaken by how inept I had been. As we taxied across an immaculate tarmac apron, people streamed out of buildings to see us. We were nervous.

The airport director, Salem Almoteri, a slim man dressed in white, could not have been kinder. He said we must pay nothing because we were 'members of a club', and he would do everything to send us on our way. He would clear us right across the desert, on a route rejected just that morning by Jeddah. I left Keith putting in fuel and preparing the Flyer for the next leg and stomped off with Mr Almoteri to drink sweet tea and negotiate our way through the paperwork.

There was one surreal moment. As my passport and documents were being photocopied, Mr Almoreri said: 'You are Mr Richard?'

I replied that I was Mr Brian, but he persisted: 'You are Mr Richard Branson?'

I was amused at the suggestion, as if there was only one Englishman left in the world with a monopoly on adventures. I gently told my host I was not Mr Branson, thinking that Keith would laugh his socks off at the suggestion. The irony was unbelievable, given the interest Branson had in racing us.

On the flight from Turayf to Ar'ar that afternoon, I meandered from one side of the road to the other, restless about falling into a pattern. We oscillated between 600 feet above the ground and 1,200 feet, depending on the weak thermal activity. I had been fearful, back in London, about being thrashed all over the sky by powerful desert thermals. Instead, we had a lazy bumbling flight, following a straight road for 145 miles. We both nearly dozed off a couple of times, and I had visions of drifting off into the desert, fast asleep, and waking to find ourselves in the middle of nowhere.

When Ar'ar came up we were surprised at how big and vibrant it looked, with another huge American-built airport. Andy McNab's SAS team, Bravo Two Zero, had flown from Ar'ar on their ill-fated mission into Iraq in the Gulf War. The head of the fire service, Mohammed Alenizi, had trained at Teesside, and found us hangarage by slinging out one of his fire engines. Keith steered the Flyer inside and we found a hotel. What we missed most at the end of the day was a beer, we were now in a country which had to be super-strict about alcohol because most of the Islamic holy places are within it. Toasting a day's flying in water or orange juice did not produce the same warm glow.

On day ten, 2 April, we ran into our first serious trouble on the flight. The day started well at Ar'ar, although we took off into another headwind. Our ground speed settled down at 43 knots and we fell into a frame of mind that was consciously patient. Our target, Qaysumah, was 340 miles away, and so long as we plodded along we would reach there before darkness.

Keith first tried the wind at height and when it showed no advantage, chose to fly one thousand feet above the desert, while he looked for ways to amuse himself. These included overtaking the occasional lorry so the driver saw an enormous shadow on the road in front of him and wondered what he was being pursued by. I sat in the back and took as many pictures as I could.

Once, when taking out a camera from my pocket, I was hit on the shoulder by something and Keith said the engine had missed a beat. I spent some time wondering what it was, as the thump had appeared substantial. But there was no apparent damage to the prop and we speculated it might have been a small bird. When we landed we discovered the lower strap of my life-jacket, which we wore at all times because there was no room to stow them, had fluttered back in the slipstream and been caught by the prop. Its remains were wrapped around the prop-shaft.

We were given 50 litres of fuel for free at Rafha, but declined the offer to stay in a local villa. We flew on. The desert slowly became lighter and more sandy and also flatter. The sky remained a brilliant blue, while the thermals were easy to cope with. Opting to fly so low, often down to 500 feet above the road, and waving to cars and lorries, meant we were thrown about a bit.

We were 60 miles from Qaysumah when Keith said: 'We have a problem.'

He had been quiet for some time, absorbed in watching the water temperature rise from its operating range of 100–120°C, to 130° and above. What was causing it? The sun had gone around to the west, behind us, and we had been filming our shadow plodding across the ground. Now we thought the sun might be warming the radiator. As temperatures climbed, we thought it prudent to land. Below us was the longest runway in the world. It was not difficult for Keith to pick his moment in the traffic, and slot in to a half-mile gap between one car and the next. We taxied to the wide shoulder by the side of the road, stopped the engine, and looked over the aircraft to see what was wrong.

All the water coolants had gone. Until then, we had had no problems with cooling the engine, which often ran at a lower temperature than other Rotax 912s. If the engine did overheat, water was forced into an overflow bottle and sucked back when the engine cooled. But the overflow bottle was full of dark, rather oily water. We carried a litre of water with us and poured it in. Some passing motorists also had water, which they donated freely, and, thinking it was just one of those things, we got back in, restarted, taxied out between cars and took off again.

Fifteen minutes later the same thing happened, this time with frightening suddenness. By now Keith was watching the temperature gauges like a hawk, but he was not prepared for the speed at which they climbed. Having settled down at around 108°C, they suddenly shot up, 120° . . . 125° . . . 130°, then down for a short while before climbing further. Again, we landed on the highway, picking our time by assessing the speed of the traffic going east, then circling to settle in behind an especially slow car which, thankfully, did not slow up when he saw a microlight appear 40 yards behind him.

By the side of the road, this time near a large puddle of water, we attracted the attention of a passing army lance-corporal who demanded to see our passports. We had to surrender them, giving a man with very little power a chance to exercise it. He developed, in the debate that followed, that small and secret smile of someone determined to have his 15 minutes in the limelight. Keith and I struggled to understand what was wrong with the engine, first filling up with water from the puddle, then running the engine at speed to see if there were leaks. We could see none. I engaged the help of passers-by to put our case to the triumphant corporal about getting our passports back, and grew to hate the 'no problem, one minute' reply he kept giving.

Keith said we should take our chances and fly on, because the sun was setting. We took the lance-corporal's car registration and told him we would see him at Qaysumah Airport with our passports, then leapt in – as much as one can with the Flyer – and took off once more. Had we fixed it this time? Would we make it through in time? We thought at first the answer was yes and then the temperature rocketed and we thought not, so we found a road near the highway and landed there, our third landing. Neither of us wanted to spend a night in the desert so close to Iraq; we were not equipped for camping.

'The manual does say that you can run without water for an hour without damaging the engine,' said Keith, 'so long as the oil temperature does not go above 140°C.'

The oil temperature had not moved significantly as we lost water and we felt we had no option but to test this theory. Again, we hustled, and were soon flying, just 20 miles from Qaysumah which we could see so clearly on our GPS. By now we were down to basics. I was navigating, as Keith had not gone through the time-consuming process of plugging in his radio or GPS, and my Skyforce GPS, for a reason I had yet to discover, was working only on internal batteries, so it had a limited life.

It was soon apparent that the manufacturer's recommendation, about being able to use the engine without water, was a load of cock. We steeled ourselves to watch the water temperatures soar, and then turned to the oil and, with sinking hearts, saw that begin to soar as well.

'If it gets above 125, we'd better land again,' I said.

Permanent damage to the engine was our nightmare.

In the gathering dusk, the sun below the horizon but the lights of Qaysumah visible in the distance, Keith set up to land once more. He turned on the landing lights we had installed, but never tested for real, and we were relieved to discover they were set right and illuminated the road from 150 feet up. Again, Keith picked his time between cars and again we hoped that the car we chased down the highway would not slam on his brakes when he discovered what had plummeted out of the sky behind him. At the side of the road two army cars swerved across to join us, but this time the soldiers knew who we were, where our passports were and, to save our lives, one of the soldiers had a large plastic bag full of water bottles. This he donated immediately. Keith tore off the seals and poured in four bottles, the engine hissed and wheezed as the hot metal steamed. I got into the back carrying the plastic bag with the remaining bottles, afraid to drop it in the propeller, and so harassed I did not do up my seat-belt. One problem was trying to capture these events on video, while also participating in them; I did neither to my own satisfaction.

Keith took off in the last vestiges of daylight and it was seriously dark as we climbed to just 500 feet, our lights blazing, heading for the bright lights of Qaysumah. By now we were down to monitoring my GPS for distance, as I called out the distance still to go: ten miles, nine, seven and a half, six – while Keith watched the instruments. Above us the stars started to appear in the black cloudless sky. Below us the countryside darkened, the more so by contrast with the town lights we were soon flying over.

'We can't land on the highway again,' said Keith, 'because of the street lighting.'

Our only reserve was the bag with three medium bottles of water which I clutched in my left hand. I was operating a video camera with my right. I had also ended up with Keith's neck-warmer threaded onto my left arm, I struggled to juggle them all without dropping them into the propeller. It was completely dark, except for the street lights and our own small headlights.

We could actually see the airfield in the distance when, despairingly, Keith said, 'They've gone again.' He shaped up for a night landing on the road, our fifth out-landing, cursing as one particular motorist seemed to slow down to watch us and worrying about another car coming up fast behind. We had, of course, no tail lights, and who knew what a motorist might do to the fragile wing of the Flyer?

The landing was full of noise, a clattering engine, sudden looming obstacles, road signs, crash barriers, but again Keith negotiated his way through. The most dangerous moment came when we were pulling off the side of the road and felt it slope away. We thought we might tumble down a gully and scuttled left as soon as our wing was clear of the highway. It left us perched, canted over, as Keith leapt out and grabbed the bag from my death-grip, something I had consciously to force myself to release. He gave me the radiator cap and poured the last of the water in. I explained to my video camera what was happening, and in the process dropped the radiator cap on the ground, which caused another minute's frantic searching and irritation. Cars were beginning to stop and friendly greetings waved, but we were not in a mood to tell them where we had come from.

Keith started the engine, scrambled up on the road, saw no one coming and we rose into the darkness. We were now committed. There was no water left. If the engine went before we reached the airport, we were in trouble. We had already taken risks flying low by night, to keep the revs down, with the chance of hitting one of the microwave towers that dotted the countryside. Our radio was not connected (talking to ATC was the last thing on our minds), we were totally alone. We relied on the grapevine to hope that the aviation authorities at Qaysumah knew we were coming and that they had left the runway lights on. As we approached the airport – four miles, two and a half, one – it was apparent they had, and Keith made his final foray right into the dark desert before turning to land. As we taxied in, fire-brigade staff clapped their hands and whistled.

What caused the problems? Why had an engine that had run so true suddenly become a rogue with water? We thought we might have blown a head gasket, so we contacted Charles Heil in London – with great difficulty, as the mobile phone did not work – and asked for a new set of engine heads and gaskets. But Nigel Beale, the

Rotax agent, who was tracked down to a pub, said there were no head gaskets on a 912! He listened to all the symptoms, then had a long discussion with Dave Simpson, and phoned back later to say that we must be leaking water from a hose.

We spent the next three days, first trying to find out what was wrong with the engine, then asking for a replacement and putting it on. Each time we tried something new, we filled the system with water, tested it and watched the temperatures soar. Sometimes we stood on the ground and watched the overflow bottle blow up. Other times we flew into the cooler air, but after about 15 minutes the engine overheated. We thought there might have been an airlock, or a water leak, and as the day went on, our frustration grew.

All our work was done in the airport fire station, and we were looked after by mostly British-trained firemen. Whoever ran that fireman's school in Teesside had created a brilliant Anglophile culture all across the Saudi Desert. The way the firemen's eyes lit up at tales of flirtatious and beautiful Newcastle girls was a revelation. One Arab gravely told me Newcastle was the most beautiful city in England.

That first night, Keith said we needed a new engine, so we phoned Charles in London. He contacted Nigel Beale, and between Nigel, his son Conrad, who worked for Pegasus, and Charles, an astonishing logistical operation was set in motion. Conrad took all the Pegasus modifications for the Rotax engine to his father's factory and they worked through Friday night and Saturday morning to prepare an engine we could swap with our own. They then took it personally to London Airport, where Charles had arranged air freight. By Saturday evening, 24 hours after we had asked for it, the replacement engine was in the Saudi capital, Riyadh. That was 300 miles from where we were and, as Sunday dawned, we were desperately worried about customs. Only one aircraft a day came from Riyadh to Qaysumah, and that was at 3.15 p.m. Could we get our engine on it?

At the same time, I was fretful about the Branson bid to race against us, and wanted to smoke him out. Not having agreed to the delay, and therefore the million-dollar prize, they were not beholden to us, nor us to them. I worried that they would announce a bid to chase after us while we were losing precious days. I asked Kay Burley if she would start teasing Will Whitehorn about his chances, but he denied on television there had ever been a Virgin attempt to race around the world by microlight. Kay had the whole story from Rory McCarthy, so she knew the truth. I could give no explanation. Whitehorn's denial certainly took the pressure off us, but I wanted another 3,000 miles under my belt in case the Branson team set off. I did not believe Rory's claim that they could go around the world in 30 days. If they followed our route, that was an average of 800 miles a day, as against our more realistic – in microlight terms – average of 300 miles a day. If Keith and I could establish a lead of 25 days, then there would be a fair competition.

The Arabs at Qaysumah were kindness itself. They found us accommodation, fed us, gave us transport when we needed to buy anything, brought us fuel. Through the intense heat we struggled to keep our minds together and our morale high.

On the Sunday, the local airport manager, Mr Al-Nabjan and his assistant, an engaging young man called Hamed Al Saife, began to work the phones. They kept bellowing: 'No customs! No customs! Just get the engine here today!' My hopes rose. Keith and I sat across the desk from the two of them and watched them in action. Keith looked quite drained of any emotions, a man facing a daunting task if the engine should arrive. He had the main responsibility for making the whole thing work. I stomped up and down the room in frustration, making barely suppressed cries of hope and despair. This seemed to have the effect of galvanising more action.

By 1 p.m. we had done all we could, so we went off to see Mr Al-Nabjan's camel, a beast called Romania. It was hobbled out in the desert, about four miles from the airport, and we bucketed over the rough grassy ground in his four-wheel drive, listening to his tales. He was an old-fashioned Arab, still steeped in the lores of the Bedouin. Keeping a camel was a way of staying in touch with his own soul. Romania seemed happy to see us at first, so we were photographed with her and heard she was pregnant again and had produced five previous babies. Seemingly at this news, Romania began to get agitated, and began a series of long, and to me agonising, coughs and roars, which had us scuttling out of spitting range whenever she swung her head.

Back at the airport we went to the director's office, caught in spasms of tension, my stomach knotted, waiting for the definitive news about our engine. Just half an hour before the daily jet was due to arrive in Qaysumah, Omar Almaki came in and, understating it a bit, but with a huge grin, said our engine would arrive within an hour. I could have exploded with noisy pressure, and the relief was tangible. It was at 3.45 p.m. that the engine was towed to us at the far end of the airfield, where we had watched the jet taxi for take-off in a lather of impatience. We tore off the cardboard, with Keith sharply telling me to get out of his way (I was videoing the process), and began to put the heart back into the Flyer. The Beales, knowing our inexperience in assembling such an engine, had left kind notes about everything, so it was really a question of looking at the old engine and seeing what it had that the new one didn't, and then transferring it over. Keith said later he had to treat it like a jigsaw; he didn't really understand the principles. I did what I could, which included laying out two mats so the constant stream of visitors could cast off their shoes, sit cross-legged and gossip over tea while watching us slaving over our task. The sun went down peacefully, with little wind, and we worked a solid five hours reassembling until the final drop of anti-freeze was in, the last nut tightened, oil topped up and pressure induced by a bicycle pump in the system.

Keith said, 'She's ready.'

We pushed the Flyer outside into the darkness and, with our hosts uncomfortably close, prepared to start the engine. It burst into life on the first revolution and spun sweetly, apparently far smoother than the good and hitherto faithful engine now lying gutted behind us. Would the new engine be better? Would it take us the remaining 21,000 miles around the world? Who could tell?

I had expected a bill, if not for the fuel, then at least for transporting the engine to Riyadh, but Mr Al-Nabjan dismissed the query with a gentle smile and a dismissive wave. I hope they felt, as they deserved to, a sense of ownership in any of our achievements. Meanwhile, a strong rumour emerged in London that Richard Branson planned to set off on 20 April. I wanted to be well past India when he did.

On day 14, 6 April, Keith took the Flyer up for a test at dawn, stripped down, not carrying any load, including the panniers which each held 25 litres of fuel. She went like a dream, with temperatures not above 90°C. We warmed up, took off at 8.10 a.m., and climbed in smooth cold air to 3,000 feet, watching the temperature gauges, CHT for water, which went up quickly to 117° and then settled, and the oil temperature, which remained safely below 100°C. Keith and I chatted amiably.

We had a following wind, strong enough to give us a ground

speed of 70 knots. But, coming to the coast after two hours in the air, I noticed the cylinder-head temperature, despite the cold air, had climbed to 127°C, and within a minute I was shaping up to land. I chose a spare road next to the highway, picking on the tarmac section, which was a mistake because it was sticky and we soon had tar everywhere. We jumped out and discovered that all the anti-freeze in the cooling system had blown away and the new overflow bottle had a hole blown in it from tremendous internal pressure.

'It's buggered,' said Keith.

He was edgy with working out why it had happened. In my own mind, I left the problem with him. We carried spare anti-freeze, so we refilled the system, checking the hoses, thinking we had had a leak. Having tightened them, we also removed the two survival suits, each tied below a pannier, believing they might block the air-flow to the radiator, and stowed the suits in the wing. We climbed back in, took off and were soon at 4,000 feet and within 70 miles of Dhahran. But the old pattern reasserted itself. The engine ran coolly for 15 minutes, then temperatures shot up. I saw what looked like a garage complex next to the highway and landed about half a mile away on a small road. Again, almost all our coolant had been blown away. We thought we needed a much bigger radiator.

Keith was beside himself. He kept saying that we could not go around the world in an aircraft like this. At one time he said the only way the flight could continue was for him to get out, and me to continue alone. I was touched by this offer, which I rejected immediately. It became very hot, climbing to 40°C, with a strong desert wind blowing plastic bags past us. I thought we would need mechanical help to stick another radiator on, so I set off through the rubbish to the complex, which I found wind-blown and tatty, though in the middle was a well-stocked Indian-owned super-market. There I found another gallon of anti-freeze, water and two Mars bars, haggling with the shopkeeper at the exchange rate for dollars into the local riyals. I walked back with these to Keith, who was wrestling with the overheating problem.

'They used 912s in Black Rock on the Thrust attempt at the world speed record,' I said. 'It can't be the aircraft itself, it's got to be something wrong with ours.'

'When they used them in the desert, they didn't have panniers on,' said Keith. 'So it must be the panniers.'

If we removed the panniers, where were they to go? Keith

transferred everything spare into the wing, which already housed all our video and stills stock. Soon, the moon boots and the two empty plastic tanks joined the survival suits, tied to the keel and prevented from bursting out by strong velcro which looked under increasing strain. I worried, as the pilot of the day, about the effect of so much weight so far forward on the aircraft's handling.

In our slimmed-down Flyer, capable if it worked of getting us to Dhahran, but without the fuel capacity to get to Abu Dhabi, we topped up our coolant and set off again. We had a bumpy take-off into strong conditions, thermals helping us climb slowly to cold air at 4,000 feet. We watched the temperature gauges all the time, and were relieved to see them climb naturally to 107°C, before settling back to hover around the 102° mark. When we landed at Dhahran we discovered no water loss at all. So it had been the panniers all the time!

We thrashed our way through the problem as we flew over salt marshes. I would put up proposals, only to have Keith worry them to death. Meanwhile, my radio conversation with Dhahran ATC turned into a farce. They harassed us all the time, asking every minute where we were, who we were and who owned the aircraft. I said reluctantly that I did, which was true but asking for trouble. Back they came a minute later, asking, 'Are you a rich man.' They seemed to be trying to work out whether to lay the red carpet out for us. Qaysumah Airport had passed on the word that we were two VIPs, because of our world-record attempt, but when we denied we were VIPs, it all settled down. In the event, they ignored us for the rest of the day, except for the local Fire Department, where we found a home.

I worried half the evening about where we were going to sleep. We had no visas for Saudi; they wouldn't issue them to us in London until we showed we had permission to fly through. It was a situation the authorities coped with by restricting us 'air-side', and therefore not technically in the country. If I had argued with airport officials, I believe I could have got us into a luxury hotel by about 11 p.m., tired, ratty, probably hungry and certainly ripped off. Not paying the bills, Keith had a royal disdain for spending money.

The main cause of his despair was the state of the engine. We contemplated mounting the panniers off the monopole, where the trike joined the wing, but rejected that because we could then never fold down the trike, which we needed to do. Keith thought about mounting the radiator on the monopole, but that would leave it above the filler and it would never hold any water. The solution he came up with, which we planned to test by flying over the Persian Gulf with him at the bar, was to take the radiator out into a clean flow of air. He tie-wrapped it to the left wheel-strut and we sent one of the firemen out with a $50 note to find us more radiator hose and a dozen jubilee clips. When the job was done, at 10 p.m., and tested, it looked good.

But who was to say it would work?

'If it doesn't work, it's your fault,' said Keith. 'If it works, of course, it's down to me. I've always felt like that.'

If it didn't work we would both fall into the Persian Gulf.

I had practice at that sort of thing.

7. DHAHRAN TO MANDALAY

Though the firemen of Dhahran were very kind in putting us up for the night, they were, to our Western sensibilities, living in squalor. Coming off the desert with dreams of a beer, clean sheets, a meal to eat at a table, reality was dirty bathrooms with mirrors missing, showers with no heads, bare mattresses with just a blanket and no pillows, the continuously echoing noise of an all-male barracks.

Yet Mansoor Salman Alsedati, head of the fire department, was a generous host, clearing the dormitory of his men when I said Keith was a light sleeper, providing food immediately when we asked if there was any. His men were full of innocent curiosity. Because there was no adequate security, we left thousands of dollars of equipment lying around – GPSs, cameras, mobile phones – with never any threat that they would be stolen

By contrast, the authorities on Dhahran Airport could not have been more indifferent. There were bureaucratic obstacles to overcome at every turn. What drove our irritation was the fear that Keith's cobbled together engine cooling system would not work, but the only way we would discover this would be over the 300-mile crossing of the Persian Gulf and the chance that we would fall into the sea. We got away on day 15, 7 April, at 11 a.m., with great relief and no small fear.

We climbed east around Bahrain and then the long trawl across the Gulf to Abu Dhabi. It was soon evident that far from running too hot, the engine was running about 15° below its most efficient temperatures. We did not care. In the back I fell into a dream-like state. Through half-closed eyes, shapes like Keith's hand on the control bar became living figures, and I would watch them, convinced they were something else, until waking again. I was glad I wasn't flying. It was absolutely smooth, misty over the sea and the sky was a washed blue with high cirrus, with the wind generally behind us. At 3,000 feet there was no life in the air at all.

It was hours of nothing until we saw the first oil rigs in the mist at around 1 p.m. When we were within 30 miles of Abu Dhabi, savouring the thought of our first beer for six days, we were diverted to an airfield called Al Ain. We got the co-ordinates, put it into the GPS and flew north of our original destination, 50 miles inland. By contrast with Saudi, The Emirates was clean, ordered and obviously civilised. Roads led everywhere, to neat square villages with good housing, or to military bases. We flew over classical desert, with rolling sand-dunes and farms with camels. Keith picked up Al Ain ATC and we landed at the airfield after six and a half hours in the air. We were greeted by the airport manager, Said Al-Yabhouni, and a delegation of locals who stood next to us for photographs, and then authorised us hangarage, fuel and hotels, at their expense.

The airport's chief engineer was Malcolm Hardie, one of that band of Englishmen who spend most of their time overseas; he had followed our progress on Sky TV. He found a place for the Flyer inside his engineering workshop, organised fuel and took us off to his own home for that first glorious lager. Keith could frame the photo I took of his look, just before he raised the glass to his lips. After that, we mellowed out.

On day 16, 8 April, we were picked up at the Hilton by Malcolm and driven to the airport. The day dawned foggy, but it soon cleared into a mist, and we manoeuvred the Flyer out of Malcolm's workshop and packed her. When connected into the electrical system, I found there was no juice in the battery. We had left the transponder on again.

Keith was disgusted with himself, as he had been the villain the previous time. He stripped off his flying clothes, pushed the Flyer to a safe place and I sat while he hand-started. When the engine roared into life, the charging light showed green at full revs, but we aborted the first take-off because we thought it was not sufficiently green. Probably nerves. Our second take-off was a success, and we headed for Muscat.

In the hot air, fully loaded, the Flyer climbed painfully. We flew over Al Ain, the most beautiful of cities, and headed east into 4,000-foot mountains, apprehensively noting the waves of heat already rising and worrying about thermal activity. Soon, we were being bounced around, but it was benign. Every time I entered a thermal I stuffed the bar out, looking for height. We were soon able to pick our way through a pass in the mountains, north of a direct route to Muscat, but avoiding the highest peaks. Where, last year, I would have been terrified at the height and the bumpiness, now I was able to cope easily. The Flyer had convinced me of the sturdiness of microlights.

Then Keith said, full of alarm: 'That's a sandstorm!'

From left to right, as far as we could see, a rolling cloud of dust was heading for us. It was not something we could dodge. I elected to climb above it, pouring on power to get us back to 4,000 feet, still a tremendous struggle in the hot air. I felt less nervous than Keith as we got closer to the musty sandstorm, more dust than actual sand, through which we could see the murky outline of the ground, but no sign of the sea which was showing up 15 miles away on our GPS. Would it be turbulent? Had I any choice anyway? I had been in sandstorms in the desert on the Dalgety Flight, and after the scariness of the first one, had endured two others without being screwed out of the sky. We could always look up at the serene washed-blue sky and know we were the right way up. It was no more turbulent when we could taste the dust than before we entered it.

After ten minutes we saw the sea, and we were soon over smooth air, and thinking of flying down the coastline. Muscat ATC had other ideas. They sent us 20 miles out to sea to avoid restricted areas on the air map; instead of getting a good look at Oman, we spent the next hour or so over a misty sea, trying to follow compass courses. It was boring and irritating, but there was no choice, and after four hours in the air we looked forward to being on the ground where our film crew from London, Debbie Davies and Barrie Bayes, were due to meet us.

We booked into the Novotel, showered, stomped our laundry and hung it up to dry and went to Debbie's room for our first beer. Relations between her and Barry were not good. Dinner was a bad-tempered affair, and that included me.

Underneath, I was worried at how the flight would be portrayed when it was over. I could not persuade Keith to use a video camera, so what we had so far was a detailed record of Keith Reynolds flying a microlight around the world. Essential parts of the flight, including the hassle of dealing with officials, the general organising, as well as my half of the flying, were just not covered. There would be no record of this when the flight was over, and pictures dictated the story for television. I had felt that my motives and actions on the flight to Australia, ten years earlier, had been mocked and cheapened during a half-hour programme about it, and I did not want that to happen again. Keith saw using the video as the lowest of priorities. When he did use it he had to be prompted, which was wearing.

On day 17, with Keith driving, we set off across the mouth of the Persian Gulf, after a bad-tempered breakfast with Barrie and Debbie. They did not seem to be able to communicate with each other, much like Newlyn and me. It was very hot, but we had to dress up because it was cold at altitude. We flew 300 miles in calm air across a smooth sea to a Pakistani town ten miles east from Iran, called Gwadar, which I had once called the 'armpit of the world'. Vijay Singhania landed there on his flight from London to Delhi in 1988 and had been charged $11 a litre for fuel. He was an Indian billionaire and had obviously rubbed someone up the wrong way. I had been through six months before him and found everyone very kind. But I was influenced by Vijay and we wanted to bypass Gwadar and make it direct along the coast to Karachi. Then a slight headwind blew up and the chance passed to do a double-jump and gain back one of the three days we had lost in the desert. Keith turned back over terrifying countryside, and we landed at Gwadar after six and a half hours' flying.

It was hot and dusty, but everyone was kind. The local fire chief, Mohammad Mansha, evicted a fire engine and the Flyer snuggled inside the station and out of the wind. He and the airport boss, Zahid Mahmoud Sheikh, found us a lift into town. It was a very run-down place where we looked for a hotel, ending up in one of the British-built guest houses next to the sea. As the sun went down, Keith and I drank sweet tea and ate a meal laboriously put together by a kind hotel manager, with the electricity generator going in the background, and lukewarm showers. The wind blew off the sea and we thought it one of the most charming places we had ever visited.

Day 18, 10 April, my turn to fly 300 miles along the coast to Karachi. There were alarms early in the morning because no one could find the customs official, and I threw half a wobbly that we might lose another day. Zahid Mahmoud was worried his country would be blamed for the delay, so patriotically tore all over the place trying to find the missing official. We tracked him down in town and hurtled over the dusty tracks to get our passports stamped, and pass through customs. Zahid also found us fuel, which was not available on the airfield, and prices were reasonable. We got away at 11 a.m., again into a headwind, and tracked along a coast described by the Australian pioneer, Ross Smith, as 'the most inhospitable in the world'.

About two hours into the flight Keith became alarmed at the way we were using fuel, so we landed at the coastal town of Ormara and, after some shuffling around, bought an extra 25 litres, which saw us through to Karachi at 6.30 p.m., after five and a half hours in the air. We found a good hotel next to the airport where prices for two rooms, dinner and beer (for medicinal purposes only in a Muslim country) came to less than $150.

For years the biggest city in Pakistan had a dreadful reputation for bureaucracy, but recently an agent called Shaheen had been operating to clear pilots through. They were not cheap, $200 a clearance, but they halved their prices for us, and when we went in to flight-plan on day 19, they got us through customs, immigration, flight planning and a number to allow us into India. The weather forecast was for north-west winds at 15–20 knots (utter crap, as it happened).

It was very hot. We had had problems with the starter solenoid, which Keith cleaned, while I refilled the cameras with film. We got away quite early, but had difficulty climbing to 3,000 feet in hot air and being fully loaded. The countryside changed slowly, from cultivated land, until suddenly at the border we were over the Rann of Kutch. It was as barren and bleak as anywhere we had flown. Keith used thermals as a hang-glider pilot would, pushing out to gain height, pulling between lift, punctuated with the occasional explosive comment about turbulence.

The Rann of Kutch had settlements amid huge salt plains which look like snow. I thought that death would be horrible down there if the engine failed. There was a wind change about 50 miles from our first destination in India, Ahmadabad, and we raced over the last few miles.

Landing at Ahmadabad was like descending into an oven. The temperature had been 43°C (109°F) earlier in the day, a heatwave, but had dropped to 102°F when we arrived. We put the Flyer into a hangar owned by the local flying academy.

On day 20, it was my turn to fly and I was ratty about the most expensive hotel we had had to date, the Trident, near the airport. I had, as was usual in India, to deal with mind-numbing bureaucracy. But it was a legacy of the Raj and everyone wanted it to work. I had five signatures to get on my flight plan – meteorology, communications, customs, immigration and the ATC. The Met was off having tea, customs were playing cards and had lost their stamp, ATC was inclined to delay and say 'sit down, have tea' – none of which improved my temper. We were in the middle of the worst April heatwave in memory and when we finally got to the Flyer a journalist was waiting! It wasn't until 11.30 a.m. that we took off.

The forecast said 20-knot winds from the north-east which would back south-west, so we were again hacking into a headwind. Colin Bodill seemed to have taken all the tailwinds. I took the Flyer up, oh so slowly, to 7,500 feet, looking for the westerly that was 'always there'. It was almost there for us, but the inversion kept us down and it was unpleasantly turbulent. I hung on at full power before a pessimistic Keith said we couldn't break through and I came down again.

During this period I had a whiff of the panics, awareness of the total space beneath me, checking my seat-belt, panicky thoughts for about a minute, casting my mind anywhere but with reality. But in a series of images Helen helped, and the moment passed.

We were heading for Nagpur but found that, with the headwind, it would be two hours after darkness when we got there, so we opted to go to Bhopal instead. Having to use so much power in the heat was gobbling petrol. It was extremely thermic and we were thrown around. There was no height we could reach beyond the effect of the thermals. But though I worked hard, I never felt I would become too weary to fly. Keith once grabbed my back wires on a really bumpy bit and swore three or four times; he said later he thought I had earned my beer. At 3,500 feet it was always hot and at 5,000 feet the colder air made the thermals vicious, so we oscillated between the two, bumped up by warm columns of air and down by the sink in between.

After five hours' flying we reached Bhopal. Fuel was immediately available and a hangar, and ATC was affable: 'No problems here, just file a flight plan and go.' A taxi was waiting downstairs and we chose the three-star Amer Palace and two cold beers each. On the way through town I marvelled at the sheer energy of India; honking traffic, cows wandering everywhere, colours and smells and hardly any rules of the road.

Over a delicious dinner, Keith confessed to having fallen in love with Pakistan and India. Gwadar had impressed him, people who had nothing, yet offered what they had as hospitality. He was struck by the lack of aggression among ordinary people.

On day 21, there had been three telephone calls from a previously affable ATC wanting to know exactly why he had not landed in Nagpur. Each time I said 'headwinds', ATC kept saying 'hello' at the end of every sentence. Irritating.

It was hot again, and I felt queasy. We filed to go to Bhudeshwar, on the forecast of a west wind, even though the wind looked north-east to us. We doubted our own flight plan, but it would have taken an hour to file again, diverting to refuel in Nagpur, so we went anyway. The flying was smooth as the heat increased to 40°C in the mountains of the central Indian plain, we made it to Nagpur in just over three hours. There we faced a two-hour hassle on the ground in tremendous heat. Our problem was we needed to contact an official in Delhi, the only man in the whole of India who could give us a flight number to proceed. If he was at lunch, or visiting a friend in hospital, as that day he was, we had to wait until he got back. We wanted to go on to Raipur, within one day's flight of Calcutta, and we were perpetually fretting about losing another day in our four-day schedule across India. Keith opted to stay outside and fry, while I hassled. When we took off again, a miracle occurred: we had a westerly. Though it was slow and painful to climb, a journey that we thought would take four hours took two and three-quarters. We began to hope we might make Calcutta the following day.

There were more delays at Raipur Airport, where we drank a lot of water and a suspect Pepsi (they put lids back on bottles there with new drinks in them). I kept the taxi windows open on the way to the hotel, where I vomited. I drank a litre of water, but half an hour later I was sick again. I felt very run down. When I heard that, as a government hotel, they did not serve beer, I threatened to leave unless they bought some, which they did. Kay Burley phoned, almost a signal to be ill again. I took lots of Immodium and, later, aspirin, and worried about being sick in the air.

On day 22, 14 April, it was extremely hot again. I could not eat breakfast, and left the hotel with a large bottle of clean water. It was a long distance to Calcutta, 443 miles and, after taking off at 8.10 a.m., we flew east over increasingly hilly country, where our speed fell away. Then I made the crucial decision to climb, though prospects of finding a westerly did not look good, yet at 6,500 feet I found one and we began to fly faster than 60 knots. I saw a restricted area marked on the GPS and skirted it, but not very carefully, and came down into a hot and humid Calcutta after six hours in the air. Barrie Bayes was there to meet us and escort us to the local airport hotel. There was beer there, and I ate carefully. Then Barrie took us out to walk around Calcutta to get his establishing shots. We all felt the heat keenly and were glad of air-conditioning.

On our 23rd day we were still three days behind schedule, but had plans to do a double-jump and avoid Bangladesh. If bureaucrats were bad in India, we had heard they were twice as bad in the former colony of Bengal. Getting out of Calcutta was the usual nightmare. We walked on to the airport at 5 a.m., prepared for a fight, but as the hours passed and we were sent from one office to another, looking for another babu to stamp the flight plan, I felt like screaming. They were all so afraid of each other. I looked at the trembling hands and fearful eyes of the man handling our processing and realised he was a creature caught in a nightmare, and that was his living. Keith sat stoically through most of the fight. At 10 a.m. we had permission to go to the Flyer, we walked across and, in dreadful heat, we looked at a thunderstorm approaching from the west, we dressed and climbed in.

Then there was a fight to get into the air, in which ATC claimed visibility was below 2,000 metres and not VFR (visual flight rules, the rules under which we were permitted to fly), while we told him we could see seven miles. We won after a wearing debate by declaring 'special VFR', we felt like two boiled lumps of meat when we finally lined up to take off. We were in the worst possible physical condition to make a 484-mile flight to Mandalay in Burma.

The Flyer climbed steadily up to 7,000 feet as we passed smoothly over the mouth of the Ganges and sped east over the sea, intending to bypass Chittagong. Keith thought he had found a gap in the 10,000-foot mountain range that divided Burma from India and Bangladesh. We flew into the mountains with the west wind tailing off, but a storm developed to the south and raced around mountains and over country, which, if we landed out, would have wrecked the Flyer. There were no roads.

It got scary just after the main peaks, turbulent with thermals and the hot wind, and we were quietly terrified of being weathered-in. But we ploughed on, committed, no going back, skirting one particularly big black rain cloud and being hit on the edges by heavy rain drops. The countryside changed again when we reached the broad Irrawaddy valley down which my father-in-law Colonel Ian

Campbell had fought in the last war with the 14th Army. It was brown and cultivated, full of temples with a huge statue of a reclining Buddha.

We landed at Mandalay, having done our first double-jump of the whole trip, and put our watches another hour forward. The airport was surprisingly free of hassles, compared to the way I remembered Rangoon from my Australia flight. I felt strong inside myself, capable of doing anything. I hated the money-grubbing attitude we were moving into; everything had a price, but no value.

Looking back, this was the peak of Keith's and my flight together. We had reduced the deficit on our 80-day schedule to just two days, but from there on the problems we ran into grew serious and caused more frictions between us than we had bargained for. The first indication was not long in coming.

8. MANDALAY TO HONG KONG

On day 24, 16 April, the hotel in Mandalay arranged to top up our tanks for $32, and we took a pick-up provided by the street concierge to the airport. Here we dripped sweat and rebuilt the hobbled Flyer. There were a few journalists, no customs or immigration, but a shocking $129 landing- and parking-fee, all to be paid in American dollars, cash. 'It is our commission charge,' I heard.

We had no indication of the wind until we were in the air, facing 411 miles of inhospitable countryside to Luang Prabang in Laos without an alternative legal airfield. Once away, the Flyer climbed slowly, at full throttle. It was soon evident that we had a small following wind, but it was extremely misty and big, brown tree-covered mountains loomed in view, first as shadows then as solid ground over which we flew. After an hour we were at 5,000 feet, the temperature settled and we picked our way eastwards.

We soon came to a number of forest fires, each generating a long deadly plume of black smoke as an obstacle for us to clear. Inside that smoke was turbulence. Thermals started to pop, helping us to climb but also slinging us around. I could only maintain height by thrashing the engine, yet it showed no signs of distress. We settled in for the hours ahead. Keith yawned loudly.

The sky looked benign through the mist with no cloud, or high cloud, for hours. Clouds began to bubble up as we crossed the border into Laos at 7,000 feet, where we had an 'English sky', with what looked like harmless white clouds. Keith suggested flying right around a big one and I noticed it turning dark. Within minutes the base had dropped, along with buckets of rain.

We flew right, bewildered at the tremendous speed the rainstorm had developed and watched another start to explode ahead of us, so I steered left and picked my way between the two. It was not very turbulent, but the threat was always there. We were dumb with apprehension and latent fear. It seemed to us (but who could tell?) that there was a way through the rainstorms. We were suspicious of everything. I watched one lovely white cloud from a respectful distance as it turned into a monster, pouring out rain and, thankfully, far enough away for us to avoid.

After six hours we reached Luang Prabang, a pretty town next to a big river between two mountain ranges. I landed well (to Keith's relief), and after we taxied in, a stream of children and adults came at us from all quarters. Luang Prabang was a tourist town and we could scarcely find an official; when we did he took our passports. As we should have landed in Vientianne (but couldn't – it was beyond our range) I was slightly worried. We stayed at a reasonable hotel (cold-water showers) run by a Frenchman called Humbert, $40 a night for a double room, cheap food and lovely beer. The Flyer was stowed away in a hangar. It was the local water festival and we were twice soaked by good-natured crowds throwing water at us as we drove by.

We were stuck for a day in Luang Prabang. Charles had not been able to get us a visa, as it had meant sending our passports to Paris and a wait of four weeks. He had expected we would be able to buy visas for $50, but the bureaucracy of actually getting accepted took half-a-day's heavy negotiation. Then clouds came in, rain poured down, and we wiped out the whole of day 25. It was the first time bureaucrats and weather had combined to down us.

On day 26, 18 April, it was Keith's turn to fly. It had rained heavily much of the night. From 7 to 9 a.m., we did little jobs on the Flyer; replacing tubes, tightening clips, cleaning her out, repairing a small weeping leak to the fuel tank. The sky looked hopeless, heavy with cloud, the surrounding mountains buried in it. We stalked about with frustration while a constantly changing crowd chattered about the Flyer.

I was watching the sky all the time and when the rain stopped I thought a stable situation had developed. At mountain-top level there was a layer of weak, black lifeless cloud clinging to the slopes, while high above another layer was shielding the earth from the sun. I felt this would probably change later in the day as the sun got to work, but it seemed to be a window of opportunity for us to go. Keith had been brooding over the maps, particularly a long ridge of mountains 7,500 feet high, about 100 miles into the 254-mile flight to Hanoi. I suggested we should take off. He asked me if I could guarantee the mountains would be free of cloud. Of course I could not give that guarantee, I said, but I thought we should take the chance.

'What if we leave and have to come back and this valley is clagged in?' he asked.

I said I didn't think that was likely but we still had the GPS. This was the first difference of opinion between us about the flight and it developed into a muted row. We didn't shout at each other, but my louder voice made him accuse me of 'shouting and screaming and trying to bulldoze me into flying. We are not within a million miles of flying!'

I tried to persuade him he was wrong. He thought I was mistaken. If I had been the pilot of the day, I would have insisted. As he was, I couldn't. I said we could be stuck here in the monsoon season and those mountains would still be there whenever we took off.

Keith insisted he wanted to fly on as much as I did, but I felt, privately, that he had worked himself up into a state about the clouds and the mountains. When he was like that he seldom budged, so I left him alone. We each walked around nursing our frustration.

The weather changed slowly as the sun got to work, making the clag expand, but still without life. I worried that in our valley we would get total cloud cover and not be able to punch through. I kicked stones and walked and thought about insisting, as the originator of the idea, that we fly, but decided that would be fatal to our relationship.

An hour after the row, Keith, who had sat with his face in his hands, started looking at the GPS and rechecking his maps. Then, without a word, he picked up his flying suit. I started preparing to fly. We said little, just the necessary words to get ready. Keith remained deeply, bitterly, pessimistic. I felt he was going to fly to prove me wrong so he could say, 'I told you so.' The watching crowd grew and chattered, as we grimly got in, started up and Keith warmed the engine. He signalled that he was ready to go, a short taxi out to the runway and we were off.

For the first hour we exchanged terse comments about the cloud. Keith picked his way skywards, the Flyer making good progress. Once he said he couldn't fly over the next cloud and I said, 'Well, fly around it.' And we did. In one way I felt Keith wanted us to be blocked by clouds, so he would have been right, but of course he also wanted to fly to Vietnam. We soared above the lower cloud and found there were, indeed, layers through which we could fly. It was lovely to find a following wind again. There were said to be the bodies of 250 young Americans in the jungles of Laos, missing from the Vietnam War. About 15 were discovered each year, identified by teeth or dog-tags. I was aware we were looking at a country which was the last thing ever seen by so many young men of my generation.

The flying was cold but technically smooth, with hardly a ripple. We reached 8,200 feet, soon lost touch with Vientianne ATC, and the mountains Keith had worried himself into a state about scarcely troubled us. They were harmless black rocks below, not the shrouded monsters of our imagination. Gradually, Keith started to talk and we were almost back to normal by the time the mountains fell away and we knew we were flying over Vietnam.

The weather changed and it rained for more than an hour. In the north Vietnamese plain the weather was misty. We found our way in on our GPS, descending into the warmth over a populous flat country with huge brown rivers. There was little forward visibility, but we could see the ground at all times. Four miles from the airport Keith saw the runway and we landed.

Airport officials were delighted to see us, allegedly the first microlight in North Vietnam. An Australian airline captain said he had seen us on TV in Saigon. Steve Crossman, second secretary at the British Embassy, saw us through formalities. We booked into the Guoman Hotel ($70 a night), and were not aware that we would spend the next six nights there, fighting to get into China.

Keith apologised in the bar about getting the weather wrong, but things did not quite go back to normal between us. Flying was the one thing which gave him an identity; getting it wrong hurt him deeply. I was, after all, the amateur, even though I had done the Australia flight, while, as an instructor, he felt he was the professional. I resolved to try and find a way to defuse things.

The Chinese authorities, unlike the Japanese, had never actually said we could not fly through their country. Their air attaché in London, Colonel Li, was very keen on the idea, but we needed permission out of Beijing and, on the day after we arrived in Hanoi, we found that was not forthcoming. It was not that the answer was no. It just wasn't yes. Our ambassador in Beijing, Mr A.C. Galsworthy, along with one of his officials, Caroline Wilson, patiently put our case to the Chinese authorities, time and again.

The key to their change of heart was the intervention of royalty,

Prince Michael of Kent, who happened to be visiting China at the time and put our case personally to the Chinese vice-premier. This proved, in the circumstances, impossible to refuse. More than once on this flight I had found the disinterested intervention of a prince was enough to see us through. There was no financial interest in their help to us, but they did it anyway. It was enough to confirm my being a Royalist and not a dull republican.

But it took five days, from 19 April to 23 April, during which time the Flyer lay open to the elements on Hanoi International Airport, before we secured permission to fly on. In London, it was Charles Heil's finest hour, and the work he did with the supportive and courageous Caroline Wilson in particular, ensured that Keith and I were the first people ever to fly a microlight across China. Our Foreign Office backed up the work in Beijing by support services in Hanoi from our ambassador, David Fall, and Steve Crossman, our host for the whole period.

Every day Keith and I checked out of the Guoman Hotel and sat in the lobby, waiting to hear if we had permission to fly on. When we heard we had not, we checked back in again and retired to our rooms. Sometimes Steve came around and took us out on the town. Otherwise, we phoned each other occasionally and met at the bar every evening for a beer and the decision on a meal. It was wearing. I spent the time reading V.M. Yeate's *Winged Victory* for the first time on this flight. I had read it three times on the flight to Australia, and was destined, though I did not know it, to read it five times altogether before arriving in the USA. It is a brilliant account of the life of a First World War fighter pilot in a Sopwith Camel squadron, in the summer of 1918, and it was always able to transport me to another world.

On the evening of 23 April, despite our only wardrobe being jeans and T-shirts, David and Gwendolyn Fall invited us to an evening reception at the British Embassy. They had already given us lunch and introduced us to their son Nathan. We arrived in the steaming heat, walking past the Hanoi Hilton, the jail where American prisoners were kept during the Vietnam War. I think the Falls were quietly amused at the contrast between our dress and that of the other guests.

Nathan suggested we end the evening in an improbably named bar, Apocalypse Now, about ten minutes' walk from the Fall's home. It was supposed to be heaving with people, but when we got there it was nearly empty. In one corner was the hollowed-out nose of an American Huey helicopter, widely used in the Vietnam War, and certainly not bought by the bar owners. Behind the screen, where young American pilots once looked down on a war-torn country-side, a disc jockey had set up a den. He was playing, very loudly, *American Pie*, the anthem of the American soldiers who went off to fight the war, and behind the bar a young Vietnamese was shouting along with Don McLean. I had missed the Vietnam War myself, though as an immigrant to the US in the early 1960s I had been eligible for the draft and just escaped it. But the experience of being in Hanoi, in a bar with such a name, listening to such music from such a source, was quite surreal. I insisted they play it again so I could sing along with it too.

There was a flurry of activity on the morning of Friday, 24 April, with Steve Crossman monitoring the slow pace of permissions taken by the Chinese. The embassy's wonderful fixer, Mr Ei, who grinned constantly despite having huge gaps in his teeth, prepared the ground for us to get past security at Hanoi Airport. It was tremendously hot and humid when we got to the Flyer, which looked careworn after days in the sun, but we rigged her and cleaned her down. Even deep into the afternoon there was doubt about our getting away, and I hung around the ATC office waiting for the final official go-ahead. Then we were cleared, and I worried that we would not be able to get over the 7,000-foot mountains and into the Chinese airport at Nanning before it got dark.

We were now eight days behind our schedule and wanted to race across China. I flew through the mist, a common feature of North Vietnam, and we had a slight following wind as we sped into the mountains, over inhospitable countryside where landing out could easily be fatal. It was a journey of only 160 miles but it was twilight when I was guided into Nanning by an excellent English speaker. We were held on the apron for two hours while the authorities decided what to do with us.

'You are not in trouble,' said one of the policemen, as I made frustrated noises. 'It is just that we do not know how to handle a private aircraft. We have never seen one before.'

Keith and I were able to get the Flyer settled in a large open-front garage inside an enormous airport building, while four local Chinese, who followed the flight on the Internet, got us into a hotel and took us to dinner.

On day 33, we spent hours in Nanning trying to get past numerous bureaucratic delays, mostly caused by curiosity, to reach the Flyer. Everyone insisted on photographs; we finally got away at 11.40 a.m.

The cloud was thick and an east wind blowing, but as we climbed it turned westerly. There were beautiful patterns to the farming countryside. Cloud base was 1,600 feet, and, with mountains of 4,000 feet ahead of us, Keith made the key decision to climb to 7,000 feet where we found vague cloud layers. I navigated from the back with the little Garmin GPS, Keith using the Skyforce only for emergencies. For two hours we could see the ground through mist, but then we lost it and flew blindly through the cloud. We always made good time, but became apprehensive as we were whited-out. I could sense Keith's helpless fears and kept chanting, in a calm voice: 'Right 10, steady, steady.' He flew with his eyes glued to the turn-and-bank and glances at the altimeter, while I kept us on course and looked for holes in the cloud. We passed through heavy rain and stayed in touch with ATC at all times, to reassure them we were indeed the clockwork aircraft of their fantasies.

There was a period when we tried to descend to find cloud base, but failed at 5,000 feet, with 4,000-foot mountains below. This was truly terrifying. We climbed again, totally committed. Our only blind-flying instrument was a turn-and-bank indicator, which told us if the wings were level. There were no opt-out fields and anyway we could not have used them. We just had to endure it.

After long desperate hours we came close to Ghangzong, with other traffic in the air (frightening), and we were still in cloud. There we turned right for Macau, and from our map we knew the mountains were behind us, so we descended, still whited-out, over a flat plain. Breaking through cloud and seeing the ground again after so long was a sweet relief.

At 2,000 feet it was sticky and wet and both our video cameras failed. We came in to Macau at 500 feet and in mist. It looked rich and prosperous. Keith was relieved to be on the ground and said it was one of the worst flights he had ever had.

Barrie Bayes and a photographer from England called Colin Edwards, hired by Newlyn, were there to meet us, along with Debbie Davies. We spent two hours being interviewed before finally getting to the Hyatt Regency Hotel. Paul Collins, a local microlight pilot, briefed me on landing in Hong Kong. Dinner was pleasant but Bayes threw a tantrum afterwards, setting up in Keith's room and not mine, having already interviewed Keith. When asked to move to my room he stormed out and resigned. Due to a personality-clash, he could not stand working with Debbie and this emotion over-rode any professional job he was required to do. I watched my investment of £40,000 stalk huffily down the corridor, I was not sympathetic. I thought he and Newlyn were a pair, two men peripheral to the flight who could destroy it with tantrums.

I did an interview with Debbie on one of my video cameras, which worked but was not well framed. In England, Andy Webb was incandescent.

I woke after only three hours' sleep to complete my journal and berate myself for being involved with so many prima donnas. Petulant resigners should be shot.

The tantrum affected my mood, and Keith's. We had a rendezvous with Bayes at 7.10 a.m. on day 34, 26 April, in the air over Hong Kong harbour, to get some of the best pictures available to us, but we were not certain he would make it. As ever, a big hotel bill – $400 – depressed me, and when we got to the Flyer, we began sweating in the heavy humidity. At 6.35 a.m., we were ready to go. It took us 40 minutes over smooth sea and low cloud to get to Green Island, south of Hong Kong, and when we rounded the island we flew the amazing low-level route past the Hong Kong waterfront. It was breathtaking, but no sign of Bayes or the helicopter. I asked ATC where it was and discovered it was still on the ground.

'I'll never forgive him if his tantrum means he doesn't get this shot,' I told Keith. We were past the waterfront when we heard he had taken off, but a kind ATC let me fly back to Green Island, where the helicopter picked us up and we had a second pass for the cameras before landing.

There was no indication then of the dreadful conditions we were going to run into later in the day.

9. HONG KONG TO YUZHNO-SAKHALINSK

Our intended route from Hong Hong was north to Shanghai, then race up Japan via Osaka and Tokyo, and pay homage to two Japanese pilots, Abe and Kawachi, who had flown to Europe in 65 days back in 1925. From Japan, I had plotted a route along the Kurile Islands to Petro-Pavlovsk and then right to cross the Aleutians, a string of volcanic islands which link Russia to Alaska.

Though we had no inkling of problems yet in Russia, we knew Japan was going to be difficult, some said impossible. Ever since the flight was planned, the Japanese Ministry of Transport had said no. They were embarrassed by our intentions, because in Japan microlights are subjected to cretinous rules, restricted to within 1.5 kms of their airport of departure and not allowed to fly above 500 feet. There were 2,500 microlight pilots in Japan, and it was as if, all over the country, thousands of little butterflies fluttered inside legal cages. We had found no resonance at all in Japan to our homage to the 1925 pilots, which I found odd. It would have saved face.

All the way up the coast of China we were fighting – me every evening on the phone and Charles back in London – to get a yes decision from Tokyo after all the negatives.

Our first destination out of Hong Kong was Fuzchou, which I hoped to make in one flight from Kai Tak Airport. Taking off behind a huge Airbus, I hurried at 400 feet to Junk Bay and stayed under cloud at 500 feet for about 30 miles, with a poor ground speed (48–50 knots). Then a gap opened in the clouds and I climbed through to 7,000 feet, heading north to the China coast.

For a while we could see the sea in gaps between the clouds, but when we reached China the cloud became more general and we lost sight of land. Soon we were flying in vague layers, not quite in or out of cloud, and at the time always aware of the horizontal. The height gave us a west wind and we cruised at 75 knots, with Fuzchou well within range. After three and a half hours, conditions deteriorated. I was having to climb and descend to find a line through the clouds and see where I was going, with Keith chanting behind me, 'left, ten', or 'right, 20', or 'smack on course'. We had one scary moment, a complete white-out, which I climbed out of.

We talked to ATC at Xiamen, which was concerned about us, but did not harass us. I stayed at 5,000 feet for a while, entering clouds above and below us, which seemed to meet ahead of us. Then, suddenly, white-out. I could not see the wing tips. Keith said, 'Let's get below this.' So I switched on the moving-map GPS again, and discovered sea to our right. I steered with just four things in sight, the turn-and-bank indicator, the altimeter, compass and GPS. I could look at nothing else or I would have become disorientated. We descended, 5,000 feet, 4,000 feet, 3,000 feet, and all the time Keith murmured, 'Believe your instruments, don't look anywhere else,' while I reported, 'Heading for the sea, it's ahead now, steering 150, down to 2,000 feet.'

Blind panic in such situations is dangerous. You are aware that you could spiral out of the sky, so you fall back on technique and suppress your fears. There is only the faintest inkling of how awesomely fearful it is, and that provides gallons of adrenaline. We were under-supplied with blind-flying instruments, but the turn-and-bank indicator paid for itself a hundred times over in those minutes of blind descent.

At 1,500 feet, still not daring to look away from my instruments, Keith said, 'We're below cloud, I can see the coast.' I looked right and saw the coast too. We plodded along, our air speed dropping to 47 knots, and realised we had no reserves to make it to Fuzchou. It began to rain. We passed over fishing villages, brown and rich and wet, with cloud descending to 1,000 feet. I discovered where we were on the map and talked to Xiamen ATC via a relay, because of 3,000-foot mountains which got in the way of our VHF transmission.

At 800 feet we rounded the headland, where it began to rain seriously. I tried to protect our naked radio and vital GPS, but they were soon sopping wet. The rain was torrential. My helmet had lost a retaining bolt and the visor was loose; I feared for it flying off into the prop and taking the full force of the rain in my face. We flew over hundreds of boats and ships, big and small, to Xiamen Island. By now conditions were atrocious. We had just enough room under the clouds to get over two huge electricity cables, we steered all the way north to finally discover the enormous runway at Xiamen. By now I was laughing out loud at how absurd we were to be in the air.

The runway appeared out of the gloom and we landed.

The Chinese were very kind. Engineers at Xiamen Airways, many of whom spoke good English, housed the Flyer in a big hangar. ATC closed our flight plan, and a giggling girl presented me with a landing charge of $850, at which I laughed scornfully. They had never seen a private aircraft at Xiamen and were just going by the book. After more scorn she reduced the bill, first to $550, then $250, all of which I refused to pay. Then a man came and asked if I would pay $50? I said I would, so long as I had a stamped receipt. We were the only guests that night in a white elephant of a hotel.

On day 35, 27 April, we got fuel with local help, 85 litres – a lot for the previous day's journey – and Keith found the exhaust loose and a small oil leak in the new oil cooler, which he fixed. We were given a tumultuous send off, journalists joining the throng and a lot of posing for photos. Keith climbed to 500 feet and headed for the coast. Cloud base was 1,300 feet and we looked down on mist and a busy brown river full of working boats. Our intention was to stay over the sea where cloud was not so developed and for a while we did so. Then Keith punched his way upwards, never quite getting whited-out, and on top it was a lot easier. Our ground speed, which had been 50 knots, went up to 58 knots.

We settled into our new routine. Our little Garmin became our main navigation instrument, and I called out headings. The bane of our life was the radio, where we were seriously harassed by ATC. They constantly wanted to know our altitude, our distance from them, our speed, our estimate of when we would reach reporting points. There were no other aircraft within 500 miles at our level and we were disturbing no one. When fighting through cloud, full of fears and tensions, or holding the wings level for hours being banged by turbulence, it was a bloody nuisance having to reply to some insistent prat who wanted to know, for the sixth time, when we would reach his airfield. Keith was given to telling them whoppers. Each time, they replied, 'Roger'.

It took us two hours to get to Fuzhou, to be met by a crowd of 200 people and the usual demand for $850. We were given free fuel by a local, but what was striking was the demand for paper. Had we been through quarantine? Passports? Customs? Every bit of paper we had, someone wanted to see it. It was not threatening, just curious. We became brusque and irritated. We did not mean to bully people, but we were in such a hurry and they were so slow, I got to clapping my hands and actually said: 'chop chop, gotta go', and they all moved a bit faster.

It took us only an hour to get refuelled, haggle the landing fee down to $100 and fly away. Keith was resigned to going into the mountains, 6,500-feet high on the way to Hangzhou. Our maps did not cover the last 30 miles, but we knew from the Skyforce that the airport was at 20 feet, so we thought we would be fine. Our worry was darkness; it would be sunset (if we were lucky) when we landed. It was a personal nightmare, descending in the dark, in cloud, in mountains, and we did not want to do it.

Keith took an early decision to go for height, despite the rising cloud base, and we went out over the sea and headed upwards. I had never deliberately gone into cloud this way, and it was eerie being whited-out by choice. It took a few minutes to climb a thousand feet to burst out of the top into glorious blue sky with scraps of cirrus. We were now technically illegal. We rode along at 7,500 feet, white cloud bubbling underneath and occasional hills of cloud breaking out. Keith turned on his Skyforce GPS from time to time to see where the sea was. We soon lost touch – thankfully – with ATC, and a new frequency given to us by relay from another aircraft remained free of that dreadful drawl, 'Golf, Mike, Golf, Tango, Golf,' which we now hated.

The flight became a race against the sun going down. Keith kept looking for the best wind by changing heights. We might have gained five mph at 8,000 feet, compared with 6,000 feet, but it cost us in a higher fuel-burn. I wasn't as fearful of the night landing as Keith. We could both do it, we had already done it, and we kept a torch ready to read the instruments. The countryside beneath us was like Vietnam, rugged, mountainous, full of scrub and tree, with few tracks and hardly any roads. The valley floor was thickly populated with great clusters of villages. I kept busy, careful about everything I did, fearful of dropping things into the prop.

Finally, ATC at Hangzhou started calling, we were obliged to reply and Keith had a series of shouted conversations, which were very wearing, as they demanded every two minutes to know our height, speed and position. It was not helped by their poor English. Keith was irate and grumbled.

We watched the sun go down from 7,000 feet, looked at the misty valley and pondered our chances. When ATC told us to descend we reasoned he must know what he was talking about, and were relieved to find ourselves over a wide valley floor. Forward visibility was poor, but Keith had the Skyforce working full time and we went straight to the airfield.

There were hassles on the ground, offers of fuel at three times the normal price and no hangars, so we left the Flyer hobbled in one corner of the airfield and got a taxi to a hotel. It took two hours between landing and getting to our rooms in a hotel. I showered, put all my gear on charge, phoned London, went down for a beer and a 'shove-in' dinner. Bed at midnight. It was a good day, 400 miles under our belts. When I woke in the middle of the night I knew we had to stop in Shanghai and start a public fight with the Japanese about getting into their country. If they continued to say no, we could try to fly up China to Vladivostok.

On day 36, we left our poor choice of hotel – too big, too busy, too foreign – but found a wonderful taxi driver who took us straight across the tarmac to the Flyer. No messing with security for him. He said he had read about us in *China Daily*, and was number-one man among the crowd jostling around the Flyer.

I replenished all our cameras with film and video, as always fearful someone would discover the amount of camerawork we were doing. We got away, in thick haze and poor visibility, at 9.30 a.m. I climbed in smooth conditions to 5,000 feet, guided by Keith and the Garmin, and we flew over a classic alluvial plain, full of rivers and clusters of villages, but flat as a pancake. There was no harassment from ATC, which was pleasant, but I recognised the conditions as similar to India when the Djinn appeared and I was fearful he would appear again. It made me nervous.

It was a short trip to Shanghai, which did not quite know how to cope with us, they were appalled at how slowly we flew, but then they took a deep breath and let us in direct. We saw seven airliners waiting to take off as I tried to get down quickly. Keith said their pilots would dine out on the story for weeks. It was windy as we taxied in and we hung around for a while, being stared at, before China Eastern Airways found us a hangar, then we took a taxi into the city and booked into a hotel.

We stayed there that night and the whole of the following day, with me exploring other routes instead of Japan. I favoured going up China to burst into Russia via Vladivostok, but the Beijing authorities thought they had done enough for us and said no. Then I looked at flying up to the north of South Korea and punting off across the sea to Vladivostok, but that would have meant risking North Korean air space, and they shoot people down. Keith did not like that option. I wanted a public fight with the Japanese, but Dallas, back in London, vetoed that, as it could harm GT Global's business interests. In the end I decided to fly on to Cheju, right next to Japan, and hammer at its door. David Crooks, first secretary at the British Embassy in Tokyo, was extremely helpful and got our ambassador there, Sir David Wright, to plead our case.

In the meantime, for reasons I never fathomed, the parcel with our spare passports and Russian visas, which had chased us across half the world and missed us in Hong Kong, was sent to our hotel in Shanghai. It was a dreadful error and costs us days of delays.

We had still not got that parcel when we left for Cheju on day 38, 30 April. Scott Shi of China Eastern Airways met us at the airport and saw us through immigration, customs and other formalities. 'This is an historic flight', he told me, 'China must learn from the outside,' and there were no charges made.

Keith flew us out to the coast over a strongly smelling Shanghai, and the first 30 miles was VFR, but gradually cloud closed in beneath us. We climbed to 7,500 feet, but could not stay above the cloud peaks and, after a while, we were whited-out. Keith persisted, blind, for 15 minutes, and we always felt we might break through, but in the end he descended down to 3,500 feet, watching the turn-and-bank, while I chanted directions from the back. We broke out between two layers of cloud, the one below us quite beautiful and wispy, hanging over the sea. Keith was fearful these layers would meet in a cloud sandwich, but they did not. And as we progressed, our speed crept up to around 65 knots.

We were happy and didn't talk much.

The sky opened up in the last 50 miles before Cheju and we saw the sea for the first time in 200 miles; it looked rough. There was a strong east wind down there, yet at 5,000 feet we had a westerly. We flew around the west of Cheju to the airport on the north of the island, but shied away when we saw a heavy rainstorm right over the runway. Keith told ATC we would wait for the storm to pass, so we circled and watched airliners plunge into the rain. ATC asked, 'Where will you land if you don't land here?'

We laughed and replied, 'We're just waiting.'

Keith took the Flyer in on approach, but as we descended our ground speed plunged from 68 knots to 23 knots, there was a huge wind shear and it got rough. We struggled in to land, airliners lined up watching, and Keith got his first '10' score. There was a 30-knot crosswind on the ground. An Australian voice said in our earphones just after touchdown, 'Nice one, digger.'

A crowd of journalists and microlight pilots met us, we had garlands put around our necks and Korean Airlines officials guided us through the formalities. The Flyer was put away safely in the firemen's garage and we booked into the KAL hotel. A local micro-light pilot, Mr Moon, a successful businessman with a face full of character, took us out to a typical Korean dinner – shoes off, cross-legged, lots of dishes, beer and a strong chaser – which was delicious. We had no stomach problems. Happiness, I wrote later, was being able to fart without fear, not something you can do in India.

Charles told me that the Japanese were not, now, saying no, but that we had to fill in a 50-page application form, in Japanese, three copies please. Ho ho. We filed a flight plan to go to Hiroshima, despite storms being forecast. All the following day, the 39th after leaving London, I conducted a long-distance battle through GT Global's Masakazu Hasagawa with the Japanese Ministry of Transport. Mr Hasagawa, after initial hesitation, was willing to help me during this fight – sections of GT Global were worried about being associated with people who might die. After the dust settled we were given permission to fly through the west side of Japan, away from all the major cities. The authorities took revenge on us for having the infernal cheek to want to fly through their country by saying we had to use a handling agent called IBAS, which would cost $4,000 every time we touched down. This was a charge on me, though they tried to introduce a red herring by saying GT Global would pay. That would have broken my contract with GT Global in London and I was not keen on having such a hostage to fortune, to Dallas in particular. I haggled the fees down to a still-dreadful $1,200 per landing, and these charges forced us, inevitably, to make dangerous decisions on our flight through Japan. Whenever we took off, we were not keen to land.

Charles told me a big Garmin GPS, plus our repaired Skyforce, would be waiting for us in Sapporo in northern Japan, along with a computer, passports and Russian visas.

Meanwhile, the local South Korean microlight community saw us as their champions and wined and dined us. All they wanted was for

The GT Global microlight

TOP LEFT: Charles Heil
MAIN PICTURE: Keith Reynolds
RIGHT: Alison Harper

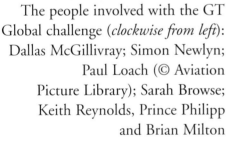

The people involved with the GT Global challenge (*clockwise from left*): Dallas McGillivray; Simon Newlyn; Paul Loach (© Aviation Picture Library); Sarah Browse; Keith Reynolds, Prince Philipp and Brian Milton

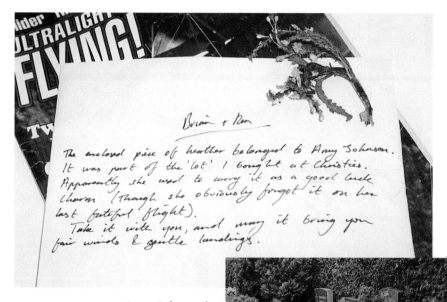

Brian + Ken

The enclosed piece of heather belonged to Amy Johnson. It was part of the 'lot' I bought at Christies. Apparently she used to carry it as a good luck charm (though she obviously forgot it on her last fateful flight).

Take it with you, and may it bring you fair winds & gentle landings.

ABOVE: Amy Johnson's lucky heather
RIGHT: Keith and Brian at Otto Lilienthal's grave in Berlin
BELOW: The pilots and photographers (*left to right*): Graham Slater, the author, Barrie Bayes and Keith

Over the Alps

By Gwadar

'No customs, no customs'

LEFT: Keith with Romania the camel, Qaysumah

BELOW: Steve Crossman

ABOVE LEFT: Our microlight was smaller than a helicopter yet we hoped it would get us around the world
ABOVE RIGHT: The flyer and the Hong Kong skyline
BELOW LEFT: Hong Kong
BELOW RIGHT: A garlanded Keith Reynolds

Valeri Kudriaveev

The Russian Consul,
Alexander Noskov

A beardless Keith says
goodbye to Lina

Keith and Brian part
company, while Lenin looks
the other way

us to succeed. We found the same simple yearning among the microlight pilots of Japan. They honoured us by their beliefs.

There was another day's hold-up in Cheju, this time because of the weather, on 2 May, the significant day 40, when we should have been at Nome, Alaska. I never minded God putting us down. It was the bureaucrats I could not stand.

On day 41, cloud was down to the ground, occasional showers, drizzle, altogether it was not inviting. At the airport I filed a flight plan and got the forecast, while Keith went to fix a puncture. He had said the previous day he could do it in 15 minutes ('trust me, trust me'), so we didn't fix it when we learned about it. In the event, he pinched the new inner tube putting it in so it punctured again and we had to use a previously repaired tube instead. Keith spent some time chiding me about whether I had removed all the air when making the repair.

I set off on runway 240, hopeful, as it meant a following wind, then headed north, climbing steadily and entering cloud at 800 feet and still catching glimpses of the ground at 1,000 feet. For the next two minutes I flew on the turn-and-bank and the compass, while Keith chanted courses in the back and I watched the altimeter. We were whited-out, rain trickling across our visors, radio and GPS protected by a shower cap. At 2,200 feet Keith said, 'You can look up now.' And I saw the rolling tops of clouds to the horizon. I turned right on course ('77 knots ground speed,' said Keith), and we set off for Japan.

Cloud remained thick over Cheju Island, but thinned out over the sea to make us uneasily legal again. I took the Flyer to 4,000 feet, a comfortable height, and lapsed into the dozing state our flight induced when there was no real work to be done. We sat, occasionally shifting for comfort, no movement to the control bar, while I tried to find a distant point to steer by, to avoid constantly monitoring the compass.

Higher up, more active cloud signalled the presence of land, and close to the first Japanese islands a gap appeared in the clouds. I went down under them to discover base was just 500 feet. For 30 miles on the way to Fukuoka I flew at 400 feet, over big fast launches criss-crossing the sea between the islands. The landing went well and IBAS showed why they were so expensive. Keith got a flight plan and all the customs and immigration formalities done for him, while I put in Avgas. We dealt with some newspaper reporters and were away within the hour.

Again, we had to climb through cloud, with 3,000-foot mountains between us and Okayama. But after we reached clean sky the next three hours were a milk run. We had passed Nagasaki, 50 miles to our right, on the way into Fukuoka, and we passed Hiroshima on our left about 100 miles later. Japan looked awesome, cultivated and thriving on every flat space, but full of rugged green mountains.

The landing at Okayama, 433 miles from Cheju, was in a stiff cross-wind, turbulent and bumpy, but it went fine. We were met by three TV crews, ten photographers and lots of journalists. Japanese microlight pilots desperately wanted us to be a success, to use as a precedent: 'If we don't fly, the MoT think we are safe,' said one flyer. Led by Onou Senta, who had helped negotiate us into the country, they put us up in a hotel overnight, fed us, including beer, and 'banzai'd' us for our flight. It seemed to be Japanese for 'three cheers'. My generation thought 'Banzai' was what Japanese soldiers shouted when conducting suicidal bayonet charges.

On day 42, 5 May, it was Keith's turn to fly the 362 miles from Okayama to Niigata. The day was beautiful with blue sky and no clouds, but Keith turned up at breakfast in a dreadful mood. He contradicted everything I said and disagreed with every decision. Senta paid our hotel bill and took us by car with a fellow-flyer to the airport. Asahi TV had arranged a helicopter to film us over Okayama, a diversion from the flight of about 20 minutes in all, and the least we could do to say thanks. Keith found every reason he could think of to say he did not want to do it and an argument developed. I wanted it done and completed the arrangements. Keith said no.

'We won't have enough fuel, we will have to land back at the airport,' he said.

'Not at $1,200 a landing,' I said.

The argument ended by him saying, 'Shut up! Just shut up! Shut up! Shut up!'

'We've got 40 more days together and we have to sort this sort of thing out,' I said.

He had developed a complex about talking to the press, as if we were on a free ride and owed nobody anything. I discovered later in the day, when replacing videotape in his camera, that it had been put in on day 24 in Laos. Andy Webb could not make a programme if he had only one hour of video covering 18 days. I could not imagine how I could cover for this.

At the airport Keith had a sudden mood change. It was as if nothing had happened. Our flight plans were done for us and TV and newspapermen were there to see us off, along with a crowd of 150 people behind a wire fence. The Asahi helicopter circled overhead, waiting for our take-off. We prepared thoroughly, depressed at the thought of another headwind, however light, and took off at 9.40 a.m. Keith confounded my fears by doing just what Asahi TV asked, to fly over downtown Okayama and circle once. They did a professional job, very close, and did not ask for more, so we set off in thermic conditions, on course, but watching our speed drop off to 45 knots.

We flew over green mountains and neatly cultivated fields, villages and numerous towns. At 5,000 feet there was little of detail to see and we soon began to get cold.

'If we keep on at this speed we will not make Niigata,' I said, after 90 minutes' flying.

Keith agreed but thought that when we broke out over the sea we could descend and perhaps find a better wind. We hit the coast, which looked like the French Riviera – beaches, power boats, yachts, marinas, holiday developments, the sparkling sea, full of bays – and we went down, avoiding clouds, to 2,000 feet. Our speed crept up to 53–55 knots, which we thought would allow us to make it to Niigata. We plotted an alternative field for refuelling at Toyama, but I was worried about yet another $1,200 landing fee.

The flight turned into a hack and was very cold. I shivered for the last two hours in the back, passing stunning, snow-covered mountains to our right as we completed a 200-mile flight over the sea. Niigata looked like it had been flooded, with miles of fields covered in water. We landed and taxied to an enthusiastic reception. Going through immigration, as we had to do daily, even though we were already in Japan, we heard that lots of media was waiting for us. But we were delayed so long that the press left and only one solitary TV crew took passive shots of the Flyer in a hangar.

We ate the fish special at the hotel restaurant, with four beers each, which cost $150. Steaks were $45 each. Keith wanted to chat cheerfully but I was wary of another eruption.

On day 43, it was my turn to steer 359 miles from Niigata to New Chitose, near Sapporo, on Hokkaido, the last island before Russia. Keith was almost cheerful at breakfast. At the Flyer, Keith put a mask around half the oil cooler to allow the engine to run at a warmer temperature. I set out all the cameras, signed some autographs, posed for photos and we got off at 9.50 a.m.

It was a beautiful high-pressure day, little wind and a washed-out sky with high curling clouds. We climbed along the rich coastline to 4,000 feet and resigned ourselves to an uneventful hack. Our ground speed settled around 60 knots, always satisfying – we felt we were making progress at such speeds – and hours went by with little to do. I hardly touched the control bar, as the coast was our course.

Our route took us over Japan's characteristic green mountains, where deer and even bears live, and the occasional majestic peak up to 7,000 feet, covered in snow. We were only 39 degrees from the equator, but on some of the mountains we flew over there was snow. We were dressed in moon boots and had our big gloves on, so cold was not the problem it had been.

At New Chitose Airport, after five hours and 40 minutes in the air, there were jumbos and other big aircraft taking off and landing, but we slotted in neatly and taxied to a reception of four TV crews, and numerous photographers. After customs and immigration, shepherded by a local agent, we put the Flyer in a large hangar all to herself and held a press conference organised by local microlight pilots.

At the hotel I discovered to my horror that the vital parcel due to have been sent on from Shanghai had not arrived. A second parcel, with a Garmin GPS, was also not there. It dawned on me that we could not go on until we got the Shanghai parcel, with our second passports, each with a Russian visa.

I got hold of Charles, at about 7.45 a.m. his time, and we had a dreadful conversation. He had no idea where the parcels were, or who to hassle about them. What was worse was that, when I asked if he had checked on any previous day, he had not. He said he had not used DHL because they could not have guaranteed getting the parcels to us on a Monday. It was now Tuesday evening. The hotel in Shanghai where the parcels were delivered had said it would 'do its best'. I found this casual attitude unbelievable and blew up. As ever, he went quiet, but it did not make the problem go away.

I asked him to discover where the parcels were, and an hour later – to his credit, because I had been spectacularly angry – he phoned back to say the GPS was stuck in Japanese customs and the much more vital Shanghai parcel was stuck in Chinese customs. That meant we would have at least a day's delay, the first that was our own fault. I should have chased Charles harder on this matter. I spent the dinner with Japanese microlight pilots outwardly full of cheer, inwardly in despair. How could this happen to us now? The weather was set good for halfway up the Kuriles and it was going to waste.

Waking up the following day was more painful than at any time on this flight. Real despair.

In all, we spent eight days in Sapporo. We did try to get Russian visas on the first day there, but the Russian consul, Alexander Noskov, though personally sympathetic, said he could not comply until we had formal permission for the flight across Siberia. I had thought this was already agreed, but buckled down and tried to get a distinct Russian yes. Noskov vetoed the route through the Kuriles, saying there was no fuel there and we should go via Magadan and the Bering Sea. Day after day we kept getting a no from Noskov, and the parcels Charles had sent us failed to appear. The GPSs arrived first, but it was not until day 49, that Hasagawa got a rocket under the parcel with our spare passports and Russian visas, which had languished for days in Shanghai and Hong Kong, and they arrived.

Keith and I were occasionally entertained by Japanese pilots, but otherwise spent the days in the airport hotel, expensive, soulless and cut off from real life. We stayed in our separate rooms, me conducting the fight to get on and watching Japanese baseball on television, Keith just watching TV or going for a walk. We knew that the East-West Association, EWA, whom we had paid £5,000 to get us through Russia, had a man waiting for us on the other side, pulling strings to get us in. Or, at least, we thought that is what he was doing. I expected that, once we had valid visas, we would be able to break into Sakhalinsk Island, come under the wing of the EWA, and then be away across Siberia.

It did not help that Sakhalinsk had the most dreadful reputation as a secret Russian base. It was from there that the jet fighter took off in 1983 and shot down a Korean jumbo jet. Noskov told us the military shot first and asked questions afterwards.

When our second passports did arrive on day 49, 12 May, a serious difference of opinion arose between Keith and me. We filed a flight plan for Yuzhno-Sakhalinsk, which the Russians did not object to, so I thought we should go because they had not turned us down. Keith held that the risk was too great. He wanted specific landing permission before flying. It was a genuine difference of opinion, reflecting our different temperaments. Keith said he was not prepared to risk his life for the flight.

'The Russians are not the French or the Germans,' he said, 'they shoot people down.'

Later, he admitted that this was an unlikely prospect, but he kept harking back to Alexander Noskov's words, 'If you go without permission, you risk being shot down.' Words later retracted by Noskov himself. But Keith was adamant: 'I do not want to break international law.'

To keep us together I did not put up a huge fight, but I was unhappy. To be honest, no one knew what would happen, but that seemed to me to be more reason for taking that risk, not less. On my side, we had Richard Creasey's man, Valeri, from EWA, there to fight for us, even if I could not get in touch with him directly. Richard said, 'Get into Russia and we will see you through.'

Keith asked me to understand his point of view. I could see it, but watched the day ebb away into rain and low cloud and was thoroughly miserable. I felt in my bones we should have gone for it, I played patience and hearts on my computer for hours. Charles phoned just before dinner to ask why we had not gone and told me Valeri had spent the day in Yuzhno-Sakhalinsk waiting for us. Charles asked how Valeri knew we were coming and Valeri said, 'The control tower told me.' Charles had also passed this news on to Keith, whose reaction, said Charles, was, 'Oh.'

I could barely contain my rage.

Over dinner, again strained, Keith explained that all he had wanted was some assurance from the Russians that they knew we were coming. Now he had it, second-hand from Charles, he agreed to fly on. The problem was that I felt that this was not the end of it. We were going to have more differences of opinion about flying and they would fall one way: he would not want to fly and I would. However tattered my ambition about flying a microlight around the world in 80 days, the core of the dream remained. I privately felt we might be lucky to do it in 100 days, but it was no use admitting that.

Another difficulty was that Keith had already made the opening moves to be paid more money for the extra time we were taking on the flight, at £800 a week. Whenever I paid heavy or excessive bills, he joked, 'It's only money.' As if that helped. It did not, of course. I had told him before we left that I had budgeted for two weeks over the 80 days in calculating his pay and above that he would have to swallow.

The weather was poor on day 51, 13 May, and I agreed with Keith that we could not fly. It was a sterile day, I spent most of it in the room. Sometimes I prowled up and down and had to calm myself down. A voice kept crying inside me, 'We should be in Russia!' Valeri phoned and said that Russian border control was now willing to let us in. I did not care very much. We were going anyway, whatever they said. The main problem had been persuading Keith. We would not know how they would react until we got there.

Keith and I were up early on day 52, 14 May. The weather looked okay but not great, the wind was forecast to be south in the south of the island, going north-east – a headwind – near Yuzhno-Sakhalinsk. Our faithful little guide from IBAS, Midori Kumaki, turned up four minutes late, full of apologies, and asked if I had got the permission number from the Russians. I told her I had not but we were going anyway.

We were heavily blown around by the wind while taxiing and waiting for take-off behind a 757 and ahead of a jumbo jet. But at 10.30 a.m. – at last, at last – we leapt into the turbulent air, turning north-west towards Sapporo, and picked our way to the coast. Clouds lifted and then cleared away as we headed north, with our ground speed above 60 knots and easily enough fuel to make it to Yuzhno-Sakhalinsk. It looked like a milk run. We cruised at about 3,000 feet, nervous about the cold – it seemed to seep into my moon boots – but not being badly inconvenienced by it.

Keith made radio contact with Wakkanai, an airfield on the north coast of Hokkaido, before being put in touch with the Russians. Yuzhno-Sakhalinsk ATC, in solemn Russian style, told us we had not obtained permission to land there and must turn back. Keith put up an argument over the radio, but had no option except to turn around and head back towards Sapporo. I sat, miserable and hollow, composing long letters in my mind to Richard Creasey about his advice to crash into Russia and let his men take care of us.

Then, after 25 miles Sapporo ATC called us and said the Russians would let us in.

'What's our permission number?' radioed Keith.

'You will get it in an hour,' Sapporo replied. 'Meanwhile, head for Sakhalinsk.'

We rejoiced, turned around and flew the distance we had already flown twice that day, up to the north-east tip of Hokkaido, and out over the strip of sea, about 30 miles across, that separates wealthy

Japan from far-east Russia. A thin blanket of cloud met us, thickening as we headed north and filling the whole of the big bay between the two arms of southern Sakhalinsk Island. In the excitement, we never chased that permission number. It would come back to haunt us.

Yuzhno-Sakhalinsk ATC asked us to descend to 2,000 feet, and cloud cover was given locally at 1,300 feet. It never, quite, got to the stage of being unflyable, and Keith followed my directions to the airport. Clouds lifted to 1,000 feet inland, we saw the airfield and did a safe landing into a blustery southerly wind.

We were met by a jovial bunch of officials in high hats and hobbled the Flyer on rough grass near the control tower. The airfield was scattered with rotting helicopters and big Russian transport aircraft. There was an air of decrepitude about everything, in the midst of which were all these attractive people with their strong faces and pleasing manners. We met EWA's man, Valeri Kudriaveev, who had been waiting for us for a week. Formalities were few and casual, our passports were almost immediately returned to us and I spent a pleasant 20 minutes in ATC, trying to file a flight plan without success.

At the Sapporo Hotel steaks were $18 each and Keith and I were full of wonder about the big blonde girls with long legs that seemed to inhabit the town. They had none of our English constraints.

The weather forecast was unbelievably good, but Valeri came to my room as I was going to bed and said the military objected to our flying on. We had an argument; that is, I said lots of things about being held up, while Valeri tried to excuse Russia for being Russia. I went to bed depressed.

10. STUCK IN YUZHNO-SAKHALINSK

It was not clear who was stopping us, the military, or the Ministry of Foreign Affairs. Whoever they were, they were in Moscow, 7,000 miles away. Arguing with them over the next two weeks was extremely difficult. It was not just that there was a seven-hour time difference. The cost of telephones in the Sapporo Hotel, where we stayed for the first nine days, was $5 a minute, and that included even short calls of three seconds. By the time we were forced to move out, my phone bill was $750.

For the first five days the Flyer lay, half-dismantled, in the mud and rain next to the tatty airport building. But then we were able to taxi her to a canvas hangar run by Australian Jet Charter, which housed a twin-engined executive jet used by the oil men. We did not see her for a week.

Every day I woke, wrote my journal, had breakfast, and tried to find someone who would allow us to fly on. All negotiations were conducted through Valeri Kudriaveev, a thick-set St Petersburg lawyer in his mid-40s, once youth boxing champion of Moscow, who had been sent to Yuzhno-Sakhalinsk by EWA. Valeri, amiable, emotional, loyal and dogged, had difficulty understanding my fast English – especially when I was emotional, which was a lot of the time. He acted as our translator during media interviews and when we met officials.

His main job was to see us through the logistics of travelling in Russia and to smooth our path. He had never been hired to get permissions. Charles, in London, thought that the EWA was handling this, and so did I. I think the EWA also thought it had the power to get Keith and me through Russia. But they had oversold themselves. They were not able to cope with the extra bureaucracy of dealing with Russian aviation, despite their experience arranging television and film shoots in Russia, specifically with the *Sharpe* series on the Napoleonic Wars. The EWA did not give up and fought with us all the way through, with Valeri in particular being a valiant ally. But our problems in Russia came down to our belief in EWA's powers and their inability to meet their own sales pitch.

It took a long time to realise this, because any dealings in Russia were difficult. You never knew who had power and who did not. Moscow had power to stop us, but who in Moscow? Where did you find someone to talk to? Valeri would turn up with people and they would assure us everything was being done to help us. But day after day nothing happened, except we were still refused permission to fly on.

If the situation was bad with us in Yuzhno-Sakhalinsk, it was even worse for Charles Heil in London. He had expended a great deal of energy in getting us through China and Japan and he could not believe the delays in Russia. And the Foreign Office, which had hitherto been quite superb, offered us a representative in Moscow – the commercial attaché, Alan Holmes – who had none of the energy or courage of the great Caroline Wilson in Beijing. Holmes was irritated by the importunings of the EWA and told Charles to resign himself to 'losing this one'. I was not, of course, resigned to anything of the sort, so Charles was caught between an unenthusiastic Mr Holmes and my fierce temper in far-east Russia. No wonder Charles sounded, at times, as if he had been beaten up.

The days dragged by, hopes rising and being dashed. On 16 May we heard it was the military who had put the block on our flight, but then the villain changed to the Ministry of Foreign Affairs. As we became a big story, locally, there was a resulting echo of publicity in Moscow, where the media started savaging the authorities. Each ministry put the blame on another and, out of the chaotic negotiations and over a period of time that almost drove us mad, a solution, of sorts, did emerge.

In Yuzhno-Sakhalinsk, Keith and I lived an odd life. I did all the fighting, using Valeri to translate my arguments. Keith came with us sometimes, or stayed in his hotel watching TV. By the third day, because of the expense of eating out or in the hotel – beer at $10 a bottle, for example – we were buying food outside and eating separately in our rooms. We bought supplies at a local market, cans of beer, apples, bananas, coke, bottled water, Mars bars and packets of nuts to snack with. I spent the long, dull afternoons writing postcards, reading *Winged Victory*, playing solitaire and hearts, or watching TV.

On 18 May, I conceded publicly on Sky TV that the 80-day dream was over, 'killed by the Russians', but that we were going to continue the flight. There were still records to fly for: as the first people to go around the world in a microlight and as the fastest open-cockpit single-engined flight around the world. That record had been established in 1924 by the Americans, at 175 days. It would take a lot more delays by the Russians to stop us beating that.

I tried pulling all sorts of strings, including faxing Downing Street and asking our princes to help, every influential friend I had was lobbied. Nothing worked. The local honorary British consul, Andrew Fox, who had just been appointed and was based in Vladivostok, became a worthy ally, and we explored his idea of asking the Americans whether we could fly out of Yuzhno-Sakhalinsk and get a piggyback from the US Pacific Fleet, who were nearby. But it was the media campaign, the EWA and Charles pulling his strings in London, that I relied upon.

We became apathetic, as if we were in prison. Hour after hour went by with nothing to do but wait. We watched TV and flirted with local girls, who should really have been dating young men my son's age. We had little power, beyond the ability to make noises to the media and send earnest faxes to our embassy in Moscow, trying to answer all the nebulous reasons we heard were being put up against our flight continuing. It was like fighting a ghostly octopus. Things only changed in Moscow when we found a new man at our embassy, Jack Thompson, who was much more upbeat than Mr Holmes.

One evening, having rejected the idea of a men's night sitting in a circle drinking vodka, we went to a restaurant with Valeri and were picked up by two girls, Lina and Arina. The women of Yuzhno-Sakhalinsk were difficult to ignore. Many were very pretty, though a western woman would find their strappy high heels and short skirts somewhat tarty. There was nothing hidden about their sexuality, which was blatant and attractive. They had one over-riding aim, and that was to find a 'strong man' to look after them – much like Jane Austen's female characters in England in the early part of the nineteenth century. In post-Communist Russia this was not an easy task because the local men seemed apathetic and fond only of vodka. One side-effect was that it made westerners like Keith and me look much more attractive than we really were.

Within ten minutes of meeting us Lina had determined Keith's marital status, and was questioning him closely about his job and his home. Within two hours, she announced that her ambition had always been to marry an Englishman and live in England. I would have been out of the restaurant and down the road at those words, but Keith was enchanted by her. Arina, the second girl – both were 25 – was more elliptical, but focused on the important matters – whether I owned my home and if I had a good job – in a way I found disconcerting. Our aim, Keith's and mine, was to continue our flight as soon as possible and, while waiting, flirting was a lovely way to pass the time. We ended that evening with a chaste goodbye kiss and a promise of dinner at a Ukrainian restaurant the following evening.

The next day I had a phone call from a man called Oleg at ATC, who said: 'File an immediate flight plan for Japan and go away.' I refused, but I did not know what the consequences would be. Lina and Arina turned up in the middle of this situation, and Keith plied them with wine while Valeri and I sorted out a polite way of telling Oleg to take a running jump. We went to the Ukrainian restaurant, the girls dressed in beautiful black dresses, us the usual scruffbags, and I spent the first hour being angry and trying not to show it.

After a while the wine and the food and the company had its effect. Both girls were terrific dancers and liked to dance together. Lina got Keith on to the dance floor, something that had last happened when he was 18. Arina's four or five dances with me were something I had never experienced before. She was tremendously sexy and quite shameless, leading me into movements I had never tried. No one seemed to mind the perambulating sex that was happening in the middle of the dance floor. I certainly didn't. We couldn't talk to each other, she had little English and I had no Russian, but being wooed by a beautiful 25-year-old was just the therapy I needed.

Four options emerged that week: firstly, we could carry on mustering forces in London and Moscow to overcome an unnamed Major-General who had taken against us. Keith was not keen on a visa fight, though I was less worried. A spell in jail, or under arrest, might focus matters.

Secondly, we could fly away to Japan. Once we did that then the flight was virtually over. The chances of getting back into Russia would be nil. It would mean everything we had flown for would be worth nothing.

Thirdly, we could pack up and air-freight the Flyer to Alaska. The flight would still be worth nothing and we would spend the next month hammering Russia with the US media.

Lastly, we could leave the Flyer, go back to London and carry on the fight there. When we got all the right permissions we would come back, pick up the aircraft and fly on.

The first faint hope came from the secretary of the Russian Aero Club, Grigory Serebrennikov, who had been lobbied in St Petersburg by Dave Simpson, Vice-Chairman of the BMAA. Serebrennikov said we must hire a Russian navigator to see us through Siberia and that the navigator would use an Antonov 2 – an 18-seater biplane which was common in Russia. He said I would have to pay 'a certain sum of money', that I had to find the AN2 and the navigator myself and if I did not succeed I should go back to Japan. At least it was an answer. Both the military and the Ministry of Foreign Affairs appeared to agree with it. The 'certain sum of money', we discovered, was likely to be around $100,000. It was a seller's market.

In the fighting that was going on between me and the authorities, the subject of our visas came up. They were due to expire on Monday, 25 May, 11 days after we flew into Yuzhno-Sakhalinsk. Initially, there was no problem getting them renewed, but then someone in Moscow objected and we were told they would not be. I laughed openly at this threat. Tony Blair was meeting Boris Yeltsin that weekend in Birmingham for a G8 meeting; would either of them really welcome two Englishmen, trying to fly around the world, getting expelled from Russia because of a visa problem? Not bloody likely, I thought.

But Keith thought differently.

He and I spent much of our time apart. He saw a lot of Lina ('I'm a sucker for blondes, Brian.'). It was a serious thing for him, unlike Arina and me. He had lost a young blonde wife in Becky, but Lina was even younger and deeply taken with him. Yet I think that spending long hours in his bedroom had a fatal effect on his mind.

On 21 May, the 59th day after leaving London, I went back to my room after breakfast and wrote: Keith and I had an argument at breakfast. It started with his usual ultimatum.

'If I haven't got my visa renewed by Monday, I am leaving the country,' he said.

'Well, I'm not,' I replied.

The argument went along the usual lines with us, and involved two genuinely opposite views. His view was that the flight was paramount, above the TV programme, above taking pictures, above anything else. To illustrate this, and his contempt for anything else, he did little filming or photography. But we would not, he believed, succeed if we broke the law.

'You cannot ask me to break international law,' he said, 'and that's what we will be doing if we stay here when our visas run out.'

I believed the Russian authorities who didn't want our flight to continue would use our visas expiring to get us on a point of law. But if we were willing to be arrested, and even jailed, that was a different matter. The story, which verged on being big, would certainly become so if we were jailed or even deported.

Keith believed, genuinely, that it was better to obey the law and leave, perhaps hanging around Anchorage and continuing the fight from there, or returning to London, than to challenge the Russian military so directly. I didn't. It was as simple as that. He thought I was wrong and that my actions were jeopardising the flight.

'I want to be able to come back here. If this flight doesn't work, then at some future time I may be on another world flight, and I don't want to be barred from Russia because of this visa issue,' he said.

As he was on this flight solely because I had organised and found the funding for it, I found this a difficult proposition to swallow, but I didn't say so. How would it have helped?

Then Keith spelled it out: 'I do not want my chances of another Russian visa put at risk. As things stand, I could always go back to London and pick up the phone to Virgin. With my experience, I've got to be in a good position to be picked for their team.'

I thought, to put it mildly, that this was quite unlikely. But it did illustrate his thinking. 'Not that I'm considering that at the moment,' he added.

The bottom line was that, as in the past, he hadn't agreed with my judgement on issues where I had responsibility, and he would make ultimatums to get his way. I didn't want him to leave, but I couldn't force him to stay – especially if he didn't agree with my reasoning. If he wanted to return home, he could, of course.

His bottom-line view was, 'You can't ask me to break the law. It isn't fair.'

I replied, 'I can ask. You must make your own choice.'

I was outraged and betrayed by the suggestion that I should not have a real fight with the Russian authorities, because it would jeopardise Keith's chances of being chosen by Richard Branson if our flight failed. In common with a great many people, Keith seemed to have made up his mind that I was going to lose this one. In that case, he was a free agent. He would, indeed, be in a position to tell Richard Branson that he knew more about flying around the world than anyone else, except me. My willingness to go down to the wire would put this scenario at risk.

I felt very lonely.

Charles called it a low blow.

I sent Keith a letter to summarise the position. He spent the day with Lina and did not see the letter until the following morning at breakfast. But he agreed that it was a fair and exact summary of the differences between us. The letter said:

> In the way we have allocated jobs on this flight, your job is to share the flying and look after the aircraft, while my job is to share the flying and everything else. But I cannot go in and negotiate on our behalf with such a major difference of opinion between us. Tactically, I am certain the best way to go is to defy the authorities. You disagree. My view is especially threatening to your long-term interests which, as you outlined them to me today, are to fly a microlight around the world. It does not have to be the GT Global Flyer, and the time scale doesn't matter, so it's okay with you to leave the Flyer here for a year and return when everything is squared away, and fly on. With me, that isn't so: this is the flight, this is the time, we either do it now or not at all.
>
> It is also in your longer-term interest not to break international law, because, as you said, you 'could always go back to London, and pick up the phone to Virgin. With my experience, I've got to be in a good position to be picked for their team.'
>
> I must admit this is not a factor which I have taken into consideration when working out how to cope with our present problems, but now you mention it, I can see where you see your interests lie. I do not want to ruin your long-term chances, as well as your short-term ones, by my current tactics, but I cannot see how to reconcile our views. We cannot sit there in front of Helena Victorovna (the Russian official at the Ministry of Foreign Affairs) with me saying, well, do your worst, and you saying, no, I'll leave when the visa expires. Both of us would look silly and both of us would suffer.
>
> So let's leave it like this: if we do not get our visas extended by Monday, I will buy you an air ticket back to London. I will stay here and intend to fight to continue the flight from here. I do not care if

they jail me or if they deport me. If they deport me, then the Flyer will be packed up and go with me, and I will have it sent to Anchorage, fly it to Nome, and then continue the journey from there. I know it will not be an official aviation record, but I will have done all that is humanly possible to fulfil the contract I made with GT Global. In my opinion it will not come to that, because of the political backlash, but I know you think differently. The way I have outlined preserves your own integrity, and allows you to make a clean approach to Virgin.

If my tactics succeed, there is a problem. How long should I wait for you to reorder your affairs in England, renew your visa and get out here? How often will such a situation occur in the future, where I face ultimatums when we have differences of opinion? And – I know it's only money – who will pay for your return trip? Do you think I should? If so, why?

If my tactics fail there is the argument that, had we both gone to Alaska or to London and continued the fight from there, maybe we would have succeeded. I think not, you think maybe. But for me this trip is everything, and it has to happen now. That's why and how I raised the money and did all the organising for it. I've staked everything on it, including £40,000 to make a film of it, and I will lose the lot if it doesn't work. I cannot think your stake is anything like as high. For you, if it doesn't work, there is always someone else to blame, and you can go back to your teaching job with lots of stories to tell and a decent lump sum in your bank account. You will be, as you say, in a good position to be chosen by the next team that wants to microlight around the world. For me, it's not as if, at 55, I can go out and raise more money with such a failure behind me.

Until Keith made that ultimatum, whatever differences of opinion we had, about whether to fly, or about tactics, were just the normal differences between two different men. We were, essentially, together. But that Branson comment gutted me. Keith later regretted he had said anything about Branson, because 'you have made rather a thing of it'. But he had, because that was what he was thinking. And I did make a thing of it, because there was a thing to be made.

There were two other comments from Keith which revealed his inner thinking. One was when he said he was young enough to have another go at the flight around the world, alluding to his own age, (46), as against mine. The other was to use the words 'Walter Mitty' about my intention to face down the Russian authorities.

Keith said, after reading my letter, that he had not changed his mind. If I could not guarantee his visa, he wanted to leave, he repeated the refrain, 'You cannot ask me to break the law.' I tried, numerous times to change his mind. He was adamant.

It was against this background that the thought occurred to me that if he did leave the country, then I had a back seat available for a Russian navigator. If I found one with the courage to fly with me, I would not need to hire an AN2.

At first, I suppressed the thought, while I waited to see if Keith fulfilled his threat, and then fill his seat. But we had been through so much together, it would have been unfair to do that. It took three days of painful thinking to reach this conclusion. I had frank discussions with friends at home like Valerie Thompson and Kay Burley, both of them taken aback by Keith's Branson option, and then fiercely opposed to it.

Andy Webb said that if we split, 'Film everything.'

On Monday, 25 May, Keith and I and Valeri walked through bucketing rain to the Ministry of Foreign Affairs' offices in Sakhalinsk Centre, to have our visas extended by a week.

This took the pressure off Keith, but put pressure on me. Had Keith left on that day's flight because his visa had not been renewed, the decision about a Russian navigator would have been easier. But I had resolved to involve him in the whole decision, however painful it was. We returned to the hotel and I asked Valeri to videotape the discussion.

I took Keith through the logic of our plight and my proposed solution, that I send him by plane to Alaska, there to wait for me while I flew across Siberia with a Russian navigator in the back. Keith thought I might have had to find $100,000 to pay the expenses of an AN2 to accompany us, and he raised the nightmare of negotiations, again beginning halfway through, with Russian demands for more money, when we could least resist them.

'You can't trust anyone in the region,' he said.

He agreed to go and put up no argument against me. I worried about his soul, his commitment to the flight, if he had to take an airliner to Alaska. At no time did Keith give any indication that he was going to abandon the flight in Alaska.

At the end of the discussion, he said he wanted to think about it on his own. When Valeri and Keith had gone to their separate rooms, I continued the search for a navigator and reviewed the prices of an AN2; $45,000 through a contact of Valeri's, $75,000 through a local pilot, Albert Braichemko. Both said the prices as if they were silly, but there was a wistful hopefulness in their voices, as if I could be persuaded to pay. I think they believed that Westerners had secret stores of millions of dollars which we kept hidden from Russians, but which, under pressure from canny negotiators, we would produce.

I spent the evening doing my paperwork. There was a knock on the door and there was Arina, who now talked about money so much I had dubbed her the 'Moneybag'. She wanted a new razorblade, but I had only two left to get me to Alaska, so I said no. I went down with her to Keith's room and found Lina in the last stages of shaving off Keith's moustache and beard. He had had that beard for 20 years, so something profound was happening.

I spent days in long-distance negotiations with the chief of all Russian navigators in the Far East, Peter Petrov, thinking Peter was negotiating on behalf of a third party; it turned out it was for himself. He wanted wages of $245 a day, plus all expenses including the air fare back to Russia from America, paid in cash. Valeri, faithful to the end, remained with us, getting poorer and more dishevelled. I used to buy him food, because of the hungry way he looked at the salami I bought at the market. Valeri took photographs of Keith and me, shaking hands under the shadow of a statue of Lenin, on a rare time when Keith was parted from Lina.

By now we were a big story locally, full-page spreads in the newspaper, a half-hour television feature built around a long interview with me. I seemed to conform to a Russian stereotype, the 'strong man', an idea which repelled me. I was very glad that none of the publicity would be seen in England.

Back home, Sarah Browse wanted to know if the flight continued with one pilot, why was it me and not Keith? My father's generation would have made a comparison between Sarah Browse and a Toc H lamp.

Sixty-six days after leaving London, and the 13th day of our internment in Russia, I saw Keith off at the airport, along with a subdued Lina, close to tears but looking very glamorous.

On 29 May Peter Kusmich Petrov arrived, with a small suitcase, and was not put off by the Flyer. He was of medium height, slim and fit, with a boxer's face – the characteristic flattened nose – which he had earned as far-east Russian boxing champion. His English was poor. I wanted to take him up for a trial flight, a suggestion which caused much sucking of teeth among the Australian air crew who were my hosts, but he swung it with the authorities and we flew for 40 minutes. He said afterwards he still wanted to fly with me.

Over dinner that night, Paul Loach called and told me that in the negotiations over Amvesco's takeover, GT Global was to die as a brand and he was out of a job. All his great power was drained away from him and he was reduced to a 'little office up the road while I consider things'. As he had been my ultimate point of appeal, my champion, I was shattered.

'So, who is looking after the flight?' I asked.

'Dallas,' said Paul, with a short laugh.

My heart sank.

Paul also said that Newlyn reported that Keith, in Anchorage, had resigned and was making preparations to go home. I said that this was dead wrong, but Newlyn swore it was true. Paul's fall and the demise of GT Global meant that all bets were off. There was no sponsor to have any loyalty to. And if Keith went home, I was truly alone. I had to rethink everything during the tough flying on the way to Alaska. Could I continue on my own?

We had two more days fighting the authorities, going right down to an exact estimate of the time we would take on each leg of the Siberian journey; Peter Petrov and Valeri did all that work. I spent the time with two Australian pilots, Murray D'ath-Weston and Dennis Wilson and their engineer, John Stewart. They played me two recorded episodes of Michael Palin's *Ripping Yarns*. There was something surreal about sitting in Yuzhno-Sakhalinsk and watching Palin's wonderful satire on British Empire attitudes. It was still an Anglo-Saxon world.

I tried phoning Keith in Alaska to find out if what Newlyn had said was true, but he was not in his room; I left a message for him to phone me, but he didn't. I was extremely nervous about the coming flight and the conditions through which I would have to fly. I knew how painful it must have been for Keith to leave, but he was party to the decision, and I still could not see any alternative. He would lose so much by going home early.

When we got formal permission for the flight to continue on 30 May, it was an anticlimax. Valeri, Peter and I went out and bought a bottle of vodka, orange juice, chocolate and radishes, and had a little feast in my bedroom. Arina phoned up, looking for her usual free dinner and more obsessive talk about her lack of money. I was not interested.

Charles phoned on 31 May to confirm that Keith had bought a ticket from Anchorage to London; he would go home in two days time.

Then came the real sickener.

Alison phoned to pass on a message from Newlyn and Browse. They said that Keith had told them he would consider continuing the flight with me if I let him fly solo from Nome to Anchorage.

I thought this was a completely stupid offer and, if true, it was disgusting. The offer seemed to have emerged from discussions between Colin Edwards, a photographer sent to Anchorage by Newlyn, and Keith, who arrived straight off the aircraft from Yuzhno-Sakhalinsk determined to go home. Newlyn had asked Edwards to do all he could to persuade Keith to stay, and there were long nightly discussions at the hotel bar. After two days, on 30 May, Edwards asked Keith: 'What would it take to make you stay?' and told me later it was Keith who made the suggestion that I get out at Nome and let him fly solo to Anchorage. The argument seemed to be: 'Neither of us would have gone around the world, but the team would have.'

Either Edwards or Keith passed this on to Newlyn. According to Alison, Newlyn turned up at the office and said there must be 'honour among pilots'. Newlyn did not have the nerve to suggest that, after struggling all across Siberia with a stranger in the back, I should then get out my own aircraft and allow Keith to fly her solo for a while. It would have had the effect of leaving neither Keith nor I as record-holders and, incidentally, meant that Richard Branson and whatever team he selected, could set the record. It would also be a direct contravention of my contract with GT Global, for whom Newlyn ostensibly worked, although only freelance. And the idea of Newlyn using the word 'honour'.

I spent most of that day in a state of deep shock at the suggestion. It was so cynical. I could not believe Keith had gone along with it. There would have been no integrity left to the flight. What public excuse did I use for getting out?

Keith did not make too much of a fuss about leaving, perhaps because he had been prepared to leave anyway if his visa had not come through, to make certain that, in future, he would be able to get another visa for the chance to fly for Branson.

With these thoughts churning in my mind, I did leave Yuzhno-Sakhalinsk that day, with Peter in the back, but after 30 minutes of flying I was told to return. A bureaucrat in Moscow did not like the weather forecast for the area I was flying through. I remember standing in the middle of the tarmac and shouting at the top of my voice, 'Fuck Russia!' It startled Peter. The day after that, 1 June, Peter thought the weather was too bad to fly. He was nervous about actually getting into the Flyer, but each day's delay was costing me $245 in pay, plus his hotel bills. I spent much of the time in an extremely bad temper. This was not made better by being unable to contact Keith in Anchorage to find out which stories about him were true, and which were not. But I mellowed out that last night, staying with the Australians in their flat, convinced that I would be able to leave in the morning.

Andrew Fox in Vladivostok and Dave Simpson, in England, both called and asked for Keith's telephone number to try and persuade him to wait for me in Nome, Alaska.

I wanted him to wait, too, but I also wanted him to do so willingly.

An hour before I was due to leave for Siberia, Keith phoned.

11. DEEPEST SIBERIA

AND THE FLYER IS BENT

It was day 71, 2 June, when Keith called. He said he fully supported the decisions I had taken and claimed that the suggestion that I should hand over the aircraft to him in Nome for a solo flight to Anchorage had come from Colin Edwards, the photographer sent out by Newlyn, and not him. How it got to me, I did not discover. I did not feel able to ask him if there had been a grey area, an indecision, about his reaction, that gave Newlyn an opportunity for mischief. Keith said he wouldn't be slagging me off when he got back to England.

'It's just that when I looked down at the landscape flying to Anchorage, I thought: I should be seeing this from a microlight and now I am not, I want to go home. As you know, flying around the world is the only thing that matters. I've never cared for the film or the publicity.'

I was in two minds about the phone call. At the time, the consensus of opinion in England was that I needed a partner, it was seen as much more dangerous for me to go on flying on my own, especially once I had dropped off Peter Petrov in Alaska. This was not a factor in Keith's decision. He was upset at not being able to go around the world. My plight afterwards did not concern him. There was, apparently, a catastrophic collapse of morale in the London office around this period, which Keith's departure did not help.

Keith rejected my pleas to stay, saying he wasn't concerned about the reaction at home. I had begun to realise the magnitude of the task he had left me to deal with alone. Was I capable of doing it?

Peter did the paperwork that I usually did, including filing a flight plan and chosing a route up the centre of the island. I was desperate to get away and no longer impose myself on the Australians, who were a model of kindness and manners. We taxied out at 10.15 a.m. and set off. The headwind was soon apparent as we went due north.

The countryside was like Scotland, pale green with rocks showing through, a sort of disguised bleakness, but the housing and road development remained truly East European. We came to an air base, Sokol, from where the fighter that shot down the Korean airliner in 1983 took off. I photographed it copiously. Flying conditions were smooth, with none of the 'moderate turbulence' forecast. I settled down to remember what it was like with Keith, putting my mind into a double state, alert for a change in weather and otherwise drifting amiably. Peter muttered in the back and gave me course changes ('steer 14 degrees right'), when I could see 50 miles and had a better GPS than him. He soon came to the conclusion that I was not obeying him as strictly as Russian pilots, so he stopped.

With Keith, I could gossip, and we would have turned over amongst ourselves the various events that had occurred in Yuzhno-Sakhalinsk. But Peter's English was not good, so small talk was out. We flew up a huge bay, 130 miles long, always curving, it was the thinnest part of the island of Sakhalinsk, and then out into a wide flat plain between two mountain ranges, where Peter steered me away from military bases.

The smooth flying changed abruptly, from calm conditions, where I steered gently to overcome a slight right-hand turn, to gorilla-gripping again. The Flyer was slung around the sky. Peter was startled at the way the Flyer plunged and leapt, but as I took no notice of it he decided he wouldn't either. It did not stop the urgent audible flow of his calculations as he estimated arrival times, passing air-space boundaries, done for the rest of us in the west by a GPS.

Hours drifted by happily. I was relieved to be in the air again. On a journey like this one felt so useless on the ground. In the air one was engaged, authentic, alive, existential. The Djinn had been thoroughly stood on. I looked for him, but could not find him, and cheekily leaned over the side, right and left, at 2,000 feet, to provoke him. The more I did this, the easier I felt. Peter, a Russian used to Siberia, commented on the cold.

We were met 30 miles outside Kiroskoye by a friend of Peter's in a battered AN2, the aircraft I was asked to hire to take Peter through Russia. It could genuinely go nearly as slowly as the Flyer, and made three passes for the wing-tip and keel cameras, before showing the way in to land. The runway surface was metal plated, of the type used by the Americans to construct temporary runways in the last war in the Pacific, and to me it felt horrible. Dozens of people turned up to meet us, and they edged closer while Peter was filing a flight plan. I could feel myself the subject of speculative glances by the women, especially when they learned I was 55 and no longer married.

'Surely he's a grandfather,' said one.

Peter came back, I rushed off to have a belated pee, we climbed in and took off again, with the wind slightly easier. I climbed to 3,000 feet and headed north-west, watching the sky anxiously. Rain showers were developing that looked thick and difficult. I stayed below the cloud, heading for the gap between the cloud and the mountains, expecting at any moment to be whacked by turbulence. Peter also murmured 'turbulence' at every little bump, but it was not as frightening as it looked. I reached the sea and smooth conditions within 30 minutes. From then on it was a smooth coastal flight, climbing slowly to 4,000 feet, trying to see if I could maintain below 4,500 revs and calculating that fuel consumption had improved now we were heading north.

We came to Nikolayevsk Na Amure over a smooth dirty-looking sea that was packed with ice for nine months of the year, and we landed smoothly on a rough-looking runway, full of cracks. Among those who met us was Fidor Zhakov, president of the local microlight club, a manufacturer in his own right. He helped hobble the Flyer, then took us to his dingy factory, of which he was obviously so proud. I was feeling the effects of nine hours in the air and wanted a shower and a beer, but the hotel we were taken to only had cold showers. There was a problem with my Russian visa, as the landlady soon discovered. In giving me what they thought was a month extra in Yuzhno-Sakhalinsk, Helena Victorovna actually gave me only a day extra, writing 1 June instead of the intended 1 July. I groaned.

Peter and I drank vodka at dinner. I was acquiring a taste for it. Like many Russian women, the young waitress disapproved.

On day 72, 3 June, I had no breakfast or hot shower, but it was a brilliant flying day, clear blue skies and little wind. Peter was keen to go but worried about the peculiar state of my visa. Fidor turned up and we tore over the roads to the airport where I rigged and Peter went off to talk to officials. There was a big crowd watching, but they had impeccable manners. Then I went down with Fidor for two hours of hell in the local immigration office. Two officials were adamant that I could not get my visa extended, but otherwise they didn't know what to do about me. Meanwhile, would I answer all sorts of questions about my flight? These included: 'Are you married?'

I brought in the name of Andrew Fox, and he was in the middle of sending faxes to get me out when Fidor returned with Peter. Within ten minutes, after a lot of shouting behind closed doors and some showing of identity cards, Peter earned all the money I was paying him. He came across as a modest and amiable man, but he was chief of navigators for the whole of the Russian far east. He took me back to the airport, where we dressed, climbed in and took off. It was 11.55 a.m. and we were late.

In the air it was bouncy as we climbed to 2,500 feet and headed north-west. Peter wanted to take us around the Sea of Okhutsk, a normally frozen area of water between Sakhalinsk Island and Magadan, about which he was nervous. I wanted to fly straight across the sea, 351 miles to Okhutsk, but Russian rules prevented single-engine aircraft doing this, so Peter banned it. Yet the drip-drip of information I kept feeding him about microlights and the extreme coldness of the flight itself, were having an effect. His proposed route to a place called Ayan was via a town called Chubican, 400 miles around the coast. There was an alternative, going 244 miles direct across still-frozen sea, a compromise between what I wanted and what he wanted. It took me time to see that he was now so committed to the flight that he was willing to break such a basic rule.

The countryside was fantastic, completely unspoiled, no roads, just the huge Amure River and thousands of square miles of forests and tundra, lakes and rivers. There were small fluffy clouds in the sky and frisky thermals; Peter had become used to them now and concentrated on his navigation and on working the wing cameras, about which he was enthusiastic. We flew over hills which grew into small mountains, then a note of concern from Peter at snow-covered peaks ahead.

'They are mountains. There will be much turbulence.'

I thought that with little wind, the only turbulence would be thermic, but my heart beat faster as we headed under clouds formed by the mountains. The mountain belt was only ten miles across and at the far side I thought the turbulence would stop, I was prepared to endure it. When we were whacked by the first violent thermal, Peter said, 'I told you,' but they were just part of flying microlights.

At the far side of the mountain range the stunning countryside fell away to the sea, which I thought was covered in a low fog. But as we flew closer, I saw that it was broken ice which lay, still and deadly, on the motionless surface. I felt, with a shudder, that if the engine stopped, we would be dead within two minutes. I was full of deep fears, constantly telling myself that this was what I was here for and if I couldn't do this I couldn't do the flight and engines don't know what's going on beneath them. This nonsense worked, and I set off across 70 miles of frozen rubble for an island landfall, followed by another 50 miles to reach the north coast of the Okhutsk Sea.

I remember looking at the bleak scene and thinking that Keith was somewhere south by now, on a big airliner, looking down from 35,000 feet, and returning to a season of summer's training in England, doing eternal circuits with students. I thought him mad not to be waiting for me in Nome.

The cold got to us. I had chamois gloves on and the big electric gloves, but they were not plugged in. A real area of cold entered my chest and no amount of exercise could quite get rid of it. But my feet were fine in the moon boots, and I had enough clothes on – we were without our survival suits, which we should have worn – to feel I had a reserve for when it got really cold around the Bering Straits. Peter was also cold, but I was not quite able to discover which part of his body was most affected. He often answered questions I never asked.

The approach to Ayan was exciting, looking down on a sloping runway covered in patches of water, suitable for an AN2 but which had a lot of dangers for my little Flyer. I chose my landing spot carefully between pools of water – who knew how deep they were? – and got down safely. Peter thumped my shoulder and shouted, 'good pilot, good pilot,' and rushed straight off to ATC, leaving me to the kind attentions of some tough-looking men. We refuelled and taxied out for the second flight of the day, continuing along the coastal mountains. I stayed ten miles out to sea, too far to make it to land if the engine stopped, but far enough to avoid any turbulence at all. Inland, I could see thunderstorms developing and black columns of rain falling.

We covered the last 30 miles with Peter shouting irritably into the radio 'Okhutsk, Okhutsk, Okhutsk,' and a debate developing between us about where my American map had put the airport, and where Peter was sure it was. The Americans were right.

We were surrounded by children when we landed, some of them remarkable mimics: I kept hearing an exaggerated echo of my English voice whenever I said anything (I hope it was exaggerated). I left the Flyer hobbled, rushed off to the loo and was then invited to a dinner with Sergei and Luna Krivoborsky, a local pilot and his wife. The food was the best I had eaten in Russia; all the cooked birds on the table had been shot by Sergei and the smoked salmon had been caught by him. We drank vodka, Russian style. I no longer demanded orange drinks to mix it with. I was tired, but was able to get a laundry done and dry out the previous wash.

Day 83 was another lovely morning, no wind, blue skies, long horizons, and a growing crowd of cheerful, chattering people around the Flyer. Three little girls, Anya, Oleysiy and Kristina, were especially charming, talking among themselves to agree English phrases they had learned at school, then one solemnly offering it to me.

We took off at 10.35 a.m., taxiing across the punishing metal-plated main runway on to gravel. I reached the coast around a headland, and turned due east along washed-out country, brown and dark green, full of lazy rivers and hundreds of glacial pools, with white-topped mountains in the background. I debated whether to refuel at Magadan and punt on to Chibuga; or should I stay overnight at Magadan, the biggest city in Siberia, which was certain to have foreign exchange facilities and a telephone, and let London know what was happening? They had not heard from me in three days. Andy Webb had been told that Magadan was the trigger for him to go to Alaska.

Peter kept steering me inland, where clouds were developing and it was turbulent. I wanted to stay over the sea, though it was a longer way around. We compromised by aiming at a mountain about 100 miles down the coast, and instead of keeping to the right of it, to turn left into a valley.

'It is the route to Magadan,' he said, meaning that this was the official way in and that's why we must go on it.

I waited for the thermals to bump us around and enjoyed the moderate trashing we got; it was a way of teasing Peter for choosing such a bumpy route. Nothing difficult happened for about four hours.

I had been watching clouds and rain develop over the mountains to our left with an air of detachment. I was glad I was not there. Our ground speed indicated a very slight tailwind, with clouds moving south across our path and I gradually became concerned. The clouds developed inexorably into rain and then thunderstorms, with lightning bolts and crashes of thunder. Magadan ATC reported rain and a local storm. Peter got agitated and started sighing.

There were villages and roads below, a contrast to the previously uninhabited countryside we had been flying over. I mentioned to Peter that if he was concerned, we could, flying a microlight, land on a road and wait the storms out. He said, as is usual in Russia, that it was impossible. But he watched more clouds develop and more lightning and, after a conversation with Magadan ATC, changed his mind.

'Land there,' he said, indicating a road below.

We descended and discovered the road was flanked by trees, which would tear the wings off the Flyer. We did a low-level examination of a number of roads, all of which had trees on either side. All the time I was aware of the storms approaching. I kept an eye on them and saw gaps developing where I could fly safely. My problem was trying to explain this to Peter. He knew there were mountains behind the storms, and did not want to fly into the mountains when storms were developing. I tried to explain that we would wait, circling, before we got to them, and find a gap to continue east, but the language was beyond him and me. I decided to land.

The place I chose looked rough but there were tracks on it, which meant it should be firm. The muddy holes in it did not show up from the air. I circled once and made a moderately fast approach, always ready to open the throttle and climb away, but it looked okay so I put down. We ran on for a short while, slowing all the time, then stopped abruptly. It did not feel as if damage had been done, though previously such incidents had broken the nose wheel off. I got out to check and found that one of the two lights Keith had installed had broken off and was dangling forlornly.

We were lucky. My nose wheel was in a wet hole; had we hit that at speed we would have turned over. Peter jumped out and celebrated the landing, watching the storm develop. We did not get the Flyer out of the hole quickly enough.

Peter wanted photographs, and as he was loading film, a gust of wind struck from behind and turned the Flyer on to the right leading edge. There were creaking and crunching noises. I was caught on the right side as the aircraft tilted over and petrol poured out of the main tank all over me. I put my finger over the tank's breathing hole and shouted to Peter to push. I wanted to lift the Flyer, now lying on its side with the leading edge of the right wing on the ground, and get it upright again. But the wind was strong and threatened to force the Flyer completely upside down. We struggled and cursed and pushed and after about two minutes of fighting, pushed the wing level again. I heaved it around so I had a wing down, into wind. In all this time I never took the one photograph that Newlyn yearned for in London. We had before-photos and after-photos, but none of her upside down.

There seemed to be no damage. I checked the leading edge from the wing-pocket, and there were, apparently, no kinks.

We held the Flyer's wings through the gusts, which were never violent. I was already thinking about taking off again, but Peter had more conventional ideas about the condition of a wing after it had been overturned. He thought it needed to be dismantled and examined by experts before he would fly again. That was not my view. In the middle of the Russian Steppes, we could have been there for weeks getting the checks. I walked over the field looking for a possible runway, and came to the conclusion that, whatever I did, I should do it solo.

There were so many wet holes in the field that I resolved to use a nearby dirt road. I walked along it, calculating the distance between the young saplings on either side. They were 30 feet apart, and 12 to 14 feet tall. The Flyer's wingspan was 33 feet, so the wingtips would brush against the saplings. Would it be fatal? I thought the Flyer would either go, or it wouldn't, but I could not find a better choice for take-off. I went back and persuaded Peter to look for a car to take him to Magadan. He was unenthusiastic, but went anyway. It began to pour with rain. He came back after ten minutes and said I should take off and he would follow me by road, but he had not found a car.

I poured away four gallons of petrol, and packed everything extra into the green bag, intending that Peter should take it with him, plus the dinghy, because I didn't want any extra weight. But Peter didn't want to carry the bag, so I put it in the passenger's seat. We heaved the Flyer the 200 yards to the dirt road, falling into wet holes half a dozen times, sweating heavily.

I found myself chanting a mantra with each pull: 'that there's some corner (heave) of a foreign field (heave) that is forever (heave) England (heave).' I became aware I was missing out the first line (was it deliberate?) 'If I should die, think only this of me,' but I just laughed harshly when I realised what I was saying.

Peter hurled himself so strongly at the propeller boss to get the Flyer on to firm ground that, days later, he was able to tear his shirt off dramatically in front of cameras and show the black markings and bruises on his shoulder.

I gave Peter the video camera to film my take-off, which would be exciting whether or not I made it. My frame of mind was detached and determined. I was not frightened. It was not something I even thought about. I had to fly. I started the engine and taxied down-wind along the dirt road, watching the trees, feeling the drag each sapling made on the wing. A particularly big one was very draggy, so that is where I decided to begin my take-off in earnest. I had about fifty yards of useful surface before the boggy field. Thirty yards beyond the big sapling I stopped the aircraft and dragged and pushed it around to face into wind. Peter left his filming place and complained the camera didn't work. I impatiently beckoned him over and pressed all the right buttons to get it working. I told him to go back to the road junction and lie low, so I would virtually fly over him. But like most amateurs, he thought he knew a better place, and fiddled with the camera for long minutes, while I waited to take off, building up a white fury, and in complete tunnel vision.

I could not stand it and shouted angrily. He turned, I waved, he waved, and I started taxiing. At faster speeds, the drag from each tree on the wing tips was so much stronger than I had expected. I was forced to waddle from side to side, gathering pace, until I got past the big tree.

Then I gunned the throttle, we raced over the ground.

Drag right. Bang! Bang! Correct it, too much! Drag left! God, we're going to hit the next tree! Bang! Bang! Got enough speed? No! Don't push out! Bang! Bang! Push out! Skim over the ground, another drag right, then left, skidding! Skidding! Just above the ground, keep on speed, keep it low for speed! Bang! Now push out for real! Have we enough speed to avoid diving into the boggy field? I am flying.

But there was something wrong with the Flyer!

12. RUSSIAN ATTRITION AND

THE BERING SEA

It was a tremendous relief to be in the air, but the wing felt odd. I circled Peter twice, then waved and set off east, climbing to 1,500 feet and getting in touch with Magadan ATC. When I looked up I saw the trike was pointing one way and the wing pointing another. I had flown another trike like this in England for months after a similar accident, and repaired it by changing the hang-bracket. I had a spare with me.

On the way to Magadan I hit moderate turbulence and was anxious, in a detached way, for the integrity of the right wing. The worse the turbulence, the better the test of any kink in the wing folding I thought, as though not really involved. The weather was good, with occasional wind gusts, but I could see for miles. Magadan ATC kept me on a single frequency on the way in, with their best English-speaker, Andrei Snitco, at the microphone.

I was met, inevitably, by one of the millions of Stalin's sisters in Russia, she wanted me to stay by the wind-blown Flyer until Peter turned up, even if that took until morning. But I was able to persuade Andrei – a big man, full of charm, his skull shaved – to get me into a hangar, and, urgently, into one of the worst toilets it had been my cross to bear. I left the Flyer under wraps, and we tried to find a hotel with hot water that did not charge me the earth. Dinner was the tin of nuts I had been keeping since Muscat for just such an emergency, plus four much-needed bottles of beer.

I spent day 74 stuck in Magadan, waiting for Peter to turn up, hour after hour with nothing to do and nowhere to go. Drinkable water, which I craved, was not available. Peter phoned and said he was at ATC and would come and see me, he wanted to leave by 2 p.m. An hour passed before he arrived to tell me we had to wait a day. We rebooked into the hotel, the matrons who ran it full of admiring glances. My story had been on TV.

I went to the airport, pervaded by the smell of dried salmon, to change $700 into roubles and get back my financial power. Then Peter took me to the Flyer. I knew that being turned over had done some damage, though I thought it wasn't dangerous. I replaced the hang-bracket, re-rigged the aircraft and began negotiations to make a test flight. When she leapt into the air, I remembered her as she used to be, as she was when I first bought her, frisky and eager, relieved of the huge loads I have been putting on her. It was like a rediscovered youth, steep 360-degree turns, stalling, weaving about the sky at a touch. Coming in to land, I was confident that she was whole again and capable of taking me and Peter across the Arctic Sea. The display was as much to convince Peter not to abandon me because of his fears about the wing's integrity, as to prove to myself that the wing was strong. (In fact, as we discovered later, the keel was four inches out of alignment.)

We had a meal in the evening at the airport, overdone steak, underdone chips, salad and good smoked fish. Peter told me that when I had taken off from the field, he was so overcome with emotion that he started to cry. As he told me the story, tears again came to his eyes and he had to pull a hankie out and dab them. He also said he had to have my flight completed by the end of the following week, because he had booked a holiday in the Black Sea with his 'like-woman'. I was heartened by the thought that this was a good reason to hurry me out of Russia, so there was a limit to the money I was due to pay him.

On day 75, 6 June, I was up early, no shower but a good wash and no breakfast, Peter and I walked with all the gear to the airport. The weather, by contrast with previous days, looked dreadful and worsened as the morning went on, thick grey cloud descended into the valley in which the airport was situated and heavy rain fell.

I had repaired two of the moon boots the previous evening with sellotape, now I did the other two. They held together quite well, but would not take the wear and tear. Their real object was to stop my feet freezing. Having to do the work of two men, without Keith, took lots of time. Peter dressed quickly, surrounded by Russians all talking loudly, he as much as anyone, but when he was ready, he wanted me to hurry up. I told him sharply to wait.

I walked out of the hangar and looked dubiously at the sky. This was unusual because normally I was the one tearing around to go, whatever the weather. The minimum Russian requirement for take-off was 5 km visibility and 600 metres, 1,800 feet. It looked to me

ABOVE: The author, Arina and Peter Petrov
LEFT: The airfield from which the fighter took off to shoot down the Korean airliner
BELOW: Peter and Valeri in Yuzhno-Sakhalinsk

In a muddy field after a forced landing in Magadan
INSET: The broken light

A guard dog protecting the flyer at Nikolayevsk

Dead instruments on the way to Evensk

The stress begins to show

En route to Anadyr

Anadyr to Providenya

TOP: Children at Evensk
INSET: Stephan, my favourite drunk in Evensk
BOTTOM: Brian and Peter with the Mayor of Providenya

LEFT: Rusty fuel
BELOW: The Flyer on its last stop
before Alaska

Our last view of Providenya

Iced up over the Bering Sea

Our first view of Alaska

The author and Peter Petrov on their first night in the USA

like 1 km and 400 feet. While Peter insisted I obey Russian law, he had been propagating myths about how brave I was and my skills as a flyer, so rules were being bent. The head of ATC turned up, listened to a torrent of Russian from Peter, and said, wonder of wonders, that it was my decision. Stifling my private doubts, I said 'no problem'. I suppose real heroes go through this all the time.

The view on the runway looked bleak, mist to the ground and the outline of mountains just visible, but I did not want to bottle out. Perhaps it would be better in the air? I could always turn back. Ho ho. I opened the throttle, climbed away and Peter said, 'go to 1,700 feet'. I laughed. I thought we would be deep in cloud by then but, as we gained height I found I could still see far enough ahead to avoid nasty mountains, of which there were a lot in the area. Within ten minutes I grew accustomed to the conditions, and soon I could see clear sky ahead, even if there were numerous rain showers to negotiate first.

I was dressed in the survival suit, so I felt comfortable and dry, in contrast to Peter, who had rejected Keith's survival suit and was wet and cold. The countryside was deserted, tundra and forests, rivers, lakes and mountains, said to be great hunting country, but no trace of man at all. There was a majestic beauty to it. We headed east to the coast, avoiding a large mountain range, before turning north to follow the coastline to Evensk.

About an hour into the flight I noticed the charging light showed red.

It was the same symptom Keith and I had had leaving Corfu. Then I had elected to turn back. A fuse had gone and when replaced, everything had worked well until now. I knew that from now on the battery was dying, but I needed it to transfer fuel from the spare tanks to the main tank. I immediately transferred fuel from the 15-litre bladder tank into the main tank and I thought I could monitor the battery dying by the electronic gauges on the engine. They usually died first and I could use the time after that to transfer the bulk of the fuel across.

I thought about turning back, but continued to fly east, banged around moderately by thermals. I turned off my electric gloves, the radio, and my big GPS, relying on Peter's small GPS in the back. I hoped Peter would not notice.

After two hours we reached the spectacular coast, surrounded by snow-covered mountains, with a still, dead Sea of Okhutsk covered in broken ice. I turned left past Takloyamsk, our alternative airfield, a dirt strip at right angles to the shore, thought about landing and changing the fuse, but did not do so. Another 90 minutes into the flight, and I had made two transfers of fuel to the main tank, enough to get us to Evensk, when, quite suddenly, the electrical system died. I could no longer monitor engine revs or temperatures and the only way I knew how much fuel was left was to look at the Mickey Mouse indicator plumbed straight into the tank. I told Peter for the first time of our situation and asked him to use the GPS sparingly. He did not throw a wobbly, for which I was grateful. There was nothing else to do anyway but fly on.

Time passed quickly, and I hardly noticed the discomfort of six hours' flying before we were in contact with Evensk. I flew away from the coast to a plain surrounded by snow-covered mountains and a long gravel landing strip. As we touched down, crowds of people came streaming in from all directions, mainly children and husky dogs. They surrounded us when we stopped, and an astonishingly beautiful blonde girl of about 14 smiled at me and presented me with a flower. It was only later I discovered how rare flowers were.

The children and their excited teacher were soon replaced by rough drunken men, contradicting each other. One, called Stephan, who claimed to be an electrician, was issuing orders right, left and centre. I took exception to him, reeling away from his vodka-laden breath, but Peter said curtly that all Russian men drank. We pushed the Flyer 400 yards to see if it would fit into a barn. When it wouldn't we tethered it to some lorries, then we unpacked. I worried about the drunks, and about two chaps who were always driving off with my bags – with my dollars on board – but I wasn't robbed.

Peter and I checked into a hotel, an unheard-of luxury, until I actually saw my room, the best on offer. The toilet had no seat, or toilet paper, there was no hot water, the cold water gave me a headache in the minute I took to wash my hair and all electricity was turned off at 10 p.m. No wonder there were so many children.

Alexei Karachentsev, head of Evensk ATC, invited Peter and me to his house to drink vodka after a meal in a café. Peter alternated between extravagant praise for my courage and furious warnings that all the airfields I wanted to visit were closed. I told him I expected him to get me through. He started to cry again when telling Alexei the story of my road take-off.

On day 76, 7 June, we found the Flyer on its nose. Having been hobbled with the wing horizontal, a stiff breeze was blowing from the back, endangering her safety. With swearing and a lot of work, and the help of the previously drunk Russians, now sober – it being morning – I got her turned around and erected her. Then the wind blew so strongly that I removed the wing altogether and snuggled her into three garages owned by Stephan. I no longer disliked him; he was a rough man, yet very kind. All day the trike stood in the persistent wind, stripped of its seat, while half a dozen scruffy Russians probed interestedly at the problem of the non-charging generator, talking with animation. We found the fuse intact. I joined in the debate, trying to isolate where the fault lay, it could be with the generator, the regulator, or the actual connections to the battery.

We worked for hours, covered in drifting dust, and I grew to like my companions. They all smelled of stale vodka, their clothes were filthy, hair all matted, but there was a tough honesty in the way they approached the job that was endearing. When not working, I paced up and down, full of bleak thoughts. I wondered whether I could persuade Peter to fly on anyway, charging the battery every evening at airfields, so it started full each morning and using it only to transfer fuel?

Peter proposed this himself.

There was no reason in the world why he should take such risks. He was a married man, with children and a good job. Why should he have that vestige of savagery that drove people like me? But he did. What was more, the Russians with whom he discussed the issue thought he was right to do so. Once Peter had made that offer, all the unhappiness left me. We could fly on, taking chances that I wondered if Keith would have taken?

'Forward, always forward,' Peter said.

We did not find out that day what was wrong. Whatever it was, it could be fixed in America, but not on the dusty Russian steppes.

A local helicopter pilot, Valeri Sirotkin, who had been advising us on the repairs, joined Peter and me on the walk home, and we diverted to buy salami, cheese, onion, beer and – inevitably – our own bottle of vodka. Alexei Karachentsev, a really lovely and intelligent man, arrived and joined Peter, Valeri Sirotkin and me for our meal. I remember being asked if I could give Engineer Valeri a flight, 'only 5 minutes', and agreeing. Valeri was so overcome that he rushed off and came back to give me two large uncut pieces of opal, which had been mined '135 nautical miles from here on a bearing of 355 degrees'. At another time I rushed off to find a photo of Helen Dudley, which I had pasted into *Winged Victory*, we all agreed that she was very beautiful and that she should have one of the opals; the other would go to my daughter. We were down to basics now, all our fine technology stripped away. If I aspired to courage, the next few days would be as good a test as any.

The next morning I had to kick Peter out of bed. Valeri and Stephan turned up in a Russian Jeep and gave us a lift to the airfield. We reassembled the Flyer and I gave Valeri his ten-minute flight. He was an experienced helicopter pilot and inclined to feel that he should be at the controls, but I wrested them from him.

It was a fine day, the wind from the south, and it looked as if it would stay fine. Dozens of people saw us off, including Stephan, now a mate; like my squire, he helped me dress. We got away at 11.15 a.m., climbing and turning left. I was in a frame of mind where I was ready for anything and I unplugged all non-essential equipment, the radio, my GPS, my camera. All three had their own internal batteries if I wanted to use them.

We flew over country rarely seen by westerners, increasingly bleak and with no place to land. It was tundra: brown, full of rivers and pocket lakes, untouched except for the winter trails that were hacked out every year. Peter snuffled away, doing navigation sums. We headed over 3,000-foot mountains, still with snow on them, east to Penzhino, where there were a couple of airfields.

The weather changed slowly, blue sky vanishing until black cloud developed and started to drop serious rain. It was worrying when you could not see even the vague outline of anything through it, and you knew that in it it would be impossible to see where you were going. For two hours I tried to avoid the worst of the rainfall, getting soaked but only entering the central rain cloud once, when there was no other way through. We spent much of that time in mountains, fearful that we would be trapped there by the cloud lowering on us. But we hacked through and turned north again, where Peter began to feel the cold badly. He was so affected he never asked me to turn the radio on to assure local ATCs where we were – when we eventually landed, we learned that helicopters had been scrambled and even Moscow informed.

It was desolate countryside and I was seeing it in summer,

stripped of snow and ice. In winter it must be a cold version of hell. All my time was taken up monitoring the fuel and electrics, choosing when to transfer petrol over. The bladder tank didn't appear to work; I could not see the usual evidence that fuel was moving by splashes in the Mickey Mouse gauge. I spent an hour pressing my foot on the bladder, physically pushing petrol through, transferring ten litres that way. When the main tank was half-empty, I moved fuel over from the left spare tank and was relieved to find it transferred, though it was slower than usual.

All the time the charging light glowed red instead of green and I lived from minute to minute with the expectation that I would suddenly lose all information about the engine: rev counter, temperatures, oil pressure. The engine ran cool anyway, as low as 66° instead of around 100°.

Despite these worries I felt cheerful and sang softly. I tried half a dozen different rhythmic versions of 'Summertime', and mantras kept popping up, fragments of songs which I found myself repeating, over and over. I had no idea what Peter thought about the odd noises in front of him. He did not say anything unless prompted, except to point either north or east to tell me a different way to go. We discovered near the end of the day that he had entered the co-ordinates of Markovo wrongly into his GPS, and there was a 25-mile difference between where he was going and where I was going, that nearly started an argument. He did not see very well, which accounted for the wrong co-ordinates, so getting them right took time. But he did not lack courage.

We passed over another mountain range, heavily covered in snow, and entered country dominated by hundreds of rivers. I was beginning to feel the cold myself. The Flyer's engine never changed pitch; and despite its problems, I had confidence in it. I had to rouse Peter to talk to ATC at Markovo and they were slow to reply. By now I could risk using my own GPS to find the runway, which was long and covered in gravel and quite unsuitable for the Flyer.

When I put her down, the gravel slowed her dangerously. I was not sure how I would get off with a full load in the morning.

Markovo was the most primitive town I visited in Russia. Everything looked gimcrack, but it had great hunting and fishing. Valentine and Evgenia Ushakov, who gave us dinner, said they were able to catch enough salmon every year with a rod and line to produce 50 litres of caviar. Evgenia produced a wonderful meal, reindeer soup, battered fish, potatoes in butter, but I just wanted to spoon down caviar, followed by neat vodka. Peter ate with his head down, shovelling food in, slurping his soup noisily and quite without embarrassment.

On day 78, 9 June I found Peter on the phone trying to find fuel. The Flyer, hobbled by the ATC building, was undisturbed and sheltered from the north wind. I pulled her so one wing was in to wind. We got into flying gear and, just as I was ready, Peter told me Magadan, 700 miles away, would not give us permission to leave. No reason was given. I stomped around shouting pithy Anglo-Saxon words. Then I borrowed a motorbike to look at the runway to determine which end was best to avoid the loose gravel. A local pilot offered to swap me an AN2 for the Flyer, I declined.

Magadan eventually decided we could fly. I set off briskly, determined not to stop and risk heavy stones being churned up by the propeller and breaking it. We turned into wind with the okay to go, I put my foot down and we sped away, first with the bar in to gain speed, then with the bar out to lift off. As I had expected, the gravel had a delaying effect and it took ages to actually break away from the ground. I pulled the bar in a few millimetres to build up speed without touching down again, then pushed out to climb. Heavily laden, we struggled into the bouncy air, ahead of us the prospect of hours of freezing flying.

The countryside east of Markovo looked very dangerous to land in. It was full of winding rivers, almost marshland, with a big clump of mountains halfway to Anadyr. At first I maintained our height at 2,000 feet, but, fearful of the expected turbulence in the mountains, I soon climbed to 4,000 feet and stayed there, enduring the cold. Peter felt it more than me; I hoped his 'like-woman' bonked his head off. Our ground speed was poor, dropping to 35 knots. It did not seem to matter at what height I flew, we always battled a headwind. There had been headwinds all the way across Siberia.

I was always alert for any sign that the battery we had charged overnight had not expended all its power. I also looked for signs of life on the ground, but could find none. The mountains appeared particularly desolate, snow-covered though with dark grey patches showing through. I clapped my hands to warm them up. The further east we went, the colder it got, with more snow and ice on the ground. As we entered the long wide mouth of the Anadyr River, ice was thick on the water despite approaching Midsummer's day. Peter groaned with cold, which he felt more in his head than elsewhere, that is, his head was colder than any other part of him.

After four hours we came to Anadyr itself, a big grey city, a port, with industry and smokestacks and a long runway with airliners and AN2s and helicopters. I landed safely, despite turbulence in the 17-knot wind. As usual, we attracted a crowd. A big, fat, bearded man with a red face in a sailor's hat and with his flies undone directed us to a hangar; it was, in fact, a fish-drying hut. I unpacked the Flyer, surrounded by chattering Russians with whom Peter conversed until it was time for him to visit ATC and file a flight plan for the morning.

We ended the evening in the best hotel available, where hot water and toilet paper were promised but did not materialise. Our dinner was four hot dogs and watery, warm mashed potatoes, a Mars bar, plus three warm beers each. We were lucky to get anything at all, in Peter's opinion, because 'Everything is closed, closed, closed.' as if it was my fault. We both went to our separate rooms in a bad temper.

If I made Nome in a couple of days I resolved to spend an hour in the shower. I had not had a chance to do a laundry since Magadan. I dreamed of conversations where I could string more than half a dozen words together, where nuances mattered.

On day 79 I set the alarm for 5 a.m. to make certain I completed the previous day's journal. Peter said we had to be away at 10 a.m., otherwise Providenya would be closed when we arrived overhead. We walked our gear across to the fish-drying shed, he gave me another warning about getting away on time and rushed off to ATC, while I prepared the aircraft. By 9 a.m. I was in my survival suit and ready to go, but Peter was nowhere to be seen. I spent the next hour and a half getting into a terrible temper. It was 10.30 a.m. when he arrived with the news that the Met Office wanted $70 for telling us the weather and ATC wanted $309 for talking us in and out.

He was apprehensive about giving me this news, and with good reason. I spent five minutes abusing him loudly. I told him I expected to be robbed in Russia, but the timing was dreadful. He looked shattered and I stopped; he had been delayed because he had done the same shouting on my behalf. I paid the money, got permission to go and strapped him in. The fat man with the red face had done up his flies and saw us off. We taxied out and took off into a strong headwind from the north. It was bitterly cold.

The Met Office forecasted headwinds for the first 20 miles and then a tailwind. For this reason, I did not argue with Peter's decision to go around the Gulf of Anadyr, adding 110 miles to the journey. With a tailwind, it should have been a doddle. But no tailwind materialised, and as we crossed snow-covered tundra, with its fantastic ice shapes, and finally the open sea, our speed dropped away. Where I had been happy with 50 knots and fatalistic about 40 knots, I was soon counting my blessings whenever we bumbled along at 35 knots, and I wondered what I would do if we remained, as we did for long periods, at 25 knots. Peter thought that as we headed east our speed would be slow, but at the far end of the gulf we turned south and then should have really motored. Instead, the headwind followed us whatever direction we flew. I looked down on an awful sea full of ice fragments. Peter groaned in the back whenever the cold really hurt him. It seemed to have made him ill.

We were surrounded by white snow-covered mountains, blue, still sea with no internal life like other seas, just the surface ruffled by the weird winds. I was over land for two hours, with at least the possibility of landing out if the engine stopped. Then for three hours we were over the sea, hardly moving at all at 3,000 feet, while watching the scenery change slowly. A mountain came into distant view, an hour later it was clearer but seemed no closer.

I first noticed the strange phenomena of rising and falling air just before the sea began. The Flyer had been maintaining a steady height at 4,500 revs, and suddenly began falling out of the sky. I watched the altimeter hand unwind like the second hand on a clock, and increased the revs to full power before she stopped falling. I thought that the ice had caused the fall, for whatever reason, but out over the sea unexplained rises and falls occurred all the time. I was either at 1,500 feet at full revs, or at 4,500 feet on tickover. I tried to tell Peter what was happening, but he focused on the slow ground speed and nothing else; he was fearful we would run out of fuel before reaching Providenya.

I had been wondering why I was not overcome by fear at what was happening to me. When my mind wandered, the thought did occur that what I was doing was incredibly dangerous and I could easily die. But instead of being paralysed by fear, a natural reaction, I turned the thought over and drifted on to think of something else. Bomber pilots in the last war may have achieved the same state of mind. I remember thinking of Shakespeare and that wonderful speech by Feeble in *Henry V*: 'By my troth I care not, a man can die but once, we owe God a death: he that dies this year is quit for the next.'

We did finally make it over the mountains, but imperceptibly we had reached 8,000 feet in the process, all on revs that should have kept us at 3,000 feet. I stayed high, fearful about turbulence. The relief in Peter's voice in the last half hour before landing was tangible. We were met by the mayor of Providenya, Alexander Batura, but spent the next hour trying to find shelter for the Flyer in a gale-force wind. She was put to rest in the lee of the airport building, and a charging unit was found to recharge the battery.

The hotel had warm water and toilet paper, so that was a plus, as was the bar where we had kebabs and chips – a real feast – with beer and vodka. Peter drank his vodka and announced he didn't want to go to Nome. Tears rolled down his cheeks. I had become used to flying with him, but he was nervous about 200 miles into a headwind over the Bering Sea. I told him I could pay his wages by cheque, but if he wanted cash he had to come with me.

I looked at him and realised we had crossed the 180-degree line, and were now closer to England going forward, than going back.

13. OUT OF RUSSIA AND INTO AMERICA

On a direct line from Providenya to Nome, Alaska, only 200 nautical miles lay between me and freedom. Peter had no influence on my route, because we were moving into international waters and I was captain of my aircraft again. I could go direct and intended to do so.

On 11 June, 80 days after I had left London, I should have returned in triumph with Keith Reynolds, after having flown around the world. In fact, I had flown only halfway around the world in the time allotted, and even then I was not sure I could make it.

Peter chivvied me in the airport hotel, worried because he knew I was going to spend the day getting robbed. I could not find my document case, which included the passport with the US visa, and fretted about this for an hour before finding it lying on the trike. We tried to find 93 octane petrol; at first only 25 litres was available, but then we heard there was some at the docks. I was driven there and met a fat man with a beard who was persuaded to sell me what I wanted. He took a bucket to some rusty 50-gallon tins, and my driver knocked the rust off and began pouring petrol into the bucket. This he transferred to my spare tanks, but stopped pouring just before a river of rust particles fell out.

He threw the dregs down a hole in the floorboards.

I watched in horror as he repeated the process time and again, and thought of the terrible damage this unfiltered fuel could do to my engine over the Bering Sea. At the airport, Peter met me with his usual word, 'problem', which irritated me. I replied that our big problem was to filter every drop of the fuel we had, twice, before putting it into the Flyer. This we did with the help of a spare can Peter cleaned with a rag. I did not have full confidence in the fuel and resolved to transfer as little as possible over from the spare tanks; there were still 60 litres of clean fuel in the main and bladder tanks.

All the time a freezing wind blew, and Peter agitated about 'problems'. They turned out to be expensive. Because we had turned up late at Providenya, we had incurred $475 overtime charges. ATC wanted $250 for providing a radio service. For a long time customs men hung around, fingering my luggage. They ended up photographing each other in heroic poses next to the Flyer. I was impatient and full of fears about the flight. I had not made the best job of attaching the battery charger and, despite hitting it with four amps an hour, I was worried that we would run out of electric power before transferring fuel.

The forecast was for a north-east wind, strong, virtually a headwind, and Peter had filed a flight plan assuming an average of 40 knots. I thought this was optimistic with the forecast, but my spirits were raised by reading that Nome expected a south-west wind and low scattered cloud at 800 feet. We dressed, both of us apprehensive, but without the language or the culture to share our fears.

We got away late, at nearly 2 p.m., because of the financial demands. I had another worry, the state of the propeller. It had been battered by the rough Russian gravel runways and I feared that the imbalance would put undue strain on the engine bearings. I was not willing to put on the three spare blades I carried, because Providenya's runway was so bad, and I did not have confidence that I would be able to set all the blades at the right angle. But we got off the gravel into a moderate north wind and turned right over small snow-covered mountains and the ice-covered sea beyond. My throat was cold because the choker I wore was not adjusted correctly; I did more fiddling than usual to get comfortable.

I had flown over thousands of miles of water; why should that day be more fearful than any other? Yet it was. The ghost of the Djinn nearly appeared but was firmly squashed, hovering in the background as I measured the distance I was flying out to a cold frozen sea, before deciding that I had gone too far to get back if the engine stopped. A combination of fears, about the petrol quality, the battery charge and the propeller, whirled around in my head, each serving to cancel each other out. I was committed to the flight. Dying is something we are all going to do anyway; it is just the method and the timing that has to be decided.

There were fields of broken ice in patches *en route*; I used them to steer by. The sky started a brilliant blue, with high washed-out clouds, but ahead, low strata developed, from left to right. At first I was not worried and droned on, but then I came to that classic choice, a cloud sandwich – I was stuck between two layers and undecided whether to go up or down if they closed up. This they did, inevitably, about halfway through the 200-mile journey, when I was in touch with Anchorage ATC, which came through loud and clear, but which had difficulty hearing me.

I decided to climb above the clouds.

This was a mistake.

As I was whited-out, I glued my eyes to the GPS and the altimeter, not daring to use the turn-and-bank indicator because it gobbled electricity and that meant less for the fuel transfer. We started climbing, going from 2,000 feet, painfully, to 5,400 feet, and I retreated to the small private dreamlike world of trying to instrument-fly a weight-shift microlight. Peter said nothing at first, but after 15 minutes, when we still had not broken through, he shouted: 'Ice!' As if coming out of a private dream, it took me some moments to discover that there was ice everywhere, on my jacket, on all the flying wires, the control bar and, worst of all, on my visor. I could not see the instruments nor the GPS except by peering closely, and then only with difficulty. Peter kept saying 'blue above, blue above', and when I chanced to look up, there was, but we had not the power to break out into it. It would have been a mistake in our heavily iced condition to do so, yet I tried. The load of ice on the wing was so heavy she would not climb. I decided to descend. There was no other choice. I also turned the turn-and-bank on because we were all over the sky, disorientated.

All this time I was in touch with Anchorage ATC, to whom I tried to keep my voice calm. They grew concerned and declared an emergency; such an embarrassing way to enter America. I told them my position and that I was busy, so would they please not call me for a while? Peter reached in front of me and scraped a window on my visor with his fingernails, so I could see by cocking my head to the right and peering left. Inside myself I felt detached, fully absorbed in trying to stay alive, so much so that the paralysis of fear never struck. Peter was encouraging and helpful and did not intrude his fears on me. I realised later how much of a relief this was. When I said I was going down, he agreed and did not panic. We dropped to 3,500 feet and I kept the wings level and pointing roughly in the right direction. Peter told me layers had appeared, and I looked up and they had. I found my way east again and was soon in clearer air, though with the cloud still above and below me I was amazed at the amount of ice we were carrying. I took a number of stills pictures, but the video camera was so cold it wouldn't work.

We were not completely out of danger, but gradually the ice melted and fell away, some of it hitting the poor battered propeller, which raised more fears. Whenever I throttled back, the engine sounded as if it were knocking, but I think that was my fevered imagination. I started talking again to Anchorage ATC, which was concerned at my situation and kind without being intrusive. Hundreds of pilots in the area must have been aware I was having a bad time out over the sea. It was the first time I had ever been iced-up. All this time we were flying east, with a ground speed in the 50s, and later above 60 knots, a tailwind for the first time in days. What a welcome to America.

With 30 miles to go, more layers of cloud developed, one layer down low over the sea. I tried to fly beneath it, but at 500 feet and still with mist ahead of me, bottled out and climbed again, to stay above it for 20 miles. Then I saw a hole and descended, to come across a small island not featured on my GPS and which could have been a nasty surprise in thicker cloud. This time I went down to 400 feet and could pick my way over the calm sea.

The Alaskan coast came into view. I shouted 'America' and asked for the back camera to get put on. Peter shouted 'Alaska'. I think, like many Russians, he was sensitive about the fact that America bought Alaska from Russia for about tuppence ha'penny in the last century. The deal, seen then as one where America got the worst of it, was not seen that way now.

We flew to the coast and circled over thousands of whitened trees washed up as driftwood, and the grubby log cabins housing people who still looked for gold on the once-fabulous gold coast. It was the most delirious moment of the whole flight, and I could hardly contain my joy and relief. We flew quickly east and Nome came into view, a town like a western film set. Keith would have sniffed at my landing – I bounced – but I did not care, though I did wonder where Andy Webb and Barrie Bayes were. They appeared as I taxied to the apron, having arrived from London via Anchorage 'five seconds before you', as Andy put it.

America was bliss after Russia; toilets with seats and paper, sinks with plugs, taps marked hot water which told the truth, shops and cafés open late in the evening, where food was served cheerfully and not as if a tremendous favour was being done. I unpacked the Flyer and found she had no electric power to restart; it was that close. Big friendly Americans pushed her into a heated hangar. Andy brought me up to date with the news that GT Global was close to pulling out. I spent only three hours sleeping, infused with energy to save the public face of the flight. I talked to Kay Burley at 1.30 a.m. my time, and could feel her concern pouring down the phone. She promised to phone friends in England to tell them I was alive.

I counted my cash in my room, a total of $2,576, so I had to be careful. I intended to pay Peter all his money, just over $3,500, and use my credit card to buy him his plane fare to Khabarovsk. He earned that and more by his behaviour. There were four weeks left of Keith's contract when he went back to England; I would use that money to pay Peter.

I had flown halfway around the world in 80 days, but suffered 33 days loss because of bureaucrats. If I could do the second half in 34 days, then the original dream could have come true.

It was a tall order for one man on his own. I had to adapt the Flyer for one-man flight.

Barrie Bayes told me that Greenland would not let me through. We would see about that.

14. ALASKA TO SAN FRANCISCO

Three engineers with Smythe Air, a local airline in Nome, John Russell, Herb Rossen and Doug Deering, set about repairing the deeply wounded Flyer. They replaced the three propeller blades with the spares I carried. Doug also filled in the holes on one of the damaged blades, so I had a new spare. The failure of the engine to charge the battery took a day and a half to sort out. After a lot of tests we found it was a cheap fuse-holder, costing just a few pence, that was arcing within itself. The engineers were not impressed at the standard of such parts on the Flyer.

I paid Peter Petrov and bought him his ticket back to Khabarovsk. He took to camera work with Barrie and Andy as if he was a professional actor, with lots of Russian emotion, and if my spare GPS had not disappeared at the same time as he did, he would have been my unqualified hero.

No one from my sponsoring company contacted me after my miraculous escape from Siberia. They were said to be considering pulling out and then not. I wrote to Dallas McGillivray but received no reply. This was a constant worry to me. Without a sponsor, I had enough money to continue but no backing for marketing the flight.

When I test-flew the Flyer, my radio communications were poor. The radio was fine; it was the Lynx interface that was broken, and it was not until I got to San Francisco that I went back to decent radio communication. This meant flying thousands of miles with crackly reception and transmission, another worry.

My main problem was doubts about my nerve. I could fly virtually anywhere two-up, but alone, would I have the same courage? I thought a lot about Keith, back in England with his students. The more I did so, the more I thought his soul would corrode. I missed him. There was a big mountain range between Nome and Anchorage and serious mountains further south that I would have to negotiate alone. Yet what was the difference between flying solo and flying dual?

The cold answer was, my mind. It was my mind I was fearful

about, full of fear and the Djinn. Could I control that fear and stamp on him?

Barrie told me that Eppo Numan, the first man to fly the Atlantic in a microlight, had volunteered to take Keith's place. I turned down the suggestion. Eppo was brave but, by his own admission, he had thumped his chase plane pilot. We would be at each other's throats in hours. Andy and Barrie both expressed their fears about my workload, and the belief grew in England that I had to have a partner to continue. I could not bear the thought of any more betrayals. I trusted me. My arguments with myself were fair-minded and self-interested.

The weather had been perfect the day after I had arrived in Nome. It was 11 June again, the same date – because I had crossed the dateline – that I had left Providenya. Repairs took a second day, 12 June, but on day 83, 13 June, I set off to Fairbanks, having rejected a route via Anchorage because of high mountains and a poor weather forecast. There was low cloud and drizzle, but a good westerly wind. I headed east, acutely conscious of the ghost of the Djinn, fearful he was full of vigour because he could get to me without interruption.

A hazy Bering Sea fog drifted off the water and reached inland. I tried to climb above it, reasoning that I could always descend over the sea if I had to. But at 5,500 feet I was too cold and the haze had not gone, and anyway I was shaking and nervous, so I descended. I found a hole in the bottom layer of clouds, slipped through to 400 feet and picked my way east. It was raining, I settled in and accepted being rained on, hugging the coast and watching the GPS.

I flew over brown land with the evidence of man's eternal search for gold: wooden cabins, tracks, diggings, fields of dreams. I cautiously probed my mind to see if it was okay, but the mind appeared vigorous and not at all interested in the Djinn. It seemed easier to close him down than it once was. Otherwise, I daydreamed, leaving the coast and setting out across 60 miles of sea, south east towards Unalakleet where I knew there was a valley below clouds through the mountains to the Yukon River. Conditions deteriorated to where I could not see where I was going. I fired up the turn-and-bank and tried to climb through the cloud, but at 3,000 feet there was no sign of a top, I descended again, whited-out. I could hear the fluttering edges of fear. At 500 feet, still well over the sea, I saw the misty outline of the cold, cold water. I kept heading east, calm in my mind, committed, and watching for layers in the clouds, which eventually appeared. Then I saw the sun shining on the water in the distance and broke out into a clear sky with 20 miles to run to Unalakleet, a small fishing village with a large gravel runway.

A small group of people said hello. I took advice about the route through the mountains, and flew away into bouncy thermals between low mountain peaks. I fell into singing, uninhibitedly, which I could obviously not do with Keith on board, different rhythmic versions of 'Summertime'. It was one of the few songs to which I knew the words. It was terrific countryside, wide and beautiful. I wondered how much had been explored, or whether there were still places to look for the fabulous Mother Lode. In places it was like Scotland. There was a predominance of English, German and Scandinavian names in the signatures in my contact book. I found I was not bothered by the heights I flew, and I settled at 3,000 feet, happy to be bumped around by thermals, singing, often nodding off and waking with a start, 30 degrees or so off course.

Galena is on the huge Yukon River, which carved out a giant flat valley in the mountains over millions of years. I thought of Jack London's heroes – Burning Daylight, The Malamute Kid, Smoke Bellow – struggling down the Yukon in winter, and I reminded myself that I was seeing the land during its brief holiday from cold. I landed and refuelled at Galena, 20 gallons donated by a man called Jeff German, took off again and watched the weather develop, apprehensive about the large black clouds to the south dumping curtains of heavy rain. I cut the curves on the Yukon, calculating the distance ahead, ready to swerve around clouds rather than get caught by them. The radio had reports about thunderstorms in the area, and once, a waterspout of 500 feet was reported near the runway at Tanana. I did not want to get caught in one of those and vowed to avoid the area.

Then I saw, to my horror, that the CHT – cylinder head temperature – had soared off the clock, 205°, while the oil temperature was at 119°, they were way too high.

I pressed the 'nearest' button on the GPS, and saw my closest airfield was that same Tanana where the waterspout had occurred just a few minutes earlier. I could see it in the distance menaced by a large black cloud. I flew 14 miles there with my heart pounding, always looking for landing fields. There were none; it would have to be the tundra, which did not look inviting. When it had happened in Saudi, we had had flat desert to land-out on.

I watched the oil temperature climb to 123 and oil pressure fall, as I made a direct approach to Tanana runway, which was long and full of gravel. I came in on tickover with the temperatures plummeting, and reached the ground safely. It started to rain, then to hail and it was soon bucketing down. A local, Ralph Eller, turned up and volunteered to get me a gallon of anti-freeze. He returned and wouldn't take payment. We poured it into the now-cool engine and, in the lashing rain, tested it for half an hour. It settled at 90°, which was fine. I thought the reason it had overheated was that I had put duct tape on the radiator, which had been running too cool. I took the tape off for the flight to Fairbanks.

Most of the way I watched the temperatures, but they settled down and behaved. Was my diagnosis right? Had I damaged the engine permanently? Who could say? It seemed to work. I monitored the few landing places I passed, mine company strips and a couple of small towns, but was never alarmed. I tried new tactics to keep my mind occupied: reciting the whole of Lewis Carroll's 'Jabberwocky' in different ways and voices; and line-dancing in the air to get the circulation going.

Flying over Fairbanks Airfield I had never seen so many small aircraft, both on land and on floats. ATC guided me in for overdue negotiations with US customs and immigration. A local microlight pilot, Jerry Standefer, was waiting to help; he had followed my story on the Internet. Thanks to him I found a hotel and a meal and a beer, and had five hours' sleep.

On day 84, I set off late from Fairbanks, because of a TV interview, to try and make it to Canada. My radio gave me problems and I had garbled messages about flight plans which I could not pick up. My route followed the wide, flat Tanana River into the mountains, where it began to rain heavily. I flew to the left of a big lake to avoid a military base and to stay away from forest fires that were still smoking, despite the torrential downpour. I steered clear of clouds beneath which there was a black haze, but I did not mind about the fringes. Inside my mind, I was calm, even exultant. This was living.

All the time I looked for thunderstorms, but there were none. It was just torrential rain. On my left, cloud development in the higher mountains was black and evil-looking, and slowly heading my way. To the right, with a gap of perhaps ten miles, it was also black. Only through the valley was the route marginally clearer, in that I could see where I was going and rain showers had defined limits. My ground speed was over 70 knots and I thought the risk worth it. The temperatures behaved and I never had that heart-stopping moment of looking down and seeing them rush off the clock.

There was a particularly bad patch of rain at Tok Junction, just after picking up the Alaska Highway – which I saw as an extended runway beneath me if I was in trouble. I went over a small mountain and saw that, at last, the two dreadful weather systems on either side of me were joined in a bridge across the Tanana. I floated down one side, looking to see where I might pick out a hazy landscape beyond. At one end it looked clearer, so I plunged through heavy rain, trying to protect the GPS and hiding the radio under the windscreen. The rain grew worse, but I could always see the ground.

I hummed to myself, occasionally breaking into scat singing, words and noises meaning nothing but the rhythms calming my soul. I was comfortable in three flying suits, including Keith's thin one, and the electric gloves worked well and did not fuse the system. I kept a listening watch on the radio, but heard nothing.

After 20 minutes of rushing at 80 knots through thick rainy gloom, I saw to my right that it was lighter and headed that way. The rain stopped, and I found myself in a beautiful austere valley, full of blacks and whites and greys, under a canopy of cloud and those exhausted little puffs that mark the end of a long spell of rain. I broke into loud singing – 'Summertime' – and flew over, rather than around, more mountains, virtually daring the cloud on the peaks to come up and envelop me and flirting with their fringes.

I crossed the huge valley, full of lakes and previous courses of the Tanana River, heading for Northway Junction, just 50 miles from my destination, Beaver Creek, the airport of entry into Canada. At first I thought just to circle Northway with the cameras on, but I could see a tremendous black curtain of cloud right across my route south and decided to land. There was a strong wind close to the ground, my speed down to 35 knots and so I shouted, 'This is the danger, it's moments like this that get you, be alert, watch out for bumps!', to avoid trashing the Flyer. We got down safely and my chanting rose in volume, 'It's not the landings, it's the taxiing that does you, too much wind, danger, danger!' This all worked, and I taxied to a line of small aircraft behind a disreputable de Havilland Caribou that had seen service in Vietnam and looked like something from a Hollywood film.

The weather centre told me Beaver Creek had a huge thunderstorm sitting over it, so I thought I'd wait it out. But when the weatherman said he expected the wind to switch at Northway when the rain and clouds arrived, I grew alarmed, and resolved to break the Flyer down for the night, right to battens-out, the first time on the whole journey. This I did, solo, working fast and getting help only to move the wings on to a trailer to protect them from the dirt. I was ready to find a room just as the rain started. It rained heavily all night.

Rooms were $45 a night in a dingy trailer park, water seeping over the floor and a sink with no plug. But I loved it. The landlady, Anne Drolz, was kind and disinterested. There was a basketball game on television and a dozen people, Indians and whites, were getting drunk and yelling at a big black fellow called Michael Jordan; apparently, his team won. I showered, ate a huge beef sandwich, drank three beers and sleepily did an interview with Kay. She, too, enjoined me to be careful.

The next day there was cloud to the ground and even a puritan like me could not fly. The rain gradually petered out and I re-rigged the Flyer, helped by a local engineer called Sam Mills. He asked me if I was Brian or Keith, so I cut Keith's name badge off his flying suit. It was an act of deep psychological significance, and I resolved that I would send his gear home and remove his name from the aircraft, but not yet. I was getting happier on my own.

The weatherman said cloud was lifting to 500 feet and there seemed to be a low passage to allow me to gully-gobble through the mountains to Beaver Creek. I took off with a north-west wind blowing and headed south-east at 400 feet over well-washed green countryside unaffected by man, the tops of mountains buried in cloud, and I was only slightly worried that cloud would descend again. The Alaska Highway was my constant companion throughout the rest of the day, fascinating to look at and to make judgements about the route taken by the engineers.

Inside myself I felt at peace, happier that all the decisions were my own. I thought that Keith would have objected to the previous day's flying, and it was less wearing to convince myself than to convince

Keith as well. I cautiously explored my mind to see where the Djinn might have been, but he was not there. Having a decent night's sleep helped. He never minded flying low, anyway.

Beaver Creek was the first customs post in Canada's Yukon Territory, a small community with only 150 people but three hotels. Customs and Immigration were painless, and the ATC controller, Heather Morgan, gave me a lift into town to buy 50 litres of unleaded Mogas. I bought razors, shaving cream and candy bars, and gloated over the plastic bag to carry them in; Russian attitudes still prevailed. Only a week ago I had been in Anadyr. I filed a flight plan for Whitehorse, 230 miles away, and even though it was early evening I set off.

My course took me via an awesome valley, clouds and rain developing to my right, but I sneaked through before the cloud fell into the valley and blocked my way. Down the valley I could see 100 miles, with great towering mountains in the distance which appeared no nearer after an hour in the air. The Highway snaked from right to left, crossing the occasional big river, always picking the firmest ground.

I flew over places with English names like Burwash and Haine's Junction, and wondered idly who they were and how they had come to name the place. It was a long way from England, yet every place I landed at – as I had found in Australia – I was struck by the Englishness of the faces and the names.

Whitehorse, capital of the Yukon, unfolds in front of you as you come around the last mountain of the day. The airfield was enormous with two long strips; I found shelter for the Flyer in a big helicopter hangar. My host was Bob Cameron, who runs Trans North Ops, and was working late teaching his 16-year-old son, Kyle, to fly. They gave me a lift to the hotel where I put all my gear on charge and went off for a lovely steak dinner served by a waitress so cheerful that I left an extravagant tip.

Charles told me Fiona was to return from Dubai, and her new man, this weekend. I was acutely sensitive about this development. My divorce was not yet through; I still had papers to sign.

On 16 June, 86 days after leaving London, Charles called again. He told me a GT Global committee was worried about the dangers of me flying alone. They were thinking of pulling out publicly, citing safety as a reason and claiming my insurance was not valid because there was only me left. This was horrifying. I thought the flight was now actually against their business interests and they were looking for an excuse to cut free. I would not forgive them if they went public with their fears; it would scupper my chances of getting through Greenland. Charles had to work on the insurance issue. It could turn into a real nightmare. It would be a banal way to end this adventure, stabbed in the back by a sponsor.

Keith, meanwhile, said Charles, was absorbed with trying to get Lina out of Russia.

It was a brilliant mountain day, blue skies and meaty clouds forming just above the highest peaks. When I took off, heading east, the air was bouncy and it grew more so as I flew slowly at 45 knots into the first valley. I was prepared for the thermic thrashing the mountains gave me, once I had convinced myself they were, indeed, thermals and not wind swirling around the peaks. I videoed with the chest camera and talked to the face camera and took stills shots. I worked hard, flying and trying to produce pictures about it. The documentary was all I had left, if anyone would buy it.

The countryside was mountainous, covered in trees, with great whorled scars where, millions of years ago, rivers had taken a different course and then been cut off and died. I flew over long, brilliant-blue lakes, with the reflections of distant snow-covered mountains in them, so that I tired of the beautiful shots I could get. Once I had the nerve to record a few versions of 'Summertime', only for the sake of telling the truth about the flight and not for the beauty of my singing voice.

The thermals grew more violent, but they were not vicious. I sang lustily when the whim took me. I wished I knew the words to more songs.

I watched clouds develop, always on my right, and I saw that they were getting higher and showers were falling in places. The snow-covered mountains retreated and lower hills, more rounded but still above 5,000 feet, appeared on my left. I flew down a long lake and then due east along a valley with old mine workings. The Alaskan Highway rose to get over the last high ground and I was truly east of the Rockies. As I headed south I had to cross the Rockies again to reach the West Coast and San Francisco to pick up Phileas Fogg's route there and make a third crossing. Otherwise, I could have headed from my goal for the day, Watson Lake, diagonally across country to New York. It was not a temptation. Even if I was the only person in the whole world who cared for the integrity of the flight, aesthetically, I wanted to do it the right way.

I had studied this part of the route closely back in London, expecting to burst out into a glacial valley, full of greys and whites, but the plain on which Watson Lake is situated is flat and green, with small lakes. I had to avoid a heavy rain shower and watch others form to my right, on my way in. I was able to find a hangar with L&R Aircraft Repair.

The tourist attraction of Watson Lake is its 'sign forest': thousands of placards and place names for which it is world-famous. They were begun when a homesick American serviceman in the last war put up a sign saying how far away his home was and others copied him. Now other towns have sign forests, but Watson Lake claims to be the first. I was sustained, intellectually, by a two-month-old copy of *The Economist* which I had found and was reading cover to cover. Even EMU excited me, starved for so long of interesting conversation or always talking about the flight.

On day 87 I prepared to fly the 495 miles to Prince George. I took off from Watson Lake at 10.10 a.m. and headed over a flat green plain, steering south for a big hill which masked the entry to a 400-mile valley. It was smooth to begin with, but as turbulence started I resolved to handle it a different way than the previous day, which had left me more weary than I had expected to be. I let the Flyer plunge and toss, then steered her back on course. As I settled into the technique, which involved not bracing myself for the lumps in the air, I found it was not tiring my arms, and especially my hands, holding the bar. My course through the air, with my new technique, was squirrelly.

For the first 180 miles I saw no roads at all. It was virgin country, though I could see evidence of winter trails. I picked my way south between two ranges of mountains, looking at small lakes and never certain whether the brown bits at the edge were dry land or scum on the water. There was a continual development of dark rain clouds to the left and I avoided them by scuttling down the right side of the valley, my ground speed close to 50 knots. I watched the temperatures carefully and occasionally cast a grateful glance at the green charging light, which had caused me so many problems in Russia.

It was hard to believe it was only a week since I was there.

After four hours flying I came across the first airfield, Terminus Mountain, and there were dirt strips from then on, including mining sites and Fort Ware. I droned along, sometimes half asleep, and was shocked to find that the Djinn was still with me. Just past Terminus, I discovered suddenly that the height I was above the ground, about 3,000 feet, was causing me fear. He did not put in an appearance, as I half expected, but whatever the frisson was, it disappeared under a ton of scorn which the rest of my mind poured upon it, and which, previously, had not worked. I just contemptuously thought of something else, taking a photograph, or using the video camera, and he went away. There was a second appearance, also tentative and also dismissed quickly. The only significance about them both was that, however put-upon, the Djinn himself was not dead, just dormant.

My ground speed dropped to the mid-30s after Terminus, and I started to worry about fuel. That morning I had had hopes that I would make Prince George on one fuel load; now I worried about making it to Mackenzie, 100 miles short of my goal. After nearly seven hours in the air, the rain got me. On the last 35 miles into Mackenzie, a heavy rain cloud stretched across my path. I had no fuel or room to dodge about, and soon rain was streaming down my visor, and I was steering with one hand and trying to protect my GPS and radio with the other. But instead of being irritated at getting wet, I loved it. It was one of those rare wonderful moments when there was nowhere else in the world I wanted to be. There, 2,000 feet over a big logging river, with mountains to my left and bucketing rain, a misty view, my beautiful Flyer strong and constant beneath me, why would I change places with anyone, anywhere?

My radio chose to work on the way into Mackenzie, a clean big airfield where fuel was easy to get and I could go for a pee, and I was off within half an hour, the quickest turnaround on the whole flight. Again, I had a headwind, and I flew over low hills and a broad river where thousands of logs were floating in big rings on the water, heading for sawmills. There was high ground between Mackenzie and Prince George and long dirty lines of cloud trailed from it across my path. I dropped down to a few hundred feet and dived through a narrow gap between cloud base and the ground, keeping the turn-and-bank indicator on in case I had to climb. I felt gloriously free, and slung in 360s whenever the whim took me, as hard over as I could, singing at the top of my voice, wordless mantras which I would be conscious of occasionally and which settled my mind.

Again, the radio worked as I entered Prince George's air-space. I found fuel immediately and shelter for the night in a hangar owned by Andy Hill, and I dined well at Esther's Inn.

I phoned an old friend near Seattle, Mike Winecoff, whom I hoped to meet the following day, though I could not, for customs reasons, land on his beach. Charles told me Amvesco were definitely going to pull the plug on me. Nothing personal, just business. He had been trying to phone Rory McCarthy about Virgin picking up the sponsorship, but Rory never phoned back. I told Charles that was Rory's way of saying get lost and he should stop trying.

Alison told me that Jackie Parker, the woman who would have flown Richard Branson's microlight around the world, wanted to have dinner with me in San Francisco.

Despite nine hours' hard flying, I felt full of life.

On day 88, 18 June, a petrol leak developed from a drain plug that had been a nuisance since the flight began. The propeller also looked in poor shape, with the aluminium tape that covered the leading edges being dented and torn. I drained the fuel tank, had the plug repaired and fixed the propeller using the glue and cotton waste Doug Deering had given me in Nome. Clouds gathered low in the sky and it looked like rain. I hurried, but it was still 11.30 a.m. before I was ready to go. Prince George ATC seemed to have no problems hearing me. I set off south, delighted to find I had a following wind of sorts, and that I was doing more than 60 knots, passing over country more and more civilised in appearance, with the huge Fraser River – Canada's Grand Canyon – to my right, and farms and small towns in evidence.

I flew 2,000 feet above the ground, at first with little bumpiness but dodging around rain clouds coming from my left, low and troublesome. South of Williams Lake the countryside rose to 7,000 feet and I opted to go right with the river, into thicker cloud and more rain. The wind was light so the rain moved slowly, but twice I had to plunge in, which I did with a sort of exultation, sometimes circling in the middle with the cameras on. I felt on the edge, totally committed, quite at ease with the flying.

But my mood changed when I flew through a more difficult bunch of clouds. I was sandwiched between them and high ground, and then rushed into the spectacular granite Fraser River valley, thousands of feet deep. I became aware of all the air beneath me again, the enormous heights I could fall from, I grew fearful. I was aware of it always for the rest of the flight down to Chilliwack, a constant background threat that would have paralysed me had I let it.

It governed my flying style. Sometimes I defied it by circling in the worst possible places, a sort of two fingers to my own mind; other times I hugged one or the other side of the canyon and drew solace from being able to see the earth close to me, though inaccessible. The fears were about not being on the earth, which I saw myself falling to, time and again. My experience with the Flyer, more than 380 hours and the difficult places she had seen me through, were among the arguments I used against these nameless fears.

My ground speed, which had touched 70 knots in some gusts, dropped gradually the further south I flew, and at Hope Airfield at the bottom of the valley where it turned right to break into open country and Vancouver, I was often flying below 40 knots. My route to Seattle was taking me west, back across the Rockies, which I had crossed going east out of Whitehorse. I watched civilisation bloom beneath me, bigger roads, power lines, a railway, towns, trees and fields, and felt I was shaking free of the Northlands, an area I had to visit again to get back to England, but only after tasting America.

I struggled around a bend in the steep valley, and came to a wall of cloud which I did not want to enter. But when I was in it I saw that it was a sort of plug between the mountain weather system and Vancouver's coastal weather. At the far end of the plug it was misty and cool, with a slight headwind. I found Chilliwack airfield and landed safely, hobbled the aircraft with an onlooker called Jim Marshall and blagged a lift to a nearby hotel. I dined on pizza and beer. I was very tired.

Jim Marshall, an instant fan of the flight, picked me up from the motel the next day and got me to the Flyer. I went through the long process of getting her ready and answering his questions. I filed a flight plan, got the weather forecast, took off into a misty day and flew via Bellingham in low cloud to the coast then south towards Seattle, passing rich green countryside dotted with expensive houses with superb views of the ocean. Every now and again I circled to enjoy the view and to film. Mike Winecoff's little village of Maryville appeared in the distance on my left. He was waiting for me with some 'of the most news-hungry journalists in the world' at Boeing Field. Seattle was spectacular, but it needed a photographer in another aircraft to be really appreciated, as Hong Kong was. I approached Boeing Field, which sounded busy, scuttled in and heard the media were waiting at the terminal.

I did all the interviews they wanted; a woman TV reporter grimaced with feminist angst when I called the box on my lap the 'lady's handbag'. Afterwards I had coffee with Mike, whom I had not seen in years. He had an attractive woman called Deborah in tow whom he seemed to be courting; she had a little girl. He had not changed much over the years, except he now had liver spots; he was still slow of speech and thoughtful, and had opened a small shop to sell wood carvings. As young men, three of us had set out to be writers. Mike had remained the truest to the ideal. Jay Jeffrey Jones had moved into marketing and advertising, though he wrote plays and short stories, while I went into journalism and had adventures.

I ate a smoked salmon sandwich, said goodbye to Mike and found the Flyer's battery had run down, but it had enough power to start the engine. The charging unit glowed a weak green; on take-off it went red and stayed that way for the rest of the flight. I decided there were enough airfields between Seattle and Albany on which to land if I could not transfer fuel in the air, and I wanted to get on. It was not recklessness so much as a need to take this sort of risk, to measure my flying skills and see if my judgement deserved the confidence I was coming to have in it. On the GPS, I could see my ground speed increasing until it was in the middle 60s, and I raced low over the countryside, singing my heart out. I did not care about the red light glowing at me again, though I did swear when I discovered I had left my transponder on, which had half-drained the battery. When I turned it off the petrol gauge worked again.

Albany Airport was deserted when I landed and taxied around looking for shelter. I stopped the engine; the battery was flat. A tall attractive woman called Tanya Alderman was waiting for her brother Ryan to return by air from a fishing trip; Tanya helped me hobble the Flyer and put it into a shelter. She drove me to a nearby motel where I had a lovely mock-Chinese meal, three beers, then I did an interview with Sky TV's Anna Topping about being abandoned by GT Global. The reason they gave was that I had failed the 80-day challenge. It sounded unconvincing.

(Outside the small intense world of my flight, it is worth looking at what happened thousands of miles away in England that week.

Amvesco seemed to have been in two minds about the sponsorship of the flight right up to the end. Towards the end of May, while Keith and I were still in Russia, the PR team were asked to justify its marketing budget. Paul Loach was ousted on 29 May, after Keith had left for Anchorage. In early June, after Keith had said he was going home, Dallas told Newlyn not to spend any more money and outstanding invoices were called in. There were more consultations between Dallas and Newlyn, both employees of GT Global, but Dallas made no contact with me, the other principal in this project. Then Dallas phoned Newlyn and said it was all over.

Dallas listed four reasons for pulling the sponsorship: the 80-day target had been missed; Keith had left; there was no insurance; and I had no permission to get across Greenland.

Later, in a letter to Dallas, I pointed out that 80 days was just a target and GT Global had been particularly keen on me not taking risks to get inside that time period. My main requirement was to fly a microlight safely around the world, the first man to do so. I told him that Keith's departure was likely to make me go faster rather than slower. The insurance was a red herring; there was a period of a day when our insurance company fretted about me being on my own, but Charles sorted it out quickly. And Greenland, like China, Japan and Russia, was just another obstructive bureaucratic problem, part of the modern world.

The project was officially ended on 19 July, the day I reached Albany. Amvesco issued a press release to that effect. Charles and Alison had to clear the office in a day.

But even the day before it ended, Mike Webb told Alison it might not be over. Charles saw a letter from someone senior in Amvesco saying they would keep the project on, but only if they could sort out details about my safety, flying alone.

It is hard to avoid the conclusion that Keith's departure was the clincher.)

On day 90, 20 June, I found Tanya at the airport with her family, including her husband, Brian. A chap appeared with a big battery charger, which I connected to the Flyer and discovered the new fuse put in by Doug Deeling had blown. When replaced, the unit charged again.

I took Tanya up for a flight to thank her for the previous night's help. She was a lovely passenger, entirely without fear. She told me her family had once owned all the land around Albany, but that multiple inheritances had broken the holding up, and she now owned no land. We did some low flying – liberating after days going in a straight line.

Once back on the journey again, I found the air turbulent with thermals and climbed and climbed until I was above 5,000 feet, where the air was smooth. I was apprehensive; at any time I felt I could be struck down by screaming fears about the height I was flying and hurtle out of the sky. But I fell into my routine – singing, a form of arm dancing, even reciting 'Jabberwocky' – and somehow the fears disappeared.

Though there were roads and airports and big towns beneath me, I was aware of how rugged the country was. The mountains were covered in scrub and trees and it was easy to imagine how they had been just 200 years ago, before the white men came. I had not expected such tough country so close to northern California. I looked for anything interesting to divert my mind. The dangerous moments were when I fell into a doze and snapped awake after a ten-second snooze. It was then I became aware of the thin crust of control, to which I was adding daily, enclosing the Djinn. Yet that is not an exact description; half-way through the day he just disappeared and never even hinted he had existed. I did not think this was permanent.

After five hours I broke out of the mountains and their thermals, and flew over the northern California flatlands, past Redding to land at Red Bluff. I asked Bob Linderhill, who was walking by, if he knew of a hangar. He did not believe I had come from London and wondered if I was 'shitting' him. Then he took a key off his key ring and gave me his own hangar.

I was under no time pressure on day 91, 22 June, because I was meeting Barrie Bayes to film my flight over the Golden Gate Bridge. I drifted south the 130 miles to Petaluma, just north of San Francisco, arriving through thin cloud to a runway full of aircraft. Dick Lodge of Aeroventure put up the Flyer, and I phoned Anthony Toni, a contact of Andy Webb's, who took me to a hotel and had drinks with me while I ate. I drafted a press release and faxed it to all the local media, but there was little response. Perhaps it had something to do with American news values?

I spent day 92 servicing the Flyer and seeing if I could find another sponsor. When I looked at the spark plugs they were in a terrible state and it was a wonder they had worked at all. It must have been the Russian fuel. I cleaned the engine and checked all the wires and hoses, replacing the broken cap on the right spare tank, a job I should have done ages ago.

Charles finally phoned from my house where he had settled in. He seemed to welcome having my son, James, with him. James was full of words like 'cool' and 'sweetness', just trying to help. He told me Rory McCarthy had been trying to get hold of me. I took a deep breath and phoned Rory. For once, his secretary let me speak to him.

Rory was as charming and as understanding as ever about the flight. When we started talking about whether Virgin would be interested in picking up the sponsorship dropped by GT Global, Rory said they would.

I asked what he wanted.

'We want you to stop right there, abandon your flight, come back to England and start again under Virgin's colours!'

I believe the second word I used was 'off'.

15. CHASING PHILEAS FOGG:

SAN FRANCISCO TO NEW YORK

Rory McCarthy told me I could fly whatever I wanted, weight-shift or three-axis, if I returned home without completing the world flight. It was just the offer Keith would have wanted to hear, and I said so. Rory was not interested in Keith, but that was because I was on track for the record and Keith was not. The proposal took no notice of Colin Bodill's obvious ambitions and ability to make a world flight.

I said no, and I was sorry they would not sponsor the rest of my flight.

'I didn't say that,' said Rory, and asked about terms, which I outlined. Rory said he would talk to Branson about them. I found that I did not care which way it went.

I spent my ninety-third day bogged down by having to be filmed over the Golden Gate Bridge and trying to get a straight answer out of Rory McCarthy. Barrie Bayes arrived with a new Lynx radio interface, which he installed. Rory was constantly unavailable. Richard Branson himself was off negotiating with airlines. It was frustrating.

The weather was poor, 600-foot cloud base, but later this lifted and I set off to circle the Golden Gate Bridge. It was unpleasant in San Francisco Bay, winds coming up the valleys and inlets and churning in the middle, just where I was. All my bland reasoning about being able to cope with turbulence went out of the window. When I finally crawled around Sausilito the turbulence subsided and I spent a lovely ten minutes circling over the Bridge, looking down and remembering my youth. I had crossed that bridge first when I was a 21-year-old and looking for a boat, dreaming of being a Jack London hero.

After two hours I struggled back to Petaluma. It was too late in the day to fly to Carson City, I had still not heard a word from Rory McCarthy, but I had to get away. Until I heard differently, I was still flying around the world in the GT Global Flyer, so I set off in smooth evening air for Sacramento, just to break free. But Sacramento Airport was far too big for my little Flyer, and I was directed on to Lincoln Field. There I was able to put the Flyer in the Atkin Air hangar; and I was the guest of Gene and Margie Fincham, to whom I told my story. Gene was a charter pilot and flight instructor who once flew open-cockpit biplanes; he and Margie had married five years ago. They had a lovely house full of computer equipment, and they threw themselves into the planning of my flight east, trying to contact friends who might put me up.

I heard from Charles on the morning of 25 June that Rory had 'squeezed' an offer of £35,000 from Virgin to buy the rights to the flight, to change the livery in San Francisco and for me to continue the rest of the way in Virgin colours. Andy Webb was reported as saying he thought I should take it, as it 'might lead to other things' (in fact, Rory said that). I was strongly disinclined to sell my soul for such a figure, but I understood the story would be a bigger one if Branson was involved. I had a strong commitment to Andy, who had never once resigned. But I had no idea what I was selling for this sum, and Rory continued to be unobtainable.

Margie Fincham, a formidable lady full of feisty energy, had fallen in love with my flight and began to talk about finding me a new sponsor. I had no way of judging what she was capable of. Could she really get through to people like Ross Perot and CNN's Larry King? Would her persuasion work? Just that she was trying mattered. Having her as a champion was a boon to my soul. There had been so many betrayals that a simple clean commitment to promote it made me feel better.

As the morning wore on and the sun heated up the Sierra Nevadas, I got into a raging temper. Rory never returned any call I made to him, so there was no chance of direct talks. Should I go back to Petaluma on the off-chance of a change into Virgin colours and another dangerous flight around the Golden Gate Bridge? Or should I head out into the Rockies? It was, by now, evening in England. Did I need to throw away the beauty and purity of my adventure for someone who would not even talk to me? Margie watched me get very angry and crystallised my mind by saying, 'he's a flake'. Rory was much more complicated than a flake, but I had had enough. Every hour I dithered meant the sun had more time to heat up the mountains and make the journey east more unpleasant.

LEFT: The author in Nome, Alaska, preparing to set out on the solo leg of his journey
INSET: Northway Junction, Alaska
BOTTOM: In Nome with Herb Rossen, John Russell and Doug Deering

ABOVE: Fraser River, British Columbia
LEFT: Forest fire outside Whitehorses
BELOW: View of Seattle

The author in Prince George
INSET: The salt lakes of Utah

The New York skyline

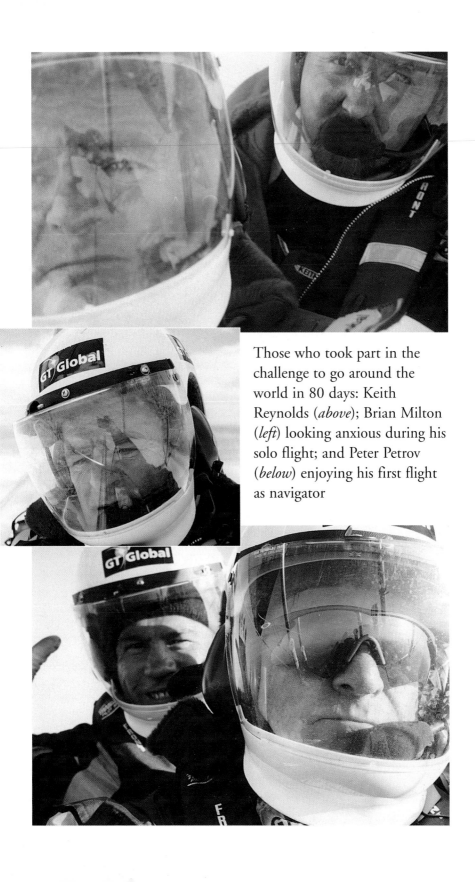

Those who took part in the challenge to go around the world in 80 days: Keith Reynolds (*above*); Brian Milton (*left*) looking anxious during his solo flight; and Peter Petrov (*below*) enjoying his first flight as navigator

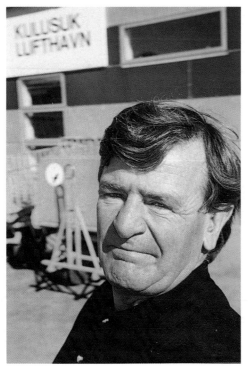

ABOVE: The first 200 miles east of Kulusuk
LEFT: The author in Greenland

ABOVE: The author celebrates his safe
arrival and the completion of the
challenge to fly around the world in a
microlight (photograph by
Margie Lindsay)
RIGHT: Jade Milton (photograph by
Margie Lindsay)

Helen Dudley

I left a message on Rory's answer-phone rejecting his offer. I felt a lot better when I did it. If I did not guard the integrity of this adventure, who would? I took off at noon.

The Rockies were my nightmare before the flight began, with their great height and the violence of their thermals in the middle of the day, but I felt I had no choice but to enter them when I did. It was always easy to call things off, put them back to another day, but I could not do it. I consciously calmed my fears as the top of the Sierra Nevadas appeared in the distant mist, and I watched the clouds above them apprehensively. The Flyer started to plunge, so I climbed above 8,000 feet, following Route 80 into the mountains. Next to it was the railway track that Phileas Fogg had taken from San Francisco to New York in Jules Verne's story.

I started to get thoroughly trashed, and retreated in my mind into a small private room. Half the time I daydreamed, half the time I acknowledged that I was hanging on to a control bar, with a strap across my lap, the only thing restraining me in a flimsy flying contraption high in turbulent mountain air, in danger of being hurled to my death. Every now and again, I was struck by gut-hollowing fear, but it was containable. It was most apparent when the control bar jerked violently right and left, back and forth, the airframe juddered and I was tossed around the sky, just about in control but trying to conserve my strength. Handling the bar in a gorilla-grip was all very well, but after a while my fingers seized into a claw and they hurt through the night. Whenever I was not being trashed, I shook my hands and exercised my fingers.

My route took me over Donnor Pass into the flatlands west of Reno, where turbulence was even worse than in the high Sierras. I longingly contemplated a landing at one of the Reno airfields, but again, it would be a tangible admission of my own cravenness and I was not sure how easy I would find it to take off again. Was I to be condemned by my cowardice to flying only when conditions were perfect? Could I get around the world flying in such a manner? These thoughts skidded around my mind as I struggled past a big mountain which I could not fly over and, trying to maintain a calm, even a bored voice, with Reno ATC, which kept calling me 'Experimental November Tango Golf'.

I thought, as I passed to the north of Reno, that conditions were getting better, so I opted not to land and headed up the valley, finding Route 80 again and setting course for a small town next to the salt flats called Lovelock. Again, there were periods when I was trashed and in which the bar rocked crazily and I was flung around, and all my rationalisations – 'these are just thermals, there is no wind to speak of, the Flyer has survived worse' – seemed banal. My mind remained detached, but I stopped singing. Singing calmed my irrational fears, but these fears were rational.

As I approached Lovelock I was telling myself that there was nothing to prove and conditions were too gross to fly. But the clincher was that I had drunk too much coffee that morning and a more pressing reason to get on to the ground was to have a pee. I circled the airfield, saw no one, landed safely, shouting at myself to be careful, taxied in and rushed off to a rest-room, tearing at my various layers of clothes. I had been in the air less than three hours. It really wouldn't do, I thought, because I had been able to fly seven hours on previous days without having to find a rest-room.

I chatted with the only inhabitant on the airfield, weatherman Terry Newman, and I convinced myself that the worst weather was over, and took off again. I followed a broad shallow valley north to the mining town of Winnemucca. I was still being trashed, the air roaring in my ears as thermals took off with me and the Flyer in them. My ground speed remained high – always in the 70-knot range – but I was doing a long dog-leg to get to my destination for the day, Elko in eastern Nevada, via Battle Mountain. The battle after which the town was named was between Red Indians – native Americans – and white settlers in the last century.

I kept an eye on the fuel gauge, and finally decided to transfer over all the petrol in the left tank to the main tank. I had already emptied the right tank. This meant reaching back and opening the stop-cock, squeezing the primer bulb and turning on the electric pump. Despite repeated priming, no fuel flowed into the main tank, I did not have enough to get to Elko. This realisation chilled me. What if it had been over the Atlantic? What was wrong? The whole system was so simple that it must be something fundamental, like a leakage in the system. I decided to land at Battle Mountain to check whether the fuel pump was working; it was. It was only later that I worked out that the fault lay in my not closing the tap on the other spare tank, to create a vacuum to enable the pump to do its job.

Half an hour later I had landed at Elko, unpacked, settled the Flyer in a hangar and was on my way by a courtesy car to a pre-booked hotel. I had been in turbulent air for six hours, but I felt good, and after a shower, three beers and – sadly – shove-in grub at the hotel restaurant, I was ready for bed.

Andy woke me and I told him I had rejected Rory's offer. The request by Rory for me to call it off so he could have an attempt at it was outrageous. Andy, in true documentary producer style, immediately accepted my reasoning, but said we had to stop for half a day in Salt Lake City, where he would meet me and we would work out how to film the flight across America.

The next day I managed to get away from the hotel and I took a courtesy bus to the airport. I took off into a decent west wind, climbing to 7,500 feet and heading east, following the road and railway through the mountains. It was occasionally turbulent. I did some singing, but my mind was now calmer than it had been. Stray thoughts entered and got pushed around, with half my attention on them. I came back again and again to the scenery below; washed granite mountains with mines dotting the landscape, and I had the work of two different engineers to muse over – the man who had laid out the railway and the road-builder who came later. In fact, the roads took the more direct route.

East of Wells the road climbed until I was above 8,200 feet and still quite close to the ground. In the distance I could see the first white patch of the salt flats, and once past Wendover I was over the salt flats proper. I expected a real hammering from the heat bubbling up, but there was not enough contrast to provide meaty thermals and the journey to Salt Lake City was quite smooth. In the City valley turbulence increased until I was being trashed all the time. I made my way in a series of wallows and wobbles to the local municipal airport and landed safely. Andy and Barrie strolled over and asked me if I would do it again for the cameras. I did, and settled the Flyer into a hangar for the night.

The weather forecast of 26 June warned of thunderstorms in the afternoon, so I was anxious to get away. I took off in a stiffening wind and flew through the mountains. The snow-covered peaks disappeared behind me and the bleak hills were covered, first in green scrub, then in brown weathered vegetation. East of Evanston I broke out into fearsome terrain, threaded by Route 80 and its accompanying railway line, and at 9,000 feet I was heavily trashed by thermals. I watched my ground speed creep up, first to 75 knots, then 85 knots. Crossing a great plain to Rock Springs I saw 96 knots on the GPS; this was 109 mph, and I only had 55 mph on the clock.

The wind below was increasing dangerously. It made me afraid of landing, but also nervous about the effect of rotor as the wind swirled around mountain peaks and threatened to pick me up and trash me into the ground.

Each time I passed airfields at Fort Bridger, Green River, Rock Springs, Rawlins and Laramie before Cheyenne, I looked down and wondered whether it might be more prudent to land. Just the possibility gave me comfort, but each time I rejected the idea. I was being slung everywhere, lifted out of my seat so violently that my plan to let the turbulence happen and guide myself back on course did not work. I wrestled with the bar for most of the day and could feel my left wrist seizing up.

Sometimes conditions were so bad I laughed out loud at the absurdity of the situation. Who cared whether I made it or not? A few friends would sympathise, but I was impressing no one else. Why was I continuing to suffer so? Because this is what life is about, my mind answered and, to be truthful, I would not have swapped places with anyone. At least the wind was with me as I roared along at 100 mph; on the occasional 360 I saw my ground speed drop to 24 knots when I faced into wind and was reminded of Anadyr Bay in Russia.

The countryside was awesome, with huge horizons and the appearance of being able to see forever. I watched the sky for signs of a build up of clouds, but it remained blue with puffy thermal markers, seemingly innocent of the churning violence it was doing to me. The major threat was the wind, especially around Elk Mountain, a peak of 11,000 feet standing on its own, behind which I had to fly. I could see in my mind's eye how the rotor would hit me, and when it joined the thermals it was particularly sickening. But I found I could endure it, and struggled on, south of Medicine Bow and Laramie, then climbing up to the highest I had ever taken the Flyer, 10,000 feet, to get on to the high plains where Cheyenne was situated.

The last 40 miles sped by as I was doing 85 knots. I talked out loud, reminding myself that my risks happened on take-off and landing. The huge runway at Cheyenne was smack into wind and I landed safely, though there was a struggle when I taxied and the wind caught the right sail and forced it to the ground, dragging it along the tarmac. ATC was concerned and asked if I needed help. I begged for a hangar and they immediately found one for me with

Sky Harbour Air Services, run by Charles Porter, right next to the control tower. A number of helpful young men stood around as I peeled off my flying clothes; they helped me refuel, gave the directions to the Hitching Post Hotel and left messages for Andy and Barrie, who were chasing across America by car. I slept for an hour before they turned up.

The day's flying had been a stern test of my physicality and aspirations to courage. My left forearm ached badly and I woke up in the night with the pain still there. The forecast was for even more windy weather, with Omaha a possible target. That might mean Chicago in two days, then New York in four. I had missed only a day's flying, in Petaluma, since leaving Nome on day 83.

The interview with Andy made me aware I could be leaving my obituary. I did not mind.

On day 97, I was nervous about flying 449 miles to Omaha, as I was still feeling the effects of the wild ride from Salt Lake City. No charge was made for the hangar but, also, no media turned up. It was as if American journalism was quite impervious, despite Margie Fincham plugging it to cities ahead of my arrival. I got the latest forecast, which played down the previous night's warning about winds, except the possibility of afternoon storms.

Heading directly east following Route 80, the countryside was completely flat; it seemed to be like that forever. I followed the road and railway line, 3,000 feet above them and at a height 8,000 feet above sea level, where I needed high revs, 4,950, just to maintain height. I did not mind as there were lots of airfields in America and it was easy to drop in on one of them to refuel. For about an hour I fought with the turbulence, resigned to my fate, but then cautiously made the judgement that it was not as bad as the previous day. The land dropped away over hundreds of miles, starting at 5,000 feet and sloping down to 2,500 feet, and with it cloud base also came down. It was impossible to climb above the inversion and calmer air at Cheyenne, but flying east and staying high, conditions became less rough.

I fell into a sleepy state of mind, that was nearly the cause of a terrible death.

East of North Platte I primed both spare tanks, the left with far more difficulty than the right, and started the electric pump to transfer fuel. I wondered why my left hand was so much weaker than the right; I thought of other things and completely forgot about the fuel transfer. Some time later, leaning back and stretching, I smelled fuel, so I looked around the landscape to see if I could find a refinery. Then the realisation hit me that it was my own aircraft venting fuel, which I could see bubbling in the Mickey Mouse gauge. I turned the pump off. Looking into the 'box' on the left, where the overflow pipe was, I found it was absolutely full and therefore venting out the back. It was being caught in the propeller and whirled around. There was at least a chance that some of it would be hurled on to the hot exhaust and ignite, causing an engine fire. The Flyer would have gone up in 30 seconds.

I sat there watching the world go by, detached and stunned, and awaited my fate. Keith had vented in a similar fashion over the Persian Gulf without causing a fire and that was the reasoning I used to carry on. What else could I do? There was about a litre and a half to vent before it stopped and as the minutes went by and I did not die, my fears subsided. It is only with hindsight I realised how close I came to burning to death. It was also a warning not to get complacent when the flying was easy. That is when the fatal mistakes occur.

The weather changed, with clouds developing at Grand Island. At first, they were sickly and without power, but they soon thickened and I saw unhealthy dangerous clouds. I was not aware of how hot it was on the ground. As cloud base fell, so did I until I was only 2,000 feet above the ground, which was by now heavily cultivated. The clouds continued to thicken, but not, in my opinion, to threaten, so I flew on without any realisation of how quickly the weather changed in this area.

I was tired in the last couple of hours, bleeding off the revs, to try and maintain height on as little power as possible, and watching the fuel gauge fall slowly. I constantly checked the gauges, backing up the electric gauge on the dashboard with the Mickey Mouse gauge actually in the tank. There was always an option to land short and top up, but I did not take it. I reached Millard, Omaha, after seven and a half hours in the air, landing safely at what looked like a deserted airport. I had found a hangar when Andy and Barrie turned up; they had driven very fast from Cheyenne. We booked into the local Sheraton and had just unpacked when a terrific storm blew up, rain bucketing down – an inch in an hour – and almost continuous lightning and thunder. I could have been up in this if I had delayed to get fuel, I thought, and was thankful I had not done so.

I woke up realising I was taking undue risks and it should not be that way. I seemed not to care very much whether I lived or died. Yet I was very happy.

On day 98 I took off from Millard with Barrie in the back to get another filming angle. We followed Route 80 through Omaha, the VFR route west to east. I stayed at 1,000 feet and twisted and turned with the highway. As soon as the GPS indicated I was clear of air space I climbed to 4,000 feet where it was smooth, despite the gathering heat, and set off to Des Moines.

It was unusual to fly with someone again after the loss of Peter and Keith. It turned out to be so smooth that Barrie commented on the fact constantly. He took 40 minutes of video on the two-hour flight to De Soto, a small microlight field 20 miles west of Des Moines, where a group of ultralight pilots greeted us. Phil Esch took Barrie up for another 30 miles to a field called Morningstar to get in-air shots, while I refuelled and set off for Chicago.

The countryside changed from the square geometric fields of the West to boundaries defined by geographical features. I stayed in touch with Barrie by radio as they raced along below. Andy led a charmed life with police patrols and was only overtaken once all day. It took nearly five hours to reach Clow International, one of dozens of small airfields in the Chicago area. The in-air refuelling went without incident; I now tied a piece of plastic on a bungee cord to flutter in front of me on the control bar whenever the pump was working, to remind me to turn it off.

I was delayed leaving the hotel the next day, because Alison Harper was trying to reset-up the Internet site in London. There had been a lot of cyberspace complaints about the sudden way the flight dropped out after Amvesco pulled the plug. It also seemed the Danish threat to bar me from flying over Greenland was a real one. Alison told me Will Whitehorn, Branson's head of corporate affairs, had phoned, but when I tried to reach him he was on holiday.

I spent the morning trying to get the transponder repaired – the aerial had been broken in Russia. Time went by slowly. A local engineer called Tony Dzicmiela who worked for Boyd Clow, the airport's owner, replaced the aerial, but the transponder still did not work, so I needed to repair or replace it. As I was getting the Flyer ready, other engineers were looking at it. One of them, John Fuling, noticed that the oil-cooler nuts had loosened and one had come off.

This could have been a disaster in the air, but why did I not notice it?

Because I was not looking as closely as I should at the engine.

'I am trained to do this,' said John.

Tony tightened both nuts and locked them with wire. John then found a loose nut on the exhaust, which Tony washered and tightened. We checked a seeping joint on the water system, an item I must look out for myself in future.

I watched in a detached way as they pronounced the engine fit to fly and I thanked them. Then I packed, climbed in, warmed up and took off to head along an advised VFR route past dozens of airfields and south of Lake Superior. It was bumpy below 1,500 feet, but not alarming, and I soon settled into watching the sky for signs of thunderstorms, but I saw only wet, fluffy clouds which carried no threat.

As soon as I was out of Chicago air space, I climbed to 3,500 feet, just below cloud base, and followed a GPS course to the south of Route 80, a line taking me to the right of Toledo and Cleveland. My goal was Kent State University, where four young students were shot dead by the National Guard in the 1960s, and which had an airfield recommended by Gene Pincham as a good place to stay. The sky remained generally benign. In the far distance I noted three huge clouds, one of which was on my course, but at least 100 miles away. This I monitored all afternoon.

The flight ended shockingly quickly. South of Toledo, I noticed the huge cloud ahead had a black and murky bottom. I tuned in to one of the local frequencies and heard pilots saying they were going to land quickly and anywhere. The word 'tornado' was used. As I got closer I saw it was heavy rain and it appeared to be coming in my direction. I looked at the nearest airfield, Fremont, just four miles ahead, and wondered if I would beat the rain to it. The air became nasty on the fringes of this storm, so I cut power and dived for the field. I saw a large open hangar, like a huge Nissan hut, next to the runway where I could stow the Flyer immediately after landing. I zoomed in and taxied straight into the hangar. The airfield was deserted.

I phoned Margie to tell her where I was and then the weatherman, Tom Du Plessis, told me the storm was a big one and stretched right across my path, and it would block me from reaching Kent State until after nightfall. He advised me to 'hunker down' and wait it out. I stayed in Fremont, while Andy and Barrie drove on to Kent

State, and I happily bought a six-pack and takeaway pizza.

That night I read about the prediction of an American pilot, Jack McCornack, that a world ultralight flight would begin on 12 April 1998. McCornack had made the first ultralight flight across America in 1979. It was difficult time. He had written his prediction in August 1997, just about the time I got the money from GT Global to set up my own attempt. Jack thought the flight would take a year to complete and the Europeans might pip the Americans. If I did not make it work, I thought, I would not get a second chance.

A hundred days after I left London, 30 June, there was an appalling weather forecast, predicting thunderstorms and rain fronts. So I packed the Flyer as quickly as I could at Fremont and taxied out in the stiffening breeze for a quick take-off. I had lost the map covering the 90 miles I wanted to fly so I could join up with Andy and Barrie at Kent State, but the GPS did an adequate job.

Conditions were claggy, with cloud base at 2,500 feet, rising to 3,500 feet as I flew further east. It was bouncy without being alarming, and I picked my way over intensively farmed countryside, almost totally flat and with dozens of airfields. I was worried about arriving late at Kent because I knew Andy wanted to get on to New York, and he was brisk when I flew in and asked for more fuel. The locals seemed almost not to believe the flight was happening. Andy and Barrie rushed off by car to Bellefonte, an airfield 186 miles away that was en route to New York, where they hoped to pick up an aircraft to film me over the Catskill Mountains.

It was raining when I went back to the Flyer and I took off in a heavy downpour. But the weather, a front moving in from the west, was not unflyable, and I actually welcomed the water streaming off my visor. I shouted with joy at times, as I found my way between two opaque showers. My ground speed touched 75 knots and I flew happily eastwards, watching the countryside change: hills and forests and deep rivers appeared, that marked the beginning of the eastern seaboard. Whenever I looked back I could see the blackness of the front racing after me, but I was ahead of it and intended to stay there.

There were bumps in the air, landing at Bellefonte, which was owned by John and Marina Elnitski. Marina had phoned the media and a press journalist and TV crew turned up quickly. I was doing the interviews when the first rumble of thunder occurred. We pushed the Flyer into a hangar and within minutes the noise of the rain on the roof, along with the thunder, made an interview virtually impossible. Andy and Barrie turned up and said they thought I might have flown on. They had been listening to the radio when an announcer broke in with a tornado warning, right where they were, and the injunction: 'Take cover! Take cover!' I was inclined not to believe in the tornado, thinking it an American journalist exaggerating, but they were adamant.

At this time I felt cut off from the world. Charles was on holiday, and Alison, just learning the media ropes, was still connected to Newlyn and Browse. I feared for the last push to get permission to cross the Atlantic and being stopped by, of all people, the civilised Danes.

My 101st day in the air, 1 July, and conditions at Bellefonte looked reasonable on the ground. People congratulated me on the prospect of a following wind, and I expected to fly around the Statue of Liberty later in the day. But as soon as I took off I knew things would be difficult, and they became more difficult as I flew east.

The countryside was full of beautiful tree-covered mountain ridges at right-angles to my line of flight, with pretty little towns in valleys, and winding rivers. Clouds piled up in frothy formations, with base about 1,500 feet above the mountain tops. But the north-west wind was fresh to strong and with the thermic activity, I was being heaved around the sky unpleasantly. There was no comparison with some of the earlier American days, when I found the thermals easy to cope with. These were not easy at all and I had to endure a wearying battle with the control bar. But I made good time over the ground, sometimes touching 85 knots, and avoided air space that came up on the GPS.

I had agreed to meet Andy and Barrie at 1 p.m. at an airfield called Caldwell in New Jersey, which was within spitting distance of the Statute of Liberty, and with just 50 miles to go I noticed that the sky directly ahead was dark. I was soon aware that it was a huge black patch of cloud and rain, frightening to look at, and which I had to avoid, if only because the winds were likely to be terrifying inside it. I diverted to the right, and tried to keep out of its influence, but sometimes I felt its violence and power and so I scurried further right to stay in the sunshine. It seemed to sit right on top of Caldwell and wherever I steered, I was no nearer my goal.

A violent series of bumps and contortions finally convinced me that I should not be in the air, and I picked an airfield I had just passed – Manville – and struggled upwind at 33 knots to reach it. Other aircraft were also diving for this safe place, and I had to circle, plunging and rearing and quite breathless with the effort of flying, before I was able to head for the runway. I was ripped all over the sky, gorilla-gripping the bar and talking to myself, barely able to cope with the fury of the air about me, crabbing sideways down to the concrete, full of fear. But I placed the Flyer safely on the ground, survived more violent seconds in which she threatened to tip over then taxied to a relatively sheltered place next to a hangar.

Other pilots came over to look at the Flyer, while I tried to cope with the weird American phone system and let Andy know where I was. Gary Anduson, of the Millstone Valley Flight School, took pity and used his own phone to ring Caldwell. I felt ready to fall asleep instantly; another pilot looked at me and commented on the effects of tiredness, comparing it to being without oxygen. But I was not keen to linger, and after an hour I thought the black cloud had gone and perhaps it would be easier in the air. I was only 25 miles from Caldwell; if I tried hard, I could defy the weather and get there. I repaired a wing-tip bungee and lined up for take-off again.

When I got into the air, surviving two wrenching tugs on the control bar just after leaving the ground, I turned right and headed into wind, north-west across two ridges. I had to stay below 1,500 feet to avoid Newark air space – airliners came in over my head – and I was tossed around the sky. I was not actively fearful, but it was something I had to endure. Close to Caldwell, I was able to raise ATC on the radio; they were expecting me, but had no information on landing conditions. If possible, it was even worse landing there than at Manville. I descended steeply, never sure which way the bar would be wrenched, crabbing right against a cross-wind that I later learned was more than 25 knots, the runway surrounded by trees and buildings which meant turbulence all the way to the ground. Again, I struggled all the way down and I was, thankfully, successful in getting on to the ground without damage. I taxied in and resolved not to fly until conditions had changed, no matter how much Andy needed to get the Statue of Liberty shot and be back in Europe.

'It is only because I love you that I was in the air at all,' I told Andy. He grinned and rushed off to rebook his ticket home.

We spent the afternoon checking the Flyer's cameras, and discovered a damaged cable was responsible for one camera taking black-and-white pictures. Barrie thought it was a legacy of the Russian turnover. I was so weary that I went to the car and fell asleep for half an hour in the back seat; when I awoke I was covered in sweat. The wind continued to blow strongly, but the forecast was that it would abate. Andy drove us to Manhattan, through long traffic jams. We booked rooms in his favourite NY hotel, the Iroquois, which cost $175 a night, and I had a view of a soot-blackened hotel wall. We went out to eat well in the open air. I left them both in a bar across from the hotel.

The following day, I flew around the Statue of Liberty in New York, pursued by Barrie and Andy who were filming me from a helicopter. The statue was green and powerful and evocative in the dappled sunshine. I could feel its power and meaning to America, and I sensed that if I got too close she would reach out and whack me, a bit like King Kong.

That afternoon I took all my kit back to the Iroquois and there, finally, removed all traces of Keith from the flight. I bought a duffel bag and put his helmet, earphones, thick flying suit, lifejacket and moon boots in it, to be carried back to London by Andy. I kept his thin flying suit as an extra protection against the cold in Greenland.

Barrie flew home, but Andy could not get a flight, so we went down together to Greenwich Village and found a decent restaurant where we drank two bottles of white wine and ate well.

All I had to do now was cross the Atlantic.

16. NEW YORK TO GREENLAND

Crossing the Atlantic meant going north to Montreal, east along the St Lawrence River to Sept-Îles and then north again to Schefferville and Baffin Island before jumping to Greenland and Iceland and home. I would not be the first to make such a crossing in a microlight. The great Dutch pilot, Eppo Numan, had done it in 1990, but he had taken more than a year – wrestling with red tape and waiting for the right weather – while I intended to race across.

Andy drove me to Caldwell early on 3 July, day 103 of the journey, before catching, ironically, a Virgin flight to London. In a curious limbo, I prepared the Flyer. Stripped down, without Keith's gear, the green bag behind me was saggy. I kept it for continuity, so that library air-shots could be used flexibly. I took off at 9.30 a.m. from an extremely busy airfield and climbed into misty air, heading north over thickly forested countryside, dotted with houses. It looked rich and prosperous.

Visibility in the Hudson Valley was never brilliant, a haze obscuring the horizon and small clouds hung over the high ground and seemed not to move. I was vaguely uneasy at 3,000 feet above the ground, and sometimes let off the throttle and lost a hundred feet to make a concession to my fears. Otherwise, I sang softly, 'Summertime'; a repetitive version of 'St Louis Blues'; and tunes whose words I did not know, but which I sang in a nonsense version.

I passed Poughskeepsie in upstate New York, with room to breathe and thousands of square miles of forested hills that must be great hunting ground. The Hudson River was bigger than I had imagined, and the further north I flew, the more water there was. By the time I crossed the Canadian border, marked on Lake Champlain by a long bridge, thermals were popping, and I found my way to St Hubert, a large airfield near Montreal, and landed into a fresh wind which I had not expected. I had to grip the bar and shout at myself to ensure that I did not get tipped over.

A Russian living in Canada, Alexander Tarussov, told me there was hangarage for me at Richelieu, a small microlight field ten miles away, so I took off into the turbulent wind and scurried there. Luc Boucher and his brother Silva, microlight instructors and former hang-glider pilots, were my hosts for the night. I was starving. Luc fed me tinned asparagus, potato chips and beer, and then Silva turned up with takeaway chicken and chips and we ate this with some German wine, while I listened to their exploits and dreams. I stayed the night in Luc's bedroom but woke up with my left arm aching. No matter how much I exercised it, the pain would not go away. It felt arthritic, and I caught a glimpse of how things will be when I am older.

On day 104, 4 July, I wanted to get to Sept-Îles, 456 miles away. I taxied out behind Silva in one trike and ahead of Luc in another. We took off into still air and climbed eastwards, while they buzzed around me. They stayed until I approached a rain front, then waved goodbye. Silva threw the biggest wing-over I had ever seen in a trike, almost over vertical, to show me how well he could fly. I waved goodbye and entered the rain, heading for Quebec City, 130 miles away, staying below 2,000 feet, not minding that water was pouring on me.

Because the flying was not arduous and all I had to do was sit and steer in a straight line, I could feel the height-fears nibbling away at me. I now used singing to achieve the same calming effect on my disorderly mind that Hare Krishna chanting must have on believers. Thoughts of Helen were always a last resort; I feared that one day they might not work and then where would I be?

I flew over big, flat, green fields, geometric shapes like in America but with diagonals and strips, a legacy of the French inheritance system where all children get something. The horizon was obscured by mist and amid vague drifting clouds of light rain I could see less than ten miles. No one else appeared in the air and I lived in a dreamland. It was important to keep my mind turning over – I did it by imagining situations when I got home – otherwise I touched the fringes of madness.

Level with Quebec City, I squeezed the Flyer down low between two areas of restricted air space and fretted that my speed had dropped to 40 knots. I was fighting a headwind. I watched my fuel and decided then that it would be prudent to land at Rivières-du-Loup, on the south side of the St Lawrence, and top up. There may have been enough to make it all the way to Sept-Îles, but I opted for prudence. Two other factors in this decision were that I wanted a pee and, five minutes before arriving at du-Loup, my earphones went dead. They were supposed to be continuously charged by the Lynx intercom system, but that neither worked in the old system, nor the new one installed in Petaluma.

I landed in Rivières-du-Loup, stomped off for a pee, revised my flight plan and filled up with fuel. The wind was strong enough to be a threat, and I was nervous about a skittish helicopter that seemed to keep its blades spinning for far longer than necessary, but I got away. Five minutes into the air and the earphones went dead again. I flew the rest of the day without them working.

Without earphones, I could not hear my own voice and, there-fore, could not sing to myself. This meant that the height-fears had time to grow, so I busied myself with anything to put them off, stills camera, back camera, anything to distract myself. In a messy way it all worked and I had time to admire the brilliant panorama of washed-out blues and greens that unfolded as the river widened. I followed a straight line to Sept-Îles, despite going out to sea, but when I was over land I was amazed at how much habitation there was. I was still south of London, but there was pack ice here for months in the winter. I also suffered from the effects of the cold, and decided to use my moon boots and another flying suit from now on.

I arrived at Sept-Îles after seven and a half hours in the air, but I could only count six – not seven – islands. I had rigged up a system to communicate with ATC, which, fortunately, worked, and I got in to the airfield with just a small amount of turbulence near the ground. I parked the Flyer in the Esso hangar – at a princely $75 a night, more than twice what I paid for my hotel – had a much-needed shower, withdrew C$200 from a cash machine and went out for a good dinner, reading the latest *Business Week* from cover to cover.

By day 105, 5 July, I realised I could set a difficult record to beat with regard to the first-ever microlight flight from New York to London. In the hangar, feeling like a warrior preparing for battle, I was thankfully alone. I thought I might be able to do a double-jump past the legendary town of Schefferville – last railhead before bandit country – 546 miles to Kuujjuaq.

The earphones, now recharged, were working, so I was able to talk to ATC. I took off into an east wind, but when I turned north and joined the railway line, my speed was just 38 knots. It climbed to 45 knots as I reached cloud base, and I thought I could just about reach Schefferville for the day. For a while I followed the railway, but the pain of seeing the GPS route go one way while the railway went 30 degrees off course just to stay in a valley, was soon too much for me. I abandoned caution and set off across the trackless mountains direct for Schefferville, 314 miles away.

Why did I take needless risks so late in the game?

The answer was, I thought I might get there quicker, and if the engine failed I was going to be in trouble anyway. I could not land on the railway track, which would bust up the Flyer as much as landing next to a lake in the tundra. Having committed myself to my engine, I had to take advantage of that faith and be bold. It was also undeniable that the flight was a craps game; I had laid my life on the pass line and was rolling the dice. I could not get my life off that line until my point was made, or I rolled a fatal seven.

As the sun heated the wild countryside, so cloud base lifted and thermal clouds formed and thickened. They drifted south and rain started to fall. It was easy enough to dodge the early showers, but later I flew through fringes of rain, measuring how much I had to divert against the chance of getting wet. I settled in at a height of 5,000 feet; paradoxically, I was not haunted at all throughout the day by fears of height. I could see hundreds of unspoiled lakes, no roads or railway or any sign of man, just stunning country, mountains to 3,500 feet and tundra.

In my mind I drifted in and out of reality, sometimes thinking about life back in London, sorting out personal affairs, wondering if my divorce had gone through. What should I do about finding another wife? What sort of a marriage prospect would I be? Other times I drank in the scenery, but not going down low enough to see the fine detail of bear or caribou. Low flying the area would be a real charge, but I remained in a hurry to prove the original 80-day dream a possibility, and that meant flying quickly.

The sky was always changing, and as I flew over the main route of the rain clouds, so I always had to be wary. Five minutes after checking the sky and going into a dreamlike state, I would jolt awake again and find a sheet of rain falling. Later in the day, rain fell so heavily it turned the air beneath the clouds black, and was opaque. There was one huge cloud that I carefully skirted around which cruised over the countryside like a juggernaut, crushing all in front of it. It was awesome, and I alternated between appreciation of its dangerous beauty and fear that the fringes would be as dangerous as the centre looked. I felt its violent edges, but I was never close enough to get caught badly.

Coming to Schefferville in the mid-afternoon, I was in two minds whether to stay, or refuel and go on. How long would daylight last? I taxied in to a deserted and indifferent airfield, rushed off to undo zips and have a much-needed pee and then looked around to find someone to sell me fuel. Jimmy Vollant, an Inuit, found some half-empty 55-gallon tins of avgas. Using a hand-pump, I sweated out 55 litres, which he gave me for nothing. It was enough to take me on to Kuujjuaq, and when Jimmy told me night fell after 10 p.m. I thought I would go for it. Though I was tired, it had not been arduous flying and I felt able to cope.

I took off again in the early evening, facing a hack of 232 miles across absolutely trackless countryside, no winter trails, no cabins, no railways, no villages, nothing but open tundra and the prospect of meeting large unfriendly animals if I survived an out-landing. But as the sun went down there were rain showers and fascinating cloud patterns. Rainbows appeared and disappeared, the horizon in front was always red and behind me, when I circled to look, I could see darkness and heavier rain falling.

Once or twice the edges of madness tugged at my mind, threatening to send me spinning out of the sky. I could feel the pull, like my brain tottering, but was able to resist it. What beat it was a distraction; what encouraged it was hours and hours of a thumping droning engine and no sensory input. I shouted from time to time to blow away tension, but I did not find the relief Americans seem to find in it.

After ten hours' flying that day, I finally landed at Kuujjuaq and found shelter at Inuit Air. A local pilot, Robert Palfreeman, found me a room in the pilot's lodge and a steak dinner, which I heated in a microwave. No beer, though Robert offered me whisky, which I declined, but I drank seven glasses of milk.

On day 106, I wanted to go on another long flight, this time to Iqaluit to see a man called Bert Rose who had picked up the flight on the Internet and told Alison he would look after me. It took longer than usual to get ready as I was distracted by thousands of midges and mosquitoes. The weather forecaster predicted light northerlies, and when I climbed into the air from the gravel runway, my ground speed was poor. I had a full load of fuel (without the bladder tank), and for the first hour flew over deserted coastline on the left side of Ungava Bay. It was glaciated country with hundreds of small lakes, with a mixture of Scottish or French names. But I soon became cold and realised I needed more clothing. Also, after only 90 minutes in the air, I wanted a pee. I opted to land at Aupaluk, where I added a survival suit to my clothing and the huge yellow mitts that Silva Boucher sold me. But though fuel was offered by the local mayor, Johnny Ahpaharak, I did not take it, thinking I had quite enough. It was a decision I later regretted.

In the air again all the extra clothing worked, so I settled down to get through five hours of flying, in conditions which were dangerous to me because they were absolutely smooth. There was not a bump, not a tremor in the air. I reached 4,000 feet and followed a direct line for Iqaluit over the sea rather than threading around the coast. It was stunningly beautiful and quite still. I looked down with an air of detachment, between dream and reality. Once, it did strike me that I was actually there, a mortal man of 55, in a tiny aircraft over hostile country, with the real prospect of dying if the engine failed and I landed in the water. I was torn between fighting this destiny and accepting it; of course, I would fight, but my state of mind was an odd one. I did not dwell on the reality of my situation because it could have frightened me into sheer paralysis.

I flew past the Low Islands, Plover and Eider Islands, the last landfall before 110 miles of open sea, and Baffin Island, cloud-ridden and mysterious in the blue distance. It was halfway across that I saw I was cutting it fine with my fuel and two hours of fretting began. At any time I could have turned back and found an airfield near Eider Islands where I would have been able to buy motor gasoline, but each time the thought occurred I resisted it.

Why?

Because I wanted to press on.

But how could I press on if I ran out of fuel?

I'll make it, I kept whispering.

When the airspeed climbed above 50 knots, I was relieved, and when it dropped below 45 knots, I was alarmed. It was entirely my fault. I had not been using the fuel bladder, because I had not modified it to fit a turn-cock. I had also turned down the offer of extra fuel at Aupaluk. But I avoided my own guilt by falling into an unreal state of mind and rationing the transfer of fuel from the spare tanks to the main tank, as if that would help. As I drew close to the coastline of Baffin Island, I saw the whole land area covered in rainstorms; they were not violent, just black and wet and numerous. I decided to go straight to Iqaluit and not be diverted by rain, and concluded that I did have enough fuel, but only just. The ghost of Keith berated me in the back.

I concentrated on negotiating the rain clouds, which was terrifically exciting. I had to pick my way through great black sheets of falling water, descend over brown and bleak mountain peaks, with no vegetation and remnants of the winter snow still lying in places, and squeeze between clouds pregnant with moisture. I did not mind getting wet; it was being caught in rain so heavy I would not be able to see that I feared. Yet, at the same time, in the odd state of mind I had reached, I flirted with danger. Once, between two vicious downpours, I circled with the cameras on, shouting with excitement, defying the weather to do its worst. I picked my way across the Meta Incognita – what a sinister name! – to burst through a clear patch into Frobisher Bay and an unlikely cluster of islands with English names, Culbertson, Fletcher, Falk, Thompson. I had come across these remnants of Empire all over the world in the maps I used.

Iqaluit ATC was already calling for me. There was a reception committee in this former USAF air base where I met Bert Rose, a big, bearded man with a kind smile, who had picked all the teachers for schools in the region over the last 20 years and had a profound effect on local education. He had direct communication with Alison via e-mail in London, and I got rid of all the diaries I had written from California, which was a big relief. If I did die, I wanted most of the story available to be told. Alison asked Bert to slow me down because she thought I needed a rest. I was touched and bothered by this injunction; it was not up to her to decide I should slow down.

Joanne Rose provided a lovely chicken dinner and found four rare bottles of beer – it was only for sale in bars at Iqaluit, because of its effect on the Inuit population – and I was put up by Sandy Tuft, another teacher who had been given his job 20 years earlier by Bert Rose. I crashed out just after 10 p.m. and slept soundly for eight hours, which was unusual.

On day 107, 7 July, I was held up all morning by repairs. These included finally fitting a stop-cock to the bladder-tank lead, so I could fill it really tight and have it as a reserve on the Atlantic flight. We also fixed the radio aerial. I added locking wire to some of the springs on the exhaust system. This took precious time, hours drifting by, with what looked like a lovely following wind all the way to Broughton Island, the stepping-off airfield to Greenland. I realised I was nervous about the flight. It was a common state with me at that time.

It was 3 p.m. when I finished refuelling – 112 litres, the most I had ever taken – and taxied out for take-off. In the air I climbed painfully. I flew over a huge desolate plateau, brown and dotted with small lakes and patches of snow, and in the distance I saw the majestic presence of two big rainstorms moving right across my path. There was no way to avoid them, so I picked the lightest patch and headed for it, losing height to avoid touching deep, black layers of cloud. I dived right in between two thick columns of rain, water streaming off my visor, the sunlight dappled in the swirling clouds, I gloried in it, shouting and circling and driving on and circling again, fearful and yet full of confidence. The Flyer, sturdy and reliable, inspired me to risk and I now relished it.

The band of clouds soon passed and I picked my way over higher ground, scraping through 100 miles to Cumberland Sound. There I composed my mind into a state of fatalism, an acceptance of the risk taken in crossing 50 miles of freezing sea in a tiny microlight, an agreement that I would abide – as I must anyway – by the consequences. It was a reaching out to real life, and the fatal responsibility of being. The whole of the late twentieth century, in the West particularly, has been a denial of death; I was nakedly alive by accepting its proximity.

Cumberland Sound was a wide, blue, still sea, dotted with the remnants of icebergs and the far side were the outer reaches of Baffin Island: mountainous, cloud-covered and fabulous. The beauty of the whole scene was quite entrancing. It was enhanced by my being cold, apprehensive and fragile, a fleeting conscious presence flitting over land unchanged in millions of years. I kept a light hand on the control bar and made myself warm by the heavy exercise of priming and refuelling in the air, and I circled from time to time to measure my progress.

Landfall at Pangnirtung was dramatic. There were two deep bays, the second fed by a river – divided by a headland: Pangnirtung emerged as a surprisingly large town, set around a big airfield and a small bay with fishing boats. I felt twinges of nervousness at 5,000 feet, the usual urge to fall, but squashed them immediately, becoming slightly out of focus, not connected directly with reality.

Bert Rose had told me to fly through the valley north-east of Pangnirtung at 4,000 feet, and assured me – though others had disagreed – that it would not be turbulent. I did start to plunge around and braced myself for worse, but it remained light turbulence. I turned on the back camera from time to time, but as I entered the mountain pass, surrounded by peaks up to 7,000 feet and astonishingly wild and beautiful, I left the camera on and had 15 minutes of the best flying of my life.

I took Andy – in spirit – towards each of the side canyons, rugged with glaciers and old snow, and as the canyon narrowed I circled close to the mountain walls, surging with joy. Instead of racing in a straight line, I rollercoasted over the sky, diving and climbing and turning, so overcome by the terrific scenery I felt blithe and spiritual. At the same time a small voice kept saying, 'Don't take chances now, you are so close.' I was careful to give myself the five or six seconds extra time to make room before slinging in another 360-degree turn.

The rest of the flight was made in a state of relaxed contentment. The valley widened and became less rugged, and I crossed the direct line to Broughton, as indicated on the GPS. Within 30 miles of my goal I did something unique for me, I climbed to 6,000 feet and set off over the mountains, rather than staying quite low through the valleys. It was another raspberry to the Djinn.

Then I noticed that cloud was reaching out from shorelines and covering the sea. Fog. Was it real? Did it extend to the runway at Broughton? I was cautious but not alarmed. I could always turn around and make my way 90 miles back to Pangnirtung if I was fogged out of the airfield, but ATC told me I could make it. When I finally did get over the airfield I could see it mistily below. There were exciting moments when I turned and plunged into cloud – I was whited out at 400 feet – but I burst through and saw the runway at an angle to my right and twisted in for a safe landing.

There was no hangar at Broughton Island, which was an Inuit community built around an old Dew Line (Distant Early Warning) station, so I had to hobble the Flyer for the first time in weeks.

During the night I was woken at 3 a.m. by the urgent calls of an excited seal, like a dog yelping. This was the furthest north I hoped to get, 22 degrees from the North Pole. The flight to Sondrestrom was slightly south, and from then on there was always a southerly element in the way I had to go. Across the bay there was an ice-rimmed sea and three icebergs. I would see a lot more as I set off over 300 miles of open water to Greenland. This was the moment of truth, where all the flying I had done would count for nothing. There were difficult days ahead where one thing going wrong would be the last thing of consequence to happen to me, except my death.

But for the next two days, 8 and 9 July, I was stuck in Broughton Island, held up by decisions taken thousands of miles away by one Irling Neilsen, a senior Danish aviation official. Charles had started negotiations with Neilsen the previous September and had thought our way was cleared through. But Neilsen found first one matter, then another, not to his liking, and he refused permission for the flight to continue. At one time he queried the Flyer's status as a microlight and the amount of fuel she carried. At another, it was my insurance for air–sea rescue. Mr Neilsen would not accept a policy at Lloyds of London; Charles was required to track down a Danish company to offer cover, and I was to find an extra £5,000 premium. I was on a primitive dirt airstrip in Canada, six hours out of step with Copenhagen, and Mr Neilson had the charming habit of going home at 3 p.m. Whatever agreement Charles was able to get with him, by fax from London, Mr Neilsen insisted it had to be confirmed with me out in the bush, and there was only one hour when I could get to facilities before Mr Neilsen sloped off home.

Conditions on the island were difficult, and made more so because I could not find decent accommodation. There was no restaurant so I had to cook my own food and communications – though better than Russia – were troublesome. Add to that a helicopter working the airstrip, throwing up wind and dust and nearly blowing the Flyer away, and there were times when I shouted with frustration. I derigged the Flyer, despite the hassle, rather than leaving her at the mercy of the elements and the helicopter, and this decision nearly wrecked her. She was nose-down on the ground while I struggled to remove the Jesus bolt linking the wing and trike, when the helicopter took off again. The wing was caught in the wash and skidded across the gravel, shredding the front of the keel, while I hung on for grim death and I only just prevented her tumbling.

My language was dreadful; I called every curse I could on bureaucrats.

I was not kind to Charles when I tracked him down in London

and complained about the delays. But his reasoning, that many bureaucrats had hoped I would crash or give up before I got to their country and therefore they did not do anything until I banged on their door, was a sound one. This had happened in China, Japan and Russia, but it was a surprise that the Danes should join such ignoble company. I blamed Neilsen for everything and planned to sue him if the Flyer was wrecked while he consulted the rule books yet again.

On the third day of internment, 10 July, 110 days after I had left London, I was in a murderous mood. The shower in the rooms I rented did not work, and there was barely enough water for a coffee. I spent two hours waiting to hear if I had permission to go, and Alison virtually had her ear torn off when she did get through. She and Charles were ringing Danish insurance companies to take the risk. Whether or not air–sea rescue would actually manage to get me out of the water, which I thought impossible in time, was another matter.

The weatherman forecast light westerlies, but the sky looked full of hard black clouds and rain and there was a cold front coming down from the Arctic, pushing thunderstorms. The front would come at me from my left as I headed south-east, so I had to be alert. As I rigged the Flyer and dressed, I still had to cope with absurd faxed demands from Copenhagen which I referred to Charles – while I tried to keep my sense of equilibrium. I was depressed at the easy way the Danish authorities could relieve me of money. It reminded me of Russia, except the excuses were different. The local ATC man, Jerry Kakka, was kind and helpful, and this had cooled me off.

I found that one of my moon boots had the insulated sole layer breaking up, and got rid of it, leaving me with less protection against the cold; it resulted in a half-frozen right foot later in the day. I struggled into my survival suit and sweated like a pig getting into the rest of my gear, desperate to leave. I was facing a difficult flight, but my state of mind was not tuned to it. I did not look forward with curiosity, but back with a black fury.

The wind was calm when I took off and climbed away, and the engine sounded sweet. I circled and then flew over a small mountain and looked ahead at the broken ice on a flat, dead, deeply blue sea. Inside myself there was not the usual fear at the transition between land and water. I felt committed, and if I should die, then that came with the territory. Obviously, I would be terrified if it happened, but I thought back over others who must have felt the same way, Amy Johnson, Charles Lindbergh, Francis Chichester, Bert Hinkler, and said to myself that my engine was better than theirs, so why should I not succeed?

For the first hundred miles I could see the coast of eastern Canada down to Cape Dyer. It seemed close to me, but this was an optical illusion. There was little movement in the air, the sky a washed blue with the remains of a previous day's clouds and the dark patches to my left stayed far enough away never to bother me. The ice on the sea was broken into hundreds of thousands of pieces, with the occasional iceberg, which I speculated on the prospects of landing on if the engine failed. My head and body became cold, and I danced around, twisting this way and that, conjuring up an illusion of warmth. But it was not intolerable. I coped through trying to think of other things.

The frustrations of the previous two days actually helped me through the long hours over the water. I relived my blind fury, 20 minutes went by, and I was that much further on the journey. My ground speed, which started at 60 knots, peeled away, and I watched with muted fear as it dropped to around 40 and touched the 38 to 39. I understood, wrongly, that Sondrestrom Airport would close long before I arrived, so I wanted to make speed (or I could face the bill for keeping the airport open). But the wind switched in every direction in the middle of Baffin Bay and I was at its mercy.

I watched cloud develop until it covered the whole sea below me, but it was not opaque and I could see through to the sea below, now full of white horses, indicating at least 15 knots on the surface and apparently coming from the south. I thought about how much I did not want to be down there, and wondered keenly how long I would last if I went in.

Gradually, the outlines of the Greenland coast came into view, brown and not white and snow-covered, as I had expected. An hour later I could look down on mountains and arctic bays in their brief summer life without snow. I circled for the cameras, took photos and had reached for a second video camera when I was nearly thrown out of the sky!

For the next 20 minutes I struggled to make progress, as the south wind swirled among the mountains and tossed me about. My ground speed dropped to 29 knots and I surged up and down under a narrow but still solid layer of clouds. The bar jerked left and right and I dampened it down and went over to the foot throttle for more control. It was frightening, but analysing the way I was being thrown around, I thought, yes, I have been here before and coped, so why not now? I tried to understand how the winds were working and I headed off my direct course after concluding that the highest mountain in the area was stirring things up. Upwind of that, the air calmed down a bit. I picked my way over the peaks, some of them at 5,000 feet, and was occasionally hit by bursts of wind, but not that first busy, frightening wind that had hit me as I moved from the sea to the land.

On the way into Sondrestrom, where I found a decent hotel and a hangar for the Flyer, I looked at the icecap in the centre of Greenland and contemplated crossing it. In the evening light, it did not look too daunting. Local pilots doubted if I could make it without going above 10,000 feet. Whatever it took, I was going to attempt it. My major fear was that I would be pushed around again by the Danish authorities, pretending that it was for my own good.

17. CROSSING THE GREENLAND ICECAP

Crossing Greenland was a nightmare I lived with for years. When Eppo Numan did it – going the other way – he waited more than a week until he thought conditions were right, but he was not racing. On day 111, 11 July, I checked the weather forecast with Karl Mortensen and heard there was a cold front coming down from the North, but if I hurried it was clear up on the icecap and I should make it. I filed a flight plan and was presented with a bill for more than $400. It seemed that each time I had filed a flight plan to get to Greenland from Broughton Island and was stopped by the Danish authorities, I incurred costs of $100. I objected, and had the bill reduced, but only by $100. They suggested I sued Neilsen in Copenhagen . . .

Karl gave me a lift to the Greenland Air hangar where I found fuel at $2 a litre, but I was not charged the usual $125 a day hangarage charges. I was grateful and took 80 litres and paid in cash. I had $1,385 left, the remnants of the $10,000 I had set out with on 24 March. A message came through from the Met Office that I should hurry as it was clagging in. At 10.30 a.m. I started up, and in the gathering rain, I taxied out to take off.

The sky was murky and turbulent as the wind swirled around the peaks. I climbed at 43 knots but was soon motoring along at 60 knots. I could see where the black cloud and rain ended, in what looked like sunshine, and raced for it, but the nearer I got the further away it retreated.

After 20 miles the brown countryside stopped, the land rose and the permanent icecap began. I climbed with it to nearly 5,000 feet where I bumped along at cloud base. The snow below was cut about with lines where melting had occurred, but as the cloud got thicker it became hard to see ahead; I couldn't make out whether it was snow or cloud. Weird cloud formations, white and deathly, came into view, and what looked like sunlight in the distance transformed into more cloud. I saw wisps rush past me and I was afraid. What if I was caught in a cloud sandwich here? The land rose to more than 9,000 feet, but did the cloud rise with it?

I persisted, because I hated turning back, but I was hollow with fear. The engine droned on and I was not too cold, but should I really be there? Was the risk acceptable? For a long while I argued that it was and that I could bash my way through to the far side of the front, and in Kulusuk the air was said to be clear. But when I got whited-out by cloud I turned back and saw, with relief, that retreat was still possible, if only just. I turned again and saw the cloud coming at me and again turned back towards Sondrestrom.

Another day, I thought, I don't have to take these risks.

I was sick inside and had to argue with myself. There were some days, even for me, when I should not be in the air.

It was because I knew how these stories turned out, classically, that I was cautious. One gets within an ace of success and then a Fokker comes along and shoots you down. That is what happened in *Winged Victory*, and, so close to home, I could see it happening to me. All the best stories end this way. I did not want mine to.

I got back safely to Sondrestrom, taxied to the hangar in bucketing rain, and heard stories of other aircraft which reported icing conditions. One of the Danes told me that weather conditions on the icecap get so bad that pilots cannot differentiate between cloud and snow – exactly as I had found. One pilot, he said, fighting in such conditions, noticed he had hit turbulence, fought it, hit some more and when it was smooth again, looked at his air speed: zero. He looked at his engine revs and they also showed zero. He had, in fact, hit the snow but did not know it. I suspected this story was apocryphal.

I packed the Flyer away and checked with the Met Office. A nice man called Bill told me I had no chance the following day, a Sunday, and the first real possibility was Monday. The front would move slowly across Greenland before dissipating. He said the weather was often good on one side of Greenland and bad on the other. Kulusuk remained clear and free of cloud.

I spent the rest of the day talking to London then dozing until 8 p.m. I went down for a good dinner, and a bottle of wine. Jade told me that Fiona was back in Dubai with her man, and would be there until September.

I spent the next day kicking my heels in Sondrestrom. I scolded myself for planning what to do when I got home, and I wanted to remain in the apprehensive state of mind which had got me safely to Sondrestrom. I tried to get a coherent look at the weather in the evening but the forecaster, who smelled heavily of booze, carried on such an interminable telephone conversation that I walked out. I went to the rowing club for dinner and drank a bottle of half-decent red wine. The food was also good, but I yearned to be in England.

On my 113th day, 13 July, I went to the Met Office and saw that the winds seemed to start from the west at Sondrestrom, but went north-east at Kulusuk.

'They are not very strong,' the forecaster said.

Any wind could knock 20 per cent off my flying speed.

I was in a frame of mind to go, no matter how fearful I felt. The satellite picture showed a bank of thin cloud in the centre and east of the island, but the clouds seemed north of the course I wanted to take. If they were not too high, I reasoned, I could fly above them, because I had to acknowledge it was a question of taking a chance with one side of Greenland or the other.

I was wound up and fatalistic. It was hard for me to comprehend what I was doing, proposing to take my dear little Flyer over more than 350 miles of trackless ice and snow. I had moments of lucidity, but otherwise fell into the routine of preparation. It always seemed to take forever, due to the huge amount of property I had to either stow or wear, but each time I put on a suit I could see tangible proof that I was getting ready. I had a last pee and worried about whether I had had too much to drink for breakfast, I then struggled into the survival suit, jacket and last flying suit. As ever, I started to sweat.

I filled the big green bag with my luggage, secured it in the back seat, and pulled the Flyer out of the heated hangar. I shook hands with Karl, got in, and spent the usual five minutes plugging myself in, as well as getting the two GPSs, radio, cameras and microphone ready. When I started the engine I was more obsessive than ever about checking temperatures and the charging unit: they worked.

I took off heading east, where the wind came from, rolling off the icecap. I was persuaded that, if I had an easterly on take-off, the wind would be westerly off the ice on the other side of Greenland. I stayed in touch with ATC and started a slow climb over naked mountains and dark lakes and fiords, warily looking at the ice as it rolled into view. It was difficult to tell, in the distance, where the icecap ended and where low thin white cloud began. I looked at the trace of Saturday's flight on the GPS and noted I had turned back 35 miles from take-off. This time the view was clear, my ground speed 50 knots, though I had had an earlier alarm when I only reached about 38 knots, and I pressed on.

For a long time nothing significant happened, except that I kept climbing until I had reached 8,500 feet and it grew very cold. I banged my hands together to keep the feeling in my fingers, and wiggled my toes in my right boot where the insulation had crumbled. I wondered about putting my sunglasses on against the glare of the sun and the snow, but it meant opening the visor and I was not sure I could get it closed again with all the pressure of suits and neck warmers. I was fearful, because the commitment was so great.

The fears grew suddenly when the radio cut out.

The Lynx earphones were no longer being charged by the system and had run down; that meant trying to find the emergency back-up system, but not yet, because of the numbing cold. I decided not to turn back.

There was one small man-made presence in the middle of the icecap, an automatic weather station called Dye 2, sometimes manned, marked on my GPS. It came in to view 100 miles from Sondrestrom when I lost radio contact. I was comforted by knowing it was there if I wimped out. A thin layer of cloud appeared below me and I found it more difficult than ever to decide which was snow and which was cloud. I started to climb again. On my map I saw that I needed to be at least 9,000-feet high to clear any obstacle on my direct route to Kulusuk; I climbed to 10,000 feet and stayed above the cloud. As I climbed so did the land below and so did the cloud, and I was forced higher than I had ever been in a microlight, up to 12,000 feet where the light was clear, the air was thin and caused me to gasp and the cold was completely numbing.

A layer of ice formed on the right of the visor. It was my breath freezing.

Being above cloud, which was now so thick I could not see the ground below, was an all-or-nothing affair. If the engine failed, I faced a horrible few minutes plunging into it and the prospect of a ghastly death. I was conscious of this most of the time, but tried to ignore it. Was it not the same over the frozen sea in Okhutsk? I asked myself. What was so different about now? But I could not hear my own voice asking questions because of the duff intercom and this increased my sense of detachment. I measured my distance above the cloud constantly, keeping the revs up to stay high. I was nervous about being whited-out, or the cloud bubbling up casually to engulf me and cause the Flyer to be loaded with ice, or mistaking the snow for cloud. It was easy enough to believe that story about a pilot crashing without knowing it.

The cloud, which had been widespread but patchy, thickened until I could no longer see the ground. I was isolated from the earth by it, as I was insulated from the rest of the world by my silent earphones. I could only shift around to try and get warm, bang my hands, waggle my shoulders and anxiously keep an eye on my instruments. My ground speed waxed and waned, sometimes down at 44–46 knots, which made me fret about whether I had enough fuel, and at other times I travelled above 65 knots as the winds changed on a whim.

Fantastic thin cloud patterns appeared in the sky above me. The contrail of a jet airliner on its way to America made a lined shadow across snow and ice, almost pointing the way to Kulusuk; the shadow stayed with me for an hour. I lined the Flyer up on wisps of cloud in the distance, but fell away left or right when I lost concentration and had to steer her straight again.

In my mind I moved in and out of reality. Part of me thought about summer days in France, in the Dordogne, preparing for a day of writing. I dreamed of the early-morning cycle run, a wild two-mile brakeless ride downhill where I twice met wild boar, the struggle back up to the 700-year-old Bastide village, carrying a day-old copy of the *Daily Telegraph*, baguettes and butter, home for a shower and a crackly John Humphreys on Radio 4, read the newspaper cover to cover and then ten or twelve hours of writing.

If I should live, that's what I would be doing in three weeks' time. The contrast between my thoughts and reality did not strike me as surreal.

After five hours I saw the first signs in the far, far distance that the world was not completely white and featureless. A line seemed to mark a change from white to blue. As I flew closer, individual mountains and the sea emerged. I risked a descent to 9,000 feet as the cloud thinned out and I was able to discern vague lines and cloud shadows in the snow, and the brilliant cobalt colours of pools of water. I thought it was less cold and risked taking a glove off to fiddle around in one of my trouser pockets for the emergency radio interface, which I shoved into one earphone and attached to the radio; my left hand hurt for half an hour afterwards. I could hear Sondrestrom Radio again – they had superb communications across Greenland – and radioed in that I had 50 miles to go, more to reassure myself than inform them.

The height began getting to me in the old familiar way, so I started a slow descent to ward off these fears. Some rugged mountains slid by under the wing, a fiord, more rough islands half covered in snow and then the sea again with thousands of broken pieces of ice and the remains of icebergs. I dropped slowly out of the sky, relishing the feeling of being alive again, able to hope and plan once more. Sondrestrom asked me to change to the Kulusuk frequency, which picked me up immediately, and though we were separated by 30 miles, this was reassuring. I was making connections again with the world.

The gravel runway was in the lee of a formidable mountain, on the last island before 450 miles of open sea to Iceland. I came in to a quick landing which I thought was downwind, taxied past a hovering helicopter and soon had the Flyer safely bedded down inside a familiar fire-engine shed. The young air-traffic controller, Jesper Longsholm Skov, lent me a telephone to call Andy Webb in England, he also arranged a hotel and got me fuel. I filled every tank and the ten-litre plastic container, so as to be able to top up the following day. I would need every last drop to get to Iceland.

The local station manager, Arvio Thustum, asked me if I knew Eppo Numan. I said I had talked to him on the phone, but I had never met him.

'That Dutchman was mad,' said Arvio. 'He was here a week, and he asked me on the first day if there was any legal way he could kill his chase-plane pilot. He was serious. He had a temper with a fuse this short,' and he held two fingers close together.

Eppo and I would not have lasted long if I had taken up his offer in Nome, Alaska, to fly in Keith's place. I was now convinced that I was flying faster without Keith than if we had flown together. I did not have any arguments with me over whether the weather was suitable to fly. It always was, even if it wasn't.

I had heard that Kulusuk was the most primitive place in Green-land, but I found it civilised, with phones, faxes, hot showers, beer, even a good bottle of St Emilion at just over $30, which I considered a bargain and drank. I went to bed but I woke at 1.30 a.m. and was not able to sleep again.

Andy said he would meet me that evening in Reykjavik.

Everyone was getting presumptuous. I still had a thousand miles to fly to get to Scotland.

18. THE BIG ATLANTIC JUMP

The longest over-water crossing in the Atlantic, 450 statute miles from Kulusuk on the east coast of Greenland to Reykjavik in Iceland, was the stage most pilots were nervous about. I was no exception. I had dreamed of a west wind blowing which would waft me to Iceland, and when I woke up and looked out of the window on 14 July, day 114, I thought I had one. The kind carpenter at the airport, Erik Huusfeldt, gave me a lift to the Flyer, I pushed her outside from the fire-section house where Erik was laying a new floor. Sondrestrom weather bureau said winds were NW – 330 degrees – to NE – 020 degrees – and for much of the flight I would have a headwind component.

This was distressing, but I was committed to go. A local man said the prevailing wind, when there was one, was from the east, which upset all the original calculations I had made in London. He showed the common weather conditions, a low-pressure area below Greenland, producing westerlies in the mid-Atlantic, but up in our latitudes the same low produced easterlies. So I had to make a decision to go while conditions were possible, if not ideal.

I decided to risk it. I could, I reasoned, always come back.

I dressed for flight and got into the air at 10.45 a.m., pretty wound up. I had fixed the back camera, and circled twice to record the tremendous views, then rounded a mountain and set off to reach 3,000 feet over the sea, which was covered in broken pieces of ice and old icebergs. When I was high enough, I pulled the power back to 4,500 revs, adjusted the trim to ensure that I stayed at this height; in fact, I still climbed slowly and could pull power back further. I wanted to be as economical as possible to ensure better fuel consumption than 14.5 litres an hour. It was colder than I had expected.

Inside my mind was a mass of whirling emotions. There was a very strong urge to turn back and land and give up, but I could not think of an adequate excuse. I had programmed two goals into the GPSs, Reykjavik and a second airfield, Dagverdhara, which was small, out on a peninsula, and 'only' 386 miles from Kulusuk, a saving of 64 miles. I had not thought this through as I was to do later; it was just an instinct. Part of my mind parlayed between these two goals, which were separated by just four degrees. I thought I would make a choice which one to go to near the end of the flight.

Meanwhile, I watched my speed all the time, adjusting the course so there was little deviation and keeping the revs down. For someone who likes to do things all the time, to be active, it was unnatural to be urging myself to stay absolutely still and concentrate on efficiency for the next nine hours. My ground speed started at 50 knots, giving me six and a half hours to Dagverdhara, a distance and a time I had done often enough in the past. But as I crossed more miles of ocean out into the Atlantic proper, so my speed dropped off until I was flying at 43 knots, occasionally touching 41 knots. This was insupportable. I could not argue with the speed, even to myself. I could also not argue with the trend: who was to say I would not soon be doing 35 knots? Why would I want to argue?

I knew Andy Webb and Barrie Bayes were flying to Reykjavik to meet me and that weighed heavily on me. I also knew John Hunt was setting off for the Orkneys. I had a rendezvous with them and wanted to make it, and therefore carried on flying for more miles than prudence dictated. But 41 knots was the clincher, and I sadly radioed Sondrestrom ATC that I was turning back. I made the long, miserable plod back to Kulusuk at 61 knots, which indicated a solid east wind.

When I landed I was not allowed to park the Flyer back inside the fire-section house because of the work being done there, so for hours she was parked precariously on the tarmac, subject to the whims of wind and the wash of visiting aircraft. But when I topped up the fuel I saw I had used only 18.5 litres, and I had been in the air for an hour and three-quarters. That gave me a consumption of 11 litres an hour, which, with four tanks carrying a total of 120 litres, meant an endurance of 11 hours and not the nine hours I had originally calculated. At 11 hours, I could have made it to Reykjavik, even at 41 knots. I started berating myself.

But I was also studying the map again and deciding that I should make Dagverdhara a primary target, and see if I could refuel there and do the last 59 miles to Reykjavik with a full fuel load. A visiting pilot from Iceland, Ragnhadur Gudjonsd, knew Dagverdhara and said she would see if she could get fuel there for me. I reset my mind and came to terms with the new way of getting across the Atlantic, and I felt better for it. It depended on calculations which were always suspect – how did I know the 18.5 litres was a true reading, for example? – but I hoped I would have the courage to rely on my new findings when I set out in the morning, weather permitting.

I found a home for the Flyer in a garage a mile from the airport, to which I taxied over dusty roads. The weather system looked static, producing rotten weather in England, but clear blue skies in eastern Greenland. I went back into the hotel, slept, then had dinner, lovely duck and another bottle of St Emilion, which I shared with Jesper Longsholm Skov. He and I went off to look at a dance-off between local Inuits and a visiting party of elderly Danes. Jesper and I walked back to the hotel together. He wanted to be a helicopter pilot, but there was also a sense in which he was drifting through life not really knowing what he wanted to do.

On day 115, I woke up at 5 a.m., wrote, got to breakfast before anyone else and managed a very wound-up Sky TV interview pacing up and down the dining-room.

I knew I was going to make a serious attempt at the crossing to Iceland, whatever the weather forecaster said, because I was so desperate to get home.

I had to dig the hotel landlord out of bed to pay the expensive bill, and Erik Huusfeldt came down with the hotel car to give me a lift to the garage and my luggage a lift to the airport. Laurits Justesen, a nice bearded chap with glasses who worked at the airport, turned up on a motorised trike to help me manoeuvre the Flyer out of the garage and I taxied her up to the tarmac.

It was another lovely day, clear blue skies, little wind and warm. I was largely undisturbed as I prepared to fly. I was deeply apprehensive and, at the same time, determined. When I went up to ATC to talk to Alf Skoudal Friis, the wind chart he gave me was depressing, but I thought I saw – wrongly – some hope that the further east I got, the more the wind turned west. As it was, the chart showed northerly winds with an easterly component. The forecast for Reykjavik, in particular, was difficult to comprehend, north-east winds of 20 knots gusting to 38, hardly the absolute certain west winds I had contemplated waiting for before this flight began.

Why did I not stop there and say I would wait until another day? There was talk about a warm front coming down from the north-east, but nothing special was made of it. I noted absently that it was still early, so I would get to Reykjavik in good time for dinner.

The airport manager, Arvio Thastum, said Eppo Numan, was trying to get through to me, and ten minutes later I talked to him in Holland. Eppo's flight in 1990 had been an epic, and underreported in the ultralight media as well as the mainstream.

Eppo wanted to give me advice, and I allowed that I was open to it. But inside myself I was not keen on hearing anything that did not gel exactly with the way I felt. He wanted to know how much of the original 1924 record of 175 days I still had to complete. When he heard that I was well inside that, he told me I should not take chances and should wait for better days. I listened to all he had to say, and one day I would love to talk to him poperly, but not today, thanks. Flying alone, I made all the decisions. I could hear Keith's faint voice telling me that I was mad to contemplate flying when the winds were so against me, but he no longer had any influence. I told Eppo I would see him at the party at Kay Burley's to mark the end of the flight, and he rang off.

From the forecast, I expected a headwind from the start, so when I got airborne I was pleasantly surprised to find I had a tailwind, and could motor along at 65 knots. I thought this might have been a local effect and would soon fade, but the first two hours went by at this speed, and I counted the miles covered like a miser. The sky had thin cloud in it, and looking back from time to time, I found even a hundred miles away I could see the coast of Greenland clearly. Cracked it, I thought, I can beat this, but I was still wary. I was in the middle of the mighty Atlantic Ocean, which killed people so easily, and it did not do to be disrespectful.

When I came across the warm front, it happened so slowly I was not really aware of it until I was down at 500 feet, fighting for my life.

It started as a haze across the horizon, which I noted dispassionately and photographed. I was already 200 miles out to sea – whatever came my way, I had to cope with it. I was going on to Iceland now, with no choice, given my previous tailwind, of going back to Greenland. I was not to know until later that the authorities in Reykjavik wanted me to go back, because of the violence of the winds inside the weather front which was moving across my path. I could not have avoided the front, and was too committed to turn back.

When I saw the wall of advancing rain I had to make a crucial decision: did I go up and see if there was clear air above? Or go down and fly below the cloud, in the middle of the rain? I elected to go down, and saw an angry sea full of white horses and whirls, green and white, beneath me. Then the rain poured all over me, splattering my visor and instruments, GPSs and radio.

The Flyer was struck by turbulent air, and I hung on and was swung right and left by the wind. My ground speed dropped from a reassuring 63 knots, first to 50, then to the 40s, and it was soon commonplace to see 30 and then 20 knots. I was too busy to be terrified. All I could do was keep flying, try and steer her straight, monitor the gauges – especially the oil and water temperatures, which were early harbingers of trouble with the engine – and concentrate on surviving, minute by minute. The rain thickened and my horizon was reduced to half a mile, just me, the angry sea, the wind and torrential rain.

In my mind I oscillated between trying for Reykjavik and aiming at Dagverdhara, a few degrees off to the left. It was an absurd debate that could only be resolved at the exact time I got to Dagverdhara, and it depended on whether I was still fighting to stay in the air, or if conditions had changed. Oddly, it was also soothing, as if I had a choice about living or dying. I fought to stay alive, but as the weather thickened and rain poured down everywhere, the wind swirled and grew, the illusion was life-giving.

I came to a wall of heavy rain across my path, and as it approached and I could feel it engulf me, I tried to find anywhere as a refuge. It looked slightly clearer over to the left so I turned and flew that way and found my way around the thickest most opaque sheets of falling water. This happened time and again. I tried to find the clearest patches and the darker areas of low cloud that showed the bottom limits of where I could fly and still see where I was going. I was thrown up and down, rearing up to 800 feet in the dynamic lift, or falling, juddering, down to 450 feet, constantly wiping the water from my visor, peering at the GPSs to see what they told me. At one time I saw I was making 11 knots, and the estimate for getting to Reykjavik had climbed to 18 hours. Seeing 22 knots was commonplace; it meant I was heading too far north, into the teeth of the Atlantic gale. My course was erratic anyway because of the way I was being thrown around.

Sometimes the sheets of rain would stop falling and I would find a clear patch, perhaps two miles across, with the green ocean below me whipped into waves. Here, the wind was at its worse. I hung on and felt stationary in the sky, crabbing across the patch and actively looking for more rain to calm things down. I tried to miss out on the densest showers, inside which nothing could be seen, but I grew to like the rain and see it as a friend. I did check the GPSs and the radio, which got wet but never unserviceable – it would have been a total nightmare to have lost those. With that thought in mind I checked my compass; I was crabbing east on a course of 130 degrees, but the trike was actually heading 60 degrees, with the wind making up the difference.

But instead of being paralysed by fear, I found myself completely alive and up for the fight. I had no choice about it anyway, so I stuck at it, totally committed, sometimes shouting to relieve the adrenalin coursing around inside me. At other times, incongruously, I sang softly: 'Isn't it a lovely day to be going home,' time and again, like a defiant mantra. I was a Viking, stretched right out to the limits, all reserves of energy and courage thrown in. If I lost this one, I had no regrets about being there. It was always going to happen on this stage of the flight. Why should anyone be allowed a free ride across the Atlantic?

There were lucid moments when the gale was reduced to a strong breeze and my speed crept up to the upper 30s. I thought then of Ernest Hemingway's story, 'The Short Happy Life of Francis Macomber'. This was my Short Happy Life. There are moments beyond fear, as I had suspected, where life is so fulfilling that it is difficult to communicate to other people. The experience is so strong you cannot believe it and you want to go back and live it again and again. I was carried back constantly into that experience by the frontal gale, but each time I got a little closer to Iceland. I was curious myself to see where I would choose to land, if I had a choice in the matter.

Though the air was turbulent and I was thrown around the sky, the way the wing was thrashed around was not terminally exhausting, as it sometimes is with wind in mountains. I was tipped and turned, rocked, plunged and shuddered, but never beyond my capacity to cope, despite being 115 days into the flight. All I had to do was steer her straight again for a few moments and get back on course. There was a pattern to the rain, long columns of cloud and then clearer areas where the raging was not so bad. Winds reached

50 mph, certainly gale to storm force. I thought of trying to get through to Iceland Radio, but what could I have said to them? That I was in trouble? That was evident, but what could they have done about it? It would have been a hassle and a bad example for any other microlight pilot who wanted to be where I was at some time in the future.

In all, the fight lasted three hours before I slid into easier air in the lee of Iceland itself. Every moment I was stretched to the limit, but it did not seem so long until I noticed a change once more. I remained alert for more problems long after they had gone away. The sky cleared of immediate cloud and the ceiling lifted to 2,000 feet and in the distance I saw the high glacier that marked Dagverdhara. My GPS told me there were just 28 miles between me and safety, but I ignored the alarms I had suffered and elected to go on to Reykjavik and Andy Webb, at least an extra hour's flying. Throughout the ordeal I had been careful not to adjust the throttle and I had kept the revs below 4,500 to save fuel. I was able to see how efficient the engine had become, capable of flights using only 11 litres an hour. Priming the spare tanks and transferring fuel had been difficult at 500 feet while struggling to keep upright, but my private nightmare – that the electric pump would not work – never happened; each time I checked the tanks, it was evident that fuel was being transferred. I never had to pump the fuel from the bladder tank.

I motored into the huge bay that forms south west Iceland with cold hands but a contented frame of mind. I had been through as gruelling an ordeal as any peace-time pilot I knew, and had won. Guy Delage's great 26-hour microlight flight across the southern Atlantic was better, of course, and he went through worse than I had just experienced. But after 115 days' flying I could still cope and this was a comfort. I almost welcomed the fact that it had happened. If I was going to beat the Atlantic, I did not want to get away with anything cheaply; it had to be meaningful.

Barrie Bayes met me in a Supercub and filmed the last stretch into Reykjavik. There was a small crowd at the airport, as well as the intense but washed-out figure of Andy Webb. I dealt with the media interviews before sloping off to see Customs. Andy showed me an article in the *London Evening Standard* about the alleged end of the friendship between Keith Reynolds and me, which I thought contrived.

Andy said he felt that Keith, now in Russia to see Lina, was deeply unfulfilled.

I had a beer and a shower and another beer, then we went into town to find a restaurant where we ate well and drank two bottles of red wine. There were lots of good-looking young people in Iceland. I particularly appreciated the two tall girls who served us dinner; why was I attracted to big women? I think it was the length of their legs.

I had to survive.

Accepting the possibility of death, as I did in the middle of that flight, was not the same thing as welcoming it.

But I felt good.

19. REYKJAVIK TO ORKNEY

Celebrating the longest water crossing meant I only had three hours sleep, and it took a long time to write the account of the flight from Greenland. After breakfast, we paid our bills and walked over to the hangar. I could do nothing until Barrie had finished installing a wing camera again. I remember looking at my watch once and seeing it was 10.30 a.m., a time when I am normally in the air. Weather conditions looked okay but nothing great. There was menacing cloud to the north, black but not evil-looking, and I did not believe that I was going to have the tail-wind forecast. Andy interviewed me. I was again conscious it could be my obituary.

I dressed for flight, and wished I did not have so many clothes. They were beginning to smell, especially my thermal underwear which I had not washed in days, because I could not guarantee to get it dried by the following morning. I taxied out to take off. It was only when in the air that I discovered the Hi-8 camera would not record.

I went through a few moments of apprehension, left over from the days when the Djinn roared in my ears, but I was too far gone to listen to the beast any more. I headed east from Reykjavik, out over countryside which was full of small bare mountains but, compared with some of the country I had flown over, relatively civilised with roads and homesteads. There was no tailwind; my ground speed was 45 knots, falling to 40 knots. I experimented with height and was soon bumping along, just below a wide curtain of clouds, grudgingly accepting 50 knots at 3,500 feet.

The country grew wilder and more spectacular, though there always seemed to be a road going somewhere. I flew over dozens of lakes, flat winding rivers and between two ridges of mountains, those on my right were high and covered in snow. My heading was the great glacier in eastern Iceland, direct to Höfn. The more preferred route was to the south, along the coast, but I was in a hurry.

Stray thoughts wandered into my mind, hung around convivially and then sloped off to be replaced by others. It was a contented state of mind. The thoughts repeated themselves half a dozen times, each time with a small variation and with no rational pattern. Images of the drive down through France to Villefranche-du-Périgord were vivid, the view from the terrace and cooking good food. I shifted around in the seat, the usual numbness affecting my right leg, and banged my hands together when they got too cold; my left hand still suffered most.

As I looked east, I saw that there was a danger of cloud base falling and covering the tops of the mountains, so I kept a wary eye on an escape route to the right where I could see blue sky in the distance which marked the coast line. But I decided to stay where I was, scraping along a ridge of mountains and heading for a dazzling glacier. Yet as I got close and flew over dirty snow, I saw that clouds blocked my path and I could find no way through. I talked to myself, out loud: 'Come on, you can't make it through, what is the use of trying? How much time will you save? Half an hour? Is it worth it? No it isn't, so head for the coast.' I persuaded myself to turn right and follow the slope of the glacier down, across low rugged mountains and out on to the southern coastal strip. The sun shone there and it got bumpy, but bumps were a companion these days. I threw in the occasional 360, defiantly, as a sort of raspberry to the weather. My first two 360s, on a hang-glider back in 1975, resulted in crashes: once I hit the hill at Dunstable and destroyed my glider and nearly killed myself, the other time I rushed into a hedge below the Long Mynd in Shropshire. Though I had done tens of thousands of 360s since, there was still that faint air of danger to them.

The ATC man at Höfn was laconic. Later I discovered he only knew aviation English. Clouds descended to just below a thousand feet in a thick blanket over the mountains, though blue sky and sunlight could be seen further out to sea. The airfield, which I had dreamed about for so long, was much longer than I expected, and another small crowd of islanders was there to see me. One told me I had been a news story for weeks, which I could hardly believe. After the bad news that Vágar in the Faeroes was closed for the evening, I found a home for the Flyer – the wing separated from the trike – in the local fire-engine shed, which had been arranged by Jonina Kardal. All the local hotels were full up, but a freelance TV cameraman, Binni Bjynjolfsson, offered me his son Parmi's bedroom. I found I was very tired after just four hours' flying and could hardly keep awake.

The weather forecast did not look good for the flight to the Faeroes: another headwind, clouds, rain and even thunderstorms were said to be blocking my path. I was in a dream, as I took it all on board. It did not affect my decision to go on. I made verbal agreements with friends like Kay to take things easy, but I had no intention of complying. The urge to be home was very strong. I would take each flight on its merits but, if in doubt, I knew I would go rather than wait another day.

On 17 July, day 117, I had breakfast, toast and Marmite, with Binni and his wife Sigurn, while writing the journal. Sigurn had to go straight off to work, but Binni gave me a lift to the airfield. I checked the forecast: there was a weather front between Höfn and Vágar, and another front between Vágar and the Orkneys. Looking out to sea, it did not seem too threatening, though in the distance there was a low line of white foggy-looking cloud. I filed a flight plan and took off. At 3,000 feet I was below a blanket of cloud and prepared to settle down for a flight of only five hours, by the GPS estimate. I was happy with this, but the weather changed all that.

About 30 miles out I came to the foggy bank of clouds which looked, at first, like a line across my path, but I thought I could see the sea beyond. When I climbed over it, I was sandwiched between two layers of clouds, I was soon in danger of being enveloped. I grew fearful at the prospect of 230 miles of flying in such conditions, and turned back towards Iceland. I could see land, but it was like looking through a long horizontal slit, cloud above and below, which was squeezing shut. I pulled the bar in and opened the throttle and managed to get out before it closed on me, then circled and looked to see if there was another way through.

I had made my way from Greenland to Iceland low over the water; perhaps I could gully-gobble my way to the Faeroes? I dropped to 300 feet and had a second try, this time under the low cloud and scooting over the uneasy sea. For a while that seemed to work, but again I came across a wall of cloud and, at that height, I did not want to take any chances at all. One slip and I would be in the water. I turned before the cloud caught me and again saw Iceland as if through a slit. All the way back to open water, about ten miles, I was fearful of being shut down by cloud.

I started back towards Höfn, full of anger, banging the control bar. Could I try later? I thought I might, but at the same time, had I given this one my best shot? I looked at the high blanket of cloud. If I got above it I would be technically illegal, but more seriously, there was the problem of coming back down again, whited-out. As I flew closer to the Icelandic mountain range, I saw there were tears in the blanket and blue sky above. I started climbing, Keith's words about a 'fool's hole' echoing in my ears, but I thought there were too many holes to have such a title. I found one and climbed up through it, emerging at 6,500 feet above a long blanket of cloud as far as the eye could see. In the direction of Vágar, there seemed to be no obstacle.

I was in touch with a very helpful Reykjavik ATC, who checked the weather for me; there were no signs of the storms predicted that morning by Sky TV's Francis Wilson, but the major problem was that my ground speed plummeted. From 55–60 knots, it dropped to 36–40, and the more I flew out to sea, the worse it became. I lost my nerve when it touched 33 knots. There had also been one frightening moment when the engine coughed, as though a drop of water had passed through the carburettor, or one of the plugs had misfired. I had been in the air nearly two hours and had used the throttle freely, which had gobbled fuel. At 33 knots, with the prospect of even worse headwinds at Vágar, I could see myself not making it.

I began a conversation with myself, out loud: 'You are a chicken and it's your lack of nerve that is making you reluctant to go. No, it's far too dangerous to take a chance like this so close to home. What about John Hunt, sitting in Kirkwall, waiting for you? He's a nice chap and I do appreciate it, but it is still not worth the risk just to see him on time.'

In the end caution won, and sadly I turned around and flew back to Höfn. On the ground I discovered I had used 32 litres in two hours and ten minutes, far too much, but I had not been flying economically. With the help of four Germans, who had stopped on their flight through to Greenland (I bet they didn't have to pay the grasping Irling Neilsen £5,000 air–sea-rescue insurance), I dismantled the Flyer, and then in the quiet of the garage, changed her plugs and fuel filter. The plugs had last been changed in San Francisco, but had been cleaned in Broughton Island. They looked dirty but not dangerous.

Jon Rasdreksson, who ran the passenger services at the airfield, gave me a lift to a nearby guest-house where I had a large beer, a shower, a sleep, then half a bottle of wine and a good dinner.

On 18 July, day 118, I woke at 5.00 a.m. and completed all my jobs – writing the journal, charging all my electrical gear – but I was too early for breakfast at 7.30 a.m., so I lay around trying not to brood about the flight ahead. Conditions did not look ideal, dark clouds in a blanket over the mountain tops and stretching out to sea, but there was no wind. To the south-east it looked black and uninviting. I had a solitary breakfast of four pieces of toast and marmite, orange juice and coffee, and Jon Rosareksson came to give me a lift to the airport. While waiting for the latest forecast I assembled the Flyer on my own, the way one should be able to put together a microlight. I was in a detached state. Regardless of the weather, I was going anyway, to find whatever was out there and cope with it. Yesterday's cautious words meant nothing to me. I was going for it, and past a certain point, probably 50 miles out to sea, I knew I would not turn back.

When I climbed away, I was immediately confronted with a level of cloud at 1,000 feet that looked solid. I found an opening, another tear in the cloud made by nearby mountains, and climbed through it to find more layers of cloud above, but also blue sky and thin high cloud over the shifting blankets below. I set off on course, singing softly to myself: 'Isn't it a lovely day to be going home?' and kept a wary eye on conditions.

The Atlantic is one of the two great weather generators on earth, and constantly changing. The clouds shift in response to forces over thousands of miles, and in my little corner, trying to sneak through without provoking anything, I kept speaking to myself: 'Something's happening! Watch that cloud development there! Should I be above or below?' I needed the spoken word to focus on the changes, or I would watch them occurring without any alarm and then be in trouble. Great fat carpets of cloud bubbled underneath me, I climbed and they followed, and I climbed faster and then bumped into the cloud above. 'Look, there's a clearer patch to the right, go that way!' But when I got there conditions on my left had changed and there was more clag in front of me in my new position.

I flew instinctively, picking my heights without rational analysis, in tune with the sky. I looked up once, in a difficult position facing cloud barriers in all directions, and impulsively climbed and burst through to another layer where flying was easier, in that I could see where I was going.

But it was the changes, lazy and inexorable, that kept me alert, and I prodded my tired mind to keep thinking. I had run out of original thoughts and was reduced to turning over, again and again, prospects back in London if I completed the flight successfully. For every opportunity I saw three or four objections. I yearned for the comfort of GT Global, which would never be there for me again.

For the first three hours I was in danger of being whited-out, a condition I feared. I kept firing up and then closing down the turn-and-bank indicator, the only weapon I could deploy against not being able to see which way up I was. If it was turned off, I felt comforted, but then more clouds appeared and I thought I needed its assurance. When it was turned on it was like being in a state of high alert, alarming in itself. It had a delayed action and also seemed to me to exaggerate every turn.

I felt very alone, but not unhappy about that. I did not let my mind stretch out to look at the wider picture, to see myself in so tiny and fragile a craft above so immense an ocean and at the mercy of forces which, indifferently, could thrash me into the water. It did not help to let the imagination go in such a situation. Better to consciously turn it off and steer my mind elsewhere.

Each minute that passed, I had to make new decisions about the height to fly and select a way through a complicated pattern of shifting clouds. At one time I was below 1,000 feet, down in the stygian gloom and dank mist. At another, I saw a rent in the cloud blanket and climbed above it to find myself in a billowing area of mist and cloud where it was almost impossible to find a gap between one layer and another. I turned left and right, always looking for a clearer patch, not caring about being rained on but full of tension about not being able to see.

About a hundred miles from Vágar I came across a huge dark column of air and water right in my path. It took time to understand that it was a big rain cloud, and even longer to tell myself that I did not want to go into it. I turned right and picked my way around it, miles out of my way, but beyond it I could see a strip of what looked like blue sky. It was an hour before I gradually emerged into better conditions, where there were rational layers of cloud that stayed roughly still and did not puff up to engulf me.

I saw the Faeroe Islands at least 60 miles away, sticking up as a dark mass out of the banks of clouds that were not much lighter in colour. The airfield I was heading for, Vágar, had a fearsome reputation for turbulence, which I had heard about a thousand miles away. I had received all sorts of advice about how to cope and, listening to ATC announce two different winds on the runway, with opposite ends of the runway showing opposing winds, I was undecided about how to land. But a Boeing 737 went in two minutes ahead of me and I decided to follow his example and landed safely.

A small crowd of people were there to meet me, including a TV crew. Peter Denyer, a helicopter engineer with Atlantic Airways, had followed my flight on Sky TV, and gave me every help, a lift to the toilet, the use of a phone. It made things easier. I told Alison in London I was going on to Orkney immediately. Bad weather was forecast, and the thought of being so close to home and not being there was unbearable.

I rushed around paying bills, 60 litres of fuel, the landing fee, surrounded by helpful people worried that I might still be in the air when it got dark. It was too far north to get dark early, but I wanted to be gone. People asked me if I was tired; did I look tired? I felt suffused with energy. I could see rotten weather developing out to the west, and Peter told me it was possible to look in four directions in the Faeroes and see four different weather conditions, sunshine, rain, fog and high winds. I taxied out and took off at 3.45 p.m., the cameras now full of fresh tape.

This second flight was still south-east, in conditions that were almost ideal, so perfect I was suspicious. The Atlantic had sucker-punched me more than once and there was no reason for it to stop. But my ground speed was in the early 60s, the sky clear of threatening cloud and no rain in sight. When I came to a bank of low cloud I was almost relieved, revved up for another struggle, but it passed below me without menace. Every now and again the engine gave a hiccup, which at first nearly caused me heart failure, but after a while I put it down to moisture in the fuel and was not nearly so alarmed. It had happened daily on my flight to Australia.

I kept a listening watch out on the microlight frequency – 129.825 – for my friend John Hunt, and picked him up quite clearly when still 80 miles out. He reported murky conditions around Orkney, down at 300 feet below cloud. I listened to his conversations with other microlight pilots who came to greet me, and familiar feelings of home washed over me. The 80 miles seemed to rush past, and 20 miles out I came across John's low cloud and dived below it, picking my way through the mist to the island of Westray, my landfall, which I crossed at 7.23 p.m. doing more than 70 knots. John joined me first, then Ron Saunders on his Quantum, Charlie Kemp on his Cessna and Tom Sinclair in his Europa. We rushed over the sea and low-lying islands, heading for a microlight strip called Lamb Horn owned by Tom Sinclair, four miles south of Kirkwall Airport. I made one of my worst landings on the grass, about which no one commented, and taxied in for a small media gang-bang.

John helped me de-rig the Flyer and stow her in a local hangar with others of her kind, and we were given a lift to the nearby Commodore Motel, a friendly pub with superb food. I was starving. I drank two pints of lager and ate scampi and chips, and later toasted the flight in champagne donated by the landlord.

Home. Or nearly so.

20. LAST DAYS

I had hoped, once I landed in Orkney, to sweep across Scotland and England the following day and complete the journey to London with a dramatic flourish. In the event, it took three hard days of flying down our beautiful little island to get home. It did not look that way when we left the Commodore Motel, whose proprietor, Anne Sutherland, had given John Hunt and me free accommodation and free food, an extraordinary gesture of kindness in acknowledging my flight. We drove to Tom Sinclair's field and, in gentle sunshine and light northerly winds, put our various microlights together.

We headed for the turbulent waters south of Scapa Flow, over John O'Groats Hotel, and then in echelon, down the coast. It was a fantastic day, with beautiful misty sunshine but cloud coming in off the sea, and it soon became evident that we were hacking into a south-east wind. I found myself settling into a strange lassitude, letting others do the talking on the radio. All the white fury was seeping out of me. My mind was more and more in London, but I was comforted by the companions I had flying with me.

We flew past Wick, Dunbeath, Tain, Cromarty, my own country; I am not a Scot but this was home, even to an Englishman. I looked down dreamily at cars driving on the left, at the complications of small villages and roads, the way they fitted into the land. John talked us into Inverness Airport where we refuelled. South of Inverness, it looked difficult, with black clouds tumbling over the Highlands, and John decided to go east and around the high ground near Aberdeen, before heading south again to East Fortune where Graham Slater and Barrie Bayes were waiting to escort us to London. We headed east, then thought there might be a quicker way, we started into the Highlands, where the cloud descended and it began to rain. I shook myself awake again, because it was difficult flying, and for the next hour John and I hurled ourselves at the cloud, trying to find a way through the mountains to the east coast. Each time we were repulsed.

It might have been possible for me to use the turn-and-bank indicator and climb into the clouds, finding my way by GPS to the coast and then descending over the sea. But this was not possible for John, and I would not dream of leaving him.

We went slowly eastwards, diving south when we saw a gap and scuttling back again when the cloud closed in. It was glorious flying. I was full of admiration for John, who never wavered as conditions closed around us and the flying became difficult and, at times, dangerous. If the cloud descended, then we would have to find a field to land in. But this was not Russia, it was Scotland, and it abounded with such fields. We butted our heads against the Cairngorms, finding fewer and fewer options. I decided that I had not flown all the way around the world to end up splatted against a Scottish mountain.

'Do you know where that microlight field is at Insch that you were talking about?' I radioed John.

He had it on his GPS. We were in a difficult valley at the time, and needed to make a 180-degree turn, which we did in opposite directions, and crept around a ridge whose top was covered in cloud, racing down the side of it in bucketing rain. When Insch airfield appeared it looked like a bowling green, it was so perfect. John showed me the way in, and club members, who had been listening to us on the radio, were there to welcome us. John checked the weather, which looked like it would get worse, not better, and we opted to stay the night at the Premney Hotel in a nearby village.

John worried about getting out of the Highlands. We could, irony of ironies, be stuck there for days. The problem was finding land low enough not to be covered by cloud. John worked out a route north and east, right through the Aberdeen ATC, which Tom Robinson cleared for us. It was the last time I led the way, following the railway line on John's instructions, bumping along just under the blanket of cloud north of Aberdeen, until we burst out over the sea and scuttled south. The wind was so strong our ground speed was reduced to less than 30 knots at times, but we found a reasonable height out from the coastline and clear of the cloud that was bubbling off the water.

It was a hack, pleasant in John's company. We passed Montrose, Arbroath, Dundee and St Andrews. The names reminded me of football matches. We opted to go out to sea east of St Andrews and met rain clouds coming north. For the last part, into East Fortune airfield over the Firth of Forth, we both had to drop to 400 feet in bucketing rain and poor visibility. We parted before entering cloud, and found each other on the other side, where Graham Slater had told us on the radio it was clear. Slater and Barrie Bayes came out to meet us and filmed us on our way in to East Fortune. I was conscious of my landings now, under the eyes of British microlighting. One duff landing and there was sure to be a chorus: 'Well, if he flies like that then I can go around the world. Gimme the money!'

By now I had become extremely passive. Somebody said, do an interview, so I did an interview. Someone else gave me a cup of tea, so I drank it. Graham and John decided where next we were going to fly, told me and I went there. I was like a puppy dog, just scampering along thoughtlessly at their heels. They made decisions. I complied.

We made our way south via Eshott and Bagby, after the pair of them had dismantled all the extra piping Keith had installed to carry extra fuel. They were keen to get me legal again. We could do nothing about the radiator that was stuck out on the left leg, but the two side tanks were deposited in Andy Webb's car, along with piping and bladder tank, as he drove south with us and directed the filming. The Flyer was back to being an ordinary microlight. I found that, when we did climb away and settle down, the journey had got to her in ways I hadn't dreamed of. When we were filming in Malaga the previous year, she had smoked away so quickly from everyone that I had to fly with the bar right out to let Graham catch me up. Now he and John Hunt could leave me standing, and I limped along at the rear with the indignity of asking them to circle once in a while so I could catch up. Her sail was baggy after 24,000 miles, much of it overloaded.

Judy Leden was at Bagby to greet me, her baby son Cameron on her hip, her beautiful bold-eyed daughter, Yasmin, already confident with cameras. Judy had always been my champion, whether I was winning or losing. As a young girl she had knitted a jumper with the words 'Brian Milton is Innocent, OK', after I got stuffed in the Newton Aycliffe Affair. Judy was once British, European and World Women's Hang-Gliding Champion, and she had captained a British team in which every other competitor was a man. She had earned her place by skill and courage.

But I saw her, as I saw Graham Slater, another marvellous flyer, as if through the wrong end of a telescope. When they both said,

'Brilliant flight, superb,' it was like they were speaking from the other side of a long echoing hall. I knew them as great flyers, capable, if they had the chance, of doing what I had just done. It is hard to say why I found their praise so shocking. I am still trying to understand it myself.

Judy introduced me, by phone, to the man who had picked up my Internet site when GT Global legged it, Paul Hutchinson. He was a bit shy when Judy handed me the phone, and in a distracted way, I thanked him: I know a lot more now about what he had done than I did then and I promised to meet him at Kay Burley's party to celebrate the flight the following Saturday.

We flew on to Netherthorpe, with me more passive than ever. A hangar was found for us immediately. Andy Webb turned up and we found a hotel, a restaurant, ate, drank a few beers and I slept my last night on the flight. There was no come-down, I was just glad to be alive. It was a feeling that coursed through me, time and again, alive! Alive! Alive! But I couldn't talk about it, because it was a commonplace feeling to everyone else.

That night as I lay in bed and thought: *If I had failed, I would have been crucified.*

The Romans had a simple question: *cui bono* – who benefits? It is a question that leads to the real interests in any situation.

I could not see why, having abandoned me, it benefited Dallas McGillivray or Mike Webb or anyone at GT Global that the flight ended successfully. Surely, by inference, they were taking a bet that I would fail. Having taken that bet, why would it be in their interests that I succeed? Would not this just highlight their betrayal?

If I had failed, Dallas and Mike Webb could have blamed Prince Philipp or Paul Loach for making the original decision to sponsor me. The prince was in another country and Paul was out of his job and could not fight back.

If I had failed, Newlyn and Browse, far from having rude things said about them, would be able to go elsewhere and claim all sorts of knowledge about the world flight that no one could challenge, without the danger of anyone asking me for a reference.

If I had failed, Rory McCarthy would be happy as a sandboy, because with no record set, it was open to Virgin to create one, and those three Rotax 912-powered Shadows could be put to use.

If I had failed, the aviation nobodies would be able to say they had known all along and revive their sneering comments of ten years ago, while my children would suffer – *because I certainly would not have failed if there was a breath of life in me.*

And even Keith, my friend Keith, with whom I had been through so much, did he really have a genuine interest in my success?

Cui bono?

If I had failed, would that not have benefited Keith more? Why would my success be anything but ashes in his mouth? Who would ever ask him on another such adventure? If I had failed, he would indeed have had a genuine claim to the title he wanted in Yuzhno-Sakhalinsk, of knowing more about flying a microlight around the world than anyone.

I did not think any of them wished out loud for my failure. But adding up who really benefits, as against what one says in public, those were the bleak conclusions I came to.

On 21 July, day 121 for me, but 120 days for everyone else, other microlight pilots were at Netherthorpe to greet me, having flown in at dawn. They included the great Keith Ingham, who had flown a microlight around Australia; Andy Buchan, who had been on every other one of my wheezes; and Ian Bracegirdle. All three had come across the channel with me on our first day out of Brooklands. They were accompanied by Martin Mosley, Jon Pollard, Dave Concannon and Brian Sampson. I was touched that they had gone to so much trouble to get across the country and see me in, but there was little I could say, except thanks.

Still in passive mode, I wheeled the Flyer out, packed for the last day's flying, and set off in the middle of the gang, waving goodbye to the others in the air, as John Hunt and Graham Slater led me south. Near Aylesbury, more voices appeared on our microlight channel, and we were joined by a flight out of my home airfield, Plaistow, led by farmer Derek Brunt, and which included Gerry Archer, Jay Madhuani, Bill Gill, Roger Kelly, and a claimant for the title of the youngest one-eyed pilot in Britain, Robert Grimwood. Most of them were in Shadows, of the type I had flown to Australia.

In the increasing wind, we all landed safely at White Waltham, taxied in and roared welcomes at each other. Derek was nearly in tears. We had a cup of tea and a sandwich. Alison, who was master-minding the whole thing from my home in Bethnal Green, told us we had to be outside the London Control Zone, south of Brooklands, at exactly 4.45 p.m., to get in. John Fack and Billy Brooks, from Pegasus, who had seen me across the Channel on day one, flew in, and the wind went from fresh to strong, then close to being a gale.

When we climbed away on the last leg of the world flight, the wind was a complete bastard. It was not just a headwind, as we struggled south around Heathrow's air-traffic zone, but it was turbulent too. I felt a taste of all the old fears, but told myself not to be an idiot. Imagine bottling out there. Nine of us, led by Graham Slater on the radio, made it to the rendezvous point and began circling. Everyone was going to land before me, except Slater, who wanted to film the last few minutes from the air. Conditions were dreadful and worse on the ground, because when John Hunt led his band down to land, I could hear the rising tone of his voice: 'It's rough here . . . it's very rough here . . . the landing is very rough chaps, watch it.' As I circled my mind became detached again. I had got this far safely. There were only a few minutes left, one more effort, please, please, please don't cock it up.

'Someone's turned over,' said John on the radio.

Ah well, let's do it, I thought, and turned to head for Brooklands myself. The wind was tearing over some large buildings and across the runway at about 25 knots, and turning for finals, I poured every ounce of concentration I had left into the landing. I have since seen it on Sky TV. It looked terrible. The bar was all over the place and I barely got down safely. Graham, behind me, the great Graham Slater, actually put his nose-wheel on the ground first, normally a recipe for disaster.

I taxied to a halt, fighting the wind, trying to keep the wings level and waiting for someone to run up and hold the flying wires. I was safe, but the Flyer was still in danger. After an age, two pilots ran up and escorted me in to a huge crowd of press, and a blonde, sophisticated young woman standing all on her own to greet me. Without my glasses, I could not see who it was until I was quite close. It was Jade, my own daughter. Behind her, I saw familiar faces: Dave Simpson, Richard Meredith-Hardy, Roger Graham, all of whom had crossed the Channel on the first day. Kay Burley was away on holiday with her son, but I knew we would make a half-hour TV programme together the following week. Charles Heil and Alison Harper were organising things, Alison as efficient as ever, Charles looking thin and burnt-out and even haunted; this had been a tougher experience for him than for me. David Kirk, Chairman of the Dangerous Sports Club, had a bottle in his hand. Moira

Thomson arrived, late and as glamorous as ever, along with Julian Parr, one of the bravest men I know, twice told he would never walk again after accidents, and bouncing around full of energy and life.

Behind the media scrum, it took me some moments to find Helen Dudley.

'You've still got beautiful eyes,' she called out.

Not as beautiful as yours. And not as young, sadly. But you have been my guardian angel and kept me alive when the odds were against me.

Later, after interviews; champagne; being carried around; the Flyer speeding away on a trailer to Plaistow; other flyers leaving by air; I changed into a dinner jacket and with an old friend, Margie Lindsay, acting as chauffeuse, drove up to the Reform Club with Jade and Helen for a quiet drink and a toast to absent friends. I wanted to go back to where it had started. Paul Loach, still jobless, left me a message of congratulations. I hoped to have dinner with him soon.

Many of my friends were at my Cyprus Street home, where a party had been organised. I looked at them with deep affection, Margie, Valerie Thompson, Moira, her sister Julie, Helen, a gang of flyers including Derek Brunt, Jim Hill, an ebullient Dave Simpson and a brooding Richard Meredith-Hardy.

'If Brian Milton can do it,' he said, 'anyone can.'

'I don't think so,' I said. I knew Richard. He had been burning to do it himself.

'Only ten men in the world could have done it,' he said.

I didn't think that was right either.

Fiona was not there, but away in Dubai with her new man.

Dallas McGillivray and Mike Webb, despite their journey across the Channel on day one, were not there, either. This flight was a test of more than the characters of Keith and me.

But where was Keith Reynolds? His last word to me, by phone from Anchorage to Russia, was to tell me he would be there in Orkney to fly down Scotland and England with me.

He had not done that.

A couple of days before I arrived, he went back to Russia to bring Lina to England, to consider a future with her as his fourth wife. So it was not all disappointment for him.

As for me, I can still hardly believe it is over.

Being alive is lovely.

And hast thou slain the Jabberwock?
Come to my arms, my beamish boy!
Oh frabjous day! Calou! Calay!
He chortled in his joy.

But I haven't.
I do not think it is possible.

APPENDIX

For the record – the first microlight flight around the world, 1998

Date	From–To	Hours in Air	Mileage
March			
24	Brooklands–Le Touquet	2.45	102
	Le Touquet–St Die	5.15	284
25	*St Die–Constance	2.30	100
	Constance–Kempton	1.10	55
	Kempton–over Alps–Trento	2.40	150
26	Trento–Forli	2.30	115
	Forli–Bari	4.30	325
27	*Bari–Corfu	3.30	190
28	Corfu–local	0.50	
	Corfu–Marathon	4.40	280
29	*Marathon–Rhodes	4.30	303
30	Rhodes–Akrotiri	5.00	349
31	*Akrotiri–Amman (via Homs)	6.30	402
April			
1	Amman–Turayf	3.30	163
	Turayf–Ar'ar	3.00	150
2	*Ar'ar–4 road landings–		
	Qaysumah	7.00	343
3	Qaysumah–local	0.45, repairs	
4, 5	*on ground, repairs*		
6	Qaysumah–2 road landings–		
	Dhahran	5.00	282
7	*Dhahran–Al Ain	6.30	364
8	Al Ain–Muscat	4.00	173
9	*Muscat–Gwadar	6.30	275
10	Gwadar–Ormara–Karachi	5.30	291
11	*Karachi–Ahmadabad	6.00	370
12	Ahmadabad–Bhopal	5.00	295

Date	From–To	Hours in Air	Mileage
13	*Bhopal–Nagpur	3.15	184
	Nagpur–Raipur	2.45	172
14	Raipur–Calcutta	5.50	436
15	*Calcutta–Mandalay	6.25	484
16	Mandalay–Luang Prabang	6.00	411
17	*on ground, weather*		
18	*Luang Prabang–Hanoi	4.00	249
19–23	*on ground, bureaucracy*		
24	Hanoi–Nanning	3.45	178
25	*Nanning–Macau	4.50	342
26	Macau–Hong Kong	0.45	40
	Hong Kong–Xiamen	3.30	289
27	*Xiamen–Fuzhou	2.05	134
	Fuzhou–Hangzhou	5.30	302
28	Hangzhou–Shanghai	2.00	88
29	*on ground, bureaucracy*		
30 (k)	*Shanghai–Cheju	5.30	336

May

1, 2	*on ground: day 1 – bureaucracy; day 2 – weather*		
3	Cheju–Fukuoka	3.30	225
	Fukuoka–Okayama	3.30	208
4	*Okayama–Niigata	6.30	362
5	Niigata–New Chitose	5.20	359
6–13	*on ground, bureaucracy*		
14	*New Chitose–Yuzhno-Sakhalinsk	6.00	285
15 May – 1 June	*on ground, bureaucracy*		

Summary: Keith Reynolds, whose flights are indicated by an asterisk, flew 5,402 miles in 16 days' flying and for 93 hours and 40 minutes. Each day's flying averaged five hours and 51 minutes, at an average speed 57.67 mph. The average distance covered was 337 miles per flying day

Brian Milton flew 5,043 miles in 16 days' flying and for 84 hours and 55 minutes. Each day's flying averaged five hours and 18 minutes, at an average speed of 59.86 mph. The average distance covered was 315 miles per flying day

Date	From–To	Hours in Air	Mileage
June			
2	Yuzhno-Sakhalinsk–Kiroskoye	5.20	
	Kiroskoye–Nikolayevsk Na Amure	3.30	436
3	Nikolayevsk Na Amure–Ayan	4.15	244
	Ayan–Okhutsk	4.20	268
4	Okhutsk–a field in Russia	4.15	193
	A field in Russia–Magadan	1.05	70
5	*on ground, repairs*		
6	Magadan–Evensk	6.20	315
7	*on ground, repairs*		
8	Evensk–Markovo	6.50	398
9	Markovo–Anadyr	4.10	214
10	Anadyr–Providenya	5.20	265
11	Providenya–Nome	3.50	228

Summary: Brian Milton crossed Siberia to Nome, a distance of 2,631 miles, in eight flying days (ten days' elapsed time), in 40 hours and 25 minutes' flying time. Peter Petrov was the navigator. Each day's flying averaged five hours and three minutes, with an average speed of 65.1 mph. The average distance covered was 329 miles per flying day.

Date	From–To	Hours in Air	Mileage
11 (again), 12 *On ground at Nome, repairs*			
13	Nome–Unalakleet	2.40	150
	Unalakleet–Galena	2.05	125
	Galena–Tanana	2.35	143
	Tanana–Fairbanks	2.05	125
14	Fairbanks–Northway Junction	3.30	205
15	Northway Junction–Beaver Creek	1.00	
	Beaver Creek–Whitehorse	3.55	334
16	Whitehorse–Watson Lake	4.05	214
17	Watson Lake–Mackenzie	7.00	
	Mackenzie–Prince George	2.00	562
18	Prince George–Chilliwack	5.30	343
19	Chilliwack–Bellingham	1.00	
	Bellingham–Seattle	2.30	
	Seattle–Albany	3.30	305
20	Albany–Red Bluff	5.35	309
21	Red Bluff–Petaluma	2.45	131

Date	From–To	Hours in Air	Mileage
22	*Petaluma–local, repairs*		
23	Petaluma local (Golden Gate)	2.00	
	Petaluma–Lincoln	1.20	85
24	Lincoln–Lovelock	2.50	
	Lovelock–Battle Mountain	2.10	
	Battle Mountain– Elko	1.00	283
25	Elko–Salt Lake City	3.20	227
26	Salt Lake City–Cheyenne	5.00	395
27	Cheyenne–Omaha	6.15	449
28	Omaha–de Soto	2.00	
	De Soto–Morningstar	0.30	
	Morningstar–Clow International	4.50	411
29	Clow International–Fremont	3.35	261
30	Fremont–Kent State	1.40	90
	Kent State–Bellefonte	2.45	185
July			
1	Bellefonte–Mansville	2.35	
	Mansville–Caldwell	0.50	185
2	Caldwell–local (Statue of Liberty)		
3	Caldwell–St Hubert	5.20	
	St Hubert–Richelieu	0.15	315
4	Richelieu–Rivière-du-Loup	3.45	
	Rivière-du-Loup–Sept-Îles	3.30	456
5	Sept-Îles–Schefferville	6.10	314
	Schefferville–Kuujjuaq	3.55	232
6	Kuujjuaq–Aupaluk	1.25	98
	Aupaluk–Iqaluit	5.15	303
7	Iqaluit–Broughton Island	5.00	287
8, 9	*on ground, bureaucracy*		
10	Broughton Island–Sondestrum	6.00	351
11	*Sondrestrom local, weather*		
12	*on ground, weather*		
13	Sondrestrom–Kulusuk	6.10	384
14	*Kulusuk, local, weather*		
15	Kulusuk–Reykjavik	8.15	450
16	Reykjavik–Höfn	4.00	200
17	*Höfn, local, weather*		
18	Höfn–Faroe Islands	4.40	287
	Faroe Islands–Orkney	4.10	253

Date	From–To	Hours in Air	Mileage
19	Orkney–Inverness	2.15	105
	Inverness–Insch	1.15	50
20	Insch–East Fortune	3.00	107
	East Fortune–Eshott	1.35	62
	Eshott–Bagby	2.10	76
	Bagby–Netherthorpe	1.45	60
21	Netherthorpe–White Waltham	3.00	125
	White Waltham–Brooklands	0.55	22

Summary: Brian Milton completed the 10,054 miles back to London, via San Francisco and New York, in 39 days, in 177 hours and 20 minutes' flying time. He flew on 31 of those days and his average speed was 56.9mph. The average distance covered was 324 miles per flying day.

Total: Brian Milton took 121 days to finish the journey, but each of his days was, on average, 11 minutes and 54 seconds shorter than if he had been static, because he was flying east. Therefore, it was really 120 days' elapsed time.

There were 50 days going nowhere: bad weather accounted for six days; 35 days were lost to bureaucracy – in China (5), Japan (2), Russia (26) and Denmark (2); there were eight days for repairs and servicing; and one day – in New York – which was devoted to filming. He could have flown to and from San Francisco quicker, had he not had to film the Golden Gate Bridge.

He flew for 71 days: 32 of them with Keith Reynolds, which were equally split – 16 days each; 8 flying days with Peter Petrov; and 31 days flying on his own.

Total distance: 23,130 statute miles (37,223 kms)
Total flying hours: 405h10m
Average speed: 57.08mph (91.87 kph)
Average time in air: five hours and 42 minutes (just two minutes more than on the Dalgety Flyer ten years earlier).

His average speed was one mph faster with a Rotax 912 Pegasus Quantum Sport, built in 1997, than with a Rotax 447 CFM Shadow, built in 1987, but the aesthetic experience was infinitely better.